A Constitution for the European Union

CESifo Seminar Series
Edited by Hans-Werner Sinn

Inequality and Growth: Theory and Policy Implications
Theo S. Eicher and Stephen J. Turnovsky, editors

Public Finance and Public Policy in the New Century
Sijbren Cnossen and Hans-Werner Sinn, editors

Spectrum Auctions and Competition in Telecommunications
Gerhard Illing and Ulrich Kluh, editors

Managing EU Enlargement
Helge Berger and Thomas Moutos, editors

European Monetary Integration
Hans-Werner Sinn, Mika Widgrén, and Marko Köthenbürger, editors

Measuring the Tax Burden on Capital and Labor
Peter Birch Sørensen, editor

A Constitution for the European Union
Charles B. Blankart and Dennis C. Mueller, editors

A Constitution for the European Union

edited by
Charles B. Blankart and
Dennis C. Mueller

CESifo Seminar Series

The MIT Press
Cambridge, Massachusetts
London, England

© 2004 Massachusetts Institute of Technology

All rights reserved. No part of this book may be reproduced in any form by any electronic or mechanical means (including photocopying, recording, or information storage and retrieval) without permission in writing from the publisher.

MIT Press books may be purchased at special quantity discounts for business or sales promotional use. For information, please email special_sales@mitpress.mit.edu or write to Special Sales Department, The MIT Press, 5 Cambridge Center, Cambridge, MA 02142.

This book was set in Palatino on 3B2 by Asco Typesetters, Hong Kong, and was printed and bound in the United States of America.

Library of Congress Cataloging-in-Publication Data

A consitution for the European Union / edited by Charles B. Blankart and Dennis C. Mueller.
    p. cm. — (CESifo seminar series)
  ISBN 0-262-02566-3 (hardcover : alk. paper)
1. European Union. 2. Constitutional law—European Union countries. I. Blankart, Charles Beat. II. Mueller, Dennis C. III. Title. V. Series.
KJE4445.C658   2004
342.402—dc22   2004042787

10 9 8 7 6 5 4 3 2 1

Contents

List of Tables   vii
List of Figures   ix
Contributors   xi
Series Foreword   xiii
Preface   xv

1 **The European Constitution and Peace: Taking the Heat out of Politics**   1
   Geoffrey Brennan and Alan Hamlin

2 **Competitive Federalism by Default**   25
   James M. Buchanan

3 **The Assignment of Powers in an Open-Ended European Union**   37
   Pierre Salmon

4 **Rights and Citizenship in the European Union**   61
   Dennis C. Mueller

5 **Enlargements and the Principles of Designing EU Decision-Making Procedures**   85
   Mika Widgrén

6 **The Deadlock of the EU Budget: An Economic Analysis of Ways In and Ways Out**   109
   Charles B. Blankart and Christian Kirchner

7 Coordinating Sectoral Policy-Making: Searching for
   Countervailing Mechanisms in the EU Legislative Process   139
   Bernard Steunenberg

8 How to Choose the European Executive: A Counterfactual
   Analysis, 1979–1999   169
   Simon Hix, Abdul Noury, and Gérard Roland

9 The Role of Direct Democracy in the European Union   203
   Lars P. Feld and Gebhard Kirchgässner

10 Bringing the European Union Closer to Its Citizens: Conclusions
   from the Conference   237
   Charles B. Blankart and Dennis C. Mueller

   Index   257

List of Tables

Table 5.1 Impact of Nice reforms on main EU institutions' consultation procedures   92
Table 5.2 Impact of Nice reforms on main EU institutions' co-decision procedures   92
Table 5.3 Sum of squares of differences between the NBI and the square-root rule ($\times 10^{-3}$)   100
Table 6.1 Net receipts from the EU budget, 1994–2000 (in € mil)   116
Table 6.2 Percentage share of administrative expenditures and the Social Fund, 1957–1970   120
Table 6.3 Percentage share to the Agricultural Fund, 1962–1970   121
Table 6.4 Net receipts from EU budget, 1981–1984, (in € mil)   123
Table 6.5 Net receipts per capita, 1994–2000, and distribution of votes, 1995   126
Table 6.6 Status of voting power in the Council after Eastern accession   129
Table 8.1 Partisan makeup of the European Commission, 1977–2004   174
Table 8.2 Partisan makeup of the European Parliament, 1979–1999   177
Table 8.3 Mean party group NOMINATE scores, 1979–1999   180
Table 8.4 Counterfactual election of the Commission president by the fifth Parliament, using NOMINATE scores, July 1999   182
Table 8.5 Counterfactual coalition government formation in the fifth European Parliament, using NOMINATE scores, July 1999   185
Table 8.6 Counterfactual national parliamentary election of a Commission president, 1999   187
Table 8.7 Counterfactual elections of the Commission president by national parliaments   190
Table 8.8 Summary of results   191

List of Figures

Figure 4.1 Possible optimal majorities   71
Figure 5.1 Structure of the analysis   87
Figure 5.2 Consultation procedure   89
Figure 5.3 Co-decision procedure   90
Figure 5.4 Strategic power in consultation procedure   94
Figure 5.5 Strategic power in co-decision procedure   95
Figure 5.6 Impact of expanding membership on strategic power in co-decision procedure   95
Figure 5.7 Probability gatekeeping bias in co-decision procedure   98
Figure 5.8 Difference between the OPOV principle and actual power scores in two weighting schemes   102
Figure 6.1 Budgetary rules and budgetary outcomes, 1957–2000   111
Figure 6.2 Budget of the European Union in percent of GDP, 1960–2000   114
Figure 7.1 Different Council formations in the period, 1958–2002   142
Figure 7.2 Decision-making by two sectoral Council formations   145
Figure 7.3 Two sectoral Council formations in a two-dimensional policy space   146
Figure 7.4 Decision-making by sectoral Council formations coordinated by the General Affairs Council   149
Figure 7.5 Decision-making by sectoral Council formations and the European Parliament   152
Figure 7.6 Decision-making by sectoral Council formations coordinated by Coreper   154
Figure 7.7 Decision-making by sectoral Council formations and the European Council   157
Figure 8.1 NOMINATE plot of MEP locations in the fifth European Parliament   178

Contributors

Charles B. Blankart
Humboldt University, Berlin

Geoffrey Brennan
Australian National University

James M. Buchanan
George Mason University

Lars P. Feld
Philipps University of Marburg

Alan Hamlin
University of Southampton

Simon Hix
London School of Economics and Political Science

Gebhard Kirchgässner
University of St. Gallen

Christian Kirchner
Humboldt University, Berlin

Dennis C. Mueller
University of Vienna

Abdul Noury
Université Libre de Bruxelles

Gérard Roland
University of California, Berkeley

Pierre Salmon
University of Bourgogne

Bernard Steunenberg
Leiden University

Mika Widgrén
The Turku School of Economics and Business Administration

Series Foreword

This book is part of the CESifo Seminar Series in Economic Policy, which aims to cover topical policy issues in economics from a largely European perspective. The books in this series are the products of the papers presented and discussed at seminars hosted by CESifo, an international research network of renowned economists supported jointly by the Center for Economic Studies at Ludwig-Maximilians-Universität, Munich, and the Ifo Institute for Economic Research. All publications in this series have been carefully selected and refereed by members of the CESifo research network.

Hans-Werner Sinn

Preface

The heads of states of the member states of the European Union outlined the goals of a European constitution in the Declaration of Laeken of December 2001. They particularly wanted to approach the problem of the European Union's democratic foundation:

Within the Union, the European institutions must be brought closer to its citizens.... In short, citizens are calling for a clear, open, effective, democratically controlled Community approach, developing a Europe which points the way ahead for the world. An approach that provides concrete results in terms of more jobs, better quality of life, less crime, decent education and better health care. There can be no doubt that this will require Europe to undergo renewal and reform.

The issues raised by the heads of states were first discussed in a Convention of representatives of the Union and of the member states in 2002 and 2003. On the invitation of the Ifo Institute in Munich, a group of academics, mostly of economists, from Europe, the United States, and Australia met for a conference in early 2003 to contribute their ideas on what a constitution for Europe could comprise and how it could work. As the heads of states wanted the European institutions to move "closer to their citizens," the participants of the conference aimed first to study the collective choice procedures that could link citizen preferences to politcal actions at the EU level. They wanted to contribute to the discussion of a blueprint for a European constitution, such as was to emerge within the Convention and its Presidium, and their views would be presented at a Forum that is intended to take place according to the Declaration of Laeken.

The chapters in this volume address all the major issues that arise in writing a constitution. What are the goals of the state, in this case a superstate combining autonomous states? Is this superstate best organized as a confederation or a federation? Should it be a presidential state? How should taxing and spending authority be allocated across the various levels of government? What form of voting should be used for legislation? How should citizenship and basic rights be defined? What, if any, role should there be for institutions of direct democracy? The approach taken to answer these questions is in terms of public choice or political economy. That is to say, the assumption underlying the analyses in this book is that individuals are rational actors and that the goal of the state is to advance their collective interests as seen by the actors themselves. This definition of goals is quite in keeping with that set for the Convention by the heads of states.

We will not attempt to summarize the arguments of the following chapters in this short introduction. We want the reader to read each chapter unprejudiced by our summary of it. In the concluding chapter we will draw together the main arguments from each chapter and relate them to the discussion that took place in Munich, and then offer a broader set of answers to the questions posed above.

We wish to thank the Yrjö Jahnsson Foundation for its financial support, as well as the CESifo Institute for both its financial support and for providing the local organization and venue for the conference.

A Constitution for the European Union

1 The European Constitution and Peace: Taking the Heat out of Politics

Geoffrey Brennan and Alan Hamlin

1.1 Introduction

When setting out on a major project, it is normally a good idea to be clear about the objective. So, when considering the project of devising a new constitution for the European Union, the first question should be: What is a European constitution for? This leads to the equally basic question: What is the European Union for? Clearly, answers to these questions will not be simple. However, without these answers, the task of designing a European constitution—or appraising any proposed constitution—will be inchoate.

Notice that the questions posed are on the very nature of the European Union, and therefore what purpose its constitution might serve. But is there such a thing as a single (though complex) purpose relating to an organization such as the European Union? If so, how does it relate to the various aims and objectives of the institution as understood by the numerous actors that operate within the European Union? How does an organization's underlying purpose relate to the policies, behavior, and activities of the organization? A simple story about a firm, as it is usually depicted in economic models, may help elucidate some of the issues involved. From the point of view of shareholders, the fundamental purpose of the firm is to generate profits or shareholder value. However, this purpose may best be achieved if those who operate within the firm—its managers—direct their efforts toward rather more detailed and explicit objectives. And neither the fundamental purpose, nor the detailed objectives may be easily deduced by observing the behavior of the firm or its employees. If we ask the question, what does the firm do? we invite a barrage of specific answers listing the variety of goods produced and the policies in place in relation to marketing, investment, stock management, staff training, and so on.

All of these things are important, but as our intention is to question the basic design of the firm—its constitution—and ask whether it is "fit" for the fundamental purpose of the firm, we need to see through the surface patterns of behavior and policies of the firm to get a true sense of its fundamental purpose.

But what is the firm's fundamental purpose? Our simple story began from the point of view of the shareholder, and there is clear logic in this since it is the shareholders who control the constitution of the firm in a reasonably direct sense. But this is not the only possible starting point. We might have started from the point of view of the population at large (or the government, as the representative of the population) and asked about the wider social impact of the firm. This path is precisely the one we would follow if we were concerned with the design of the regulatory environment within which the firm operates. So we might be reminded that at the constitutional level, the firm is surrounded by other constituencies, implying some ambiguity as to the identification of its fundamental purpose. In this case the ambiguity arises because a firm may be seen as an organization within a larger organization—the state. Therefore the constitution of the firm has to be fitted within the constitution of the state. In the case of an autonomous and fully independent state, this source of ambiguity should not arise. If a state is truly and fully sovereign, its constitution will not be subject to any surrounding constitution (though, of course, the state may enter into binding commitments and treaties with other states). The European case is clearly a case in which the ambiguities arising from the nature of the relationship between constitutions are important.

Our initial questions were designed to cut through to the basic constitutional level and so complement the more descriptive questions asked, for example, by Alesina, Angeloni, and Schuknecht (2001) in their paper entitled "What Does the European Union Do?" and by Tabellini (2002) in a recent discussion of the "Principles of Policymaking in the European Union." While both papers explicitly take up the issue of the reform of the European constitution, both start from discussions of what the European Union actually does in a number of policy areas—trade policy, public goods policy, agricultural policy, regional policy, and so on—in order to identify potential areas of improvement in policy and in the structure of decision making. While we recognize the value in this approach, we also recognize a danger. The danger is that a vital part of the rationale and purpose of the European Union might be missed if we focus only on its policies and practices.

A somewhat negative way of approaching this point, adopted by Mueller (1996), is to argue that the European Union lacks the standard rationale that public economics would provide for the formation of a federal union. Thus, if we consider the spatial properties of public goods provided (or as might be provided) within the European Union, it is difficult to see why the formation of a larger more encompassing political entity is needed. Even more difficult to rationalize is the need for the further enlargement of the European Union. Where exactly, Mueller asks, are the public goods with European Union–wide scope? Where are the transnational externalities that make construction of a larger polity necessary? While there are advantages in constructing a free-trade area in Europe the same advantages might be expected to follow from the abolition of trade barriers anywhere, so that there is nothing distinctively European here.[1] Similarly, while there are some advantages in constructing a currency union in Europe (although these advantages are yet unclear to many both inside and outside of the euro zone) they can hardly be claimed as the rationale of the European Union as a whole. The essential point is that conventional public economics provides little by way of a basic rationale for the European Union in terms of the standard set of economic policies. This point may be taken to provide indirect support for the view that the conventional public economics approach is missing at least one vital ingredient.

A more positive way of approaching the idea of a "missing ingredient" is to take seriously the rhetorical and political claims that often surround the European Union. We will make no attempt to analyze Jean Monnet's foundational rhetoric, nor the writings and speeches of more recent European Union supporters, but it is clear that the most repeated and heavily stressed theme is that of the European Union as a force for peace in Europe. Over time, as the EU has become more firmly established, and the memory of European war has faded, this line of argument has remained—at least implicitly—in almost all EU proclamations. The official Web site of the European Constitutional Convention,[2] for example, opens its discussion of the issues to be addressed by the Convention with the statement "For over half a century the countries of the European Union have lived in peace." Similarly its discussion of the question of the enlargement of the European Union opens with the statement: "Fifty years on the Union stands at a crossroads, a defining moment in its existence. The unification of Europe is near. The Union is about to expand to bring in more than ten new Member States, predominantly Central and Eastern European.

This will finally bring to a close one of the darkest chapters in the continent's history. At long last, Europe is on its way, peacefully, to becoming a coherent whole." As a final example, the Draft text of the articles of the treaty establishing a constitution for Europe issued in February 2003 also maintains, as the very first item in the statement of the Union's objectives, "The Union's aim is to promote peace."[3] Just as the two world wars provide the essential backdrop to the formation of the European Union, so the cold war provides the essential backdrop to its current enlargement. In both cases a key aspect of the essential and continuing motivation of the European Union is the institutionalization of peace.

Peace in Europe was clearly a necessary condition for the foundation of the European project to ensure lasting cooperation among the major nations of Europe, particularly France and Germany. Our point is simply that it was the recognition of the potential fragility of this peace in the face of European history over the preceding 150 years that played a vital role in the design of the European project, and has remained its main motivation.

Now, the conventional public economist could respond that if peace is the "missing ingredient," it should be incorporated into the conventional analysis as an international public good. A sharp public choice theorist might then point out that war and peace relate directly to the political sphere rather than the marketplace. So, in this view, the analysis should be of political failure rather than market failure as the appropriate starting point for understanding the constitutional requirements of peace.

Here, at least, we have a plausible thesis: political failure in a state can produce a disposition toward war. The threat of war induces each state to engage in self-protective measures of which war itself is a likely final outcome. The initial warlike propensities in country A create, as we might put it, a negative externality for countries B, C, and D. Bad things can "spill over" the borders, and they are matters of political rather than of market failure.

We think that this thesis deserves to be taken seriously in trying to understand both the rationale offered by the architects of the European Union and the animating spirit of the project among the populace. The determination to prevent European conflict should be seen not just as a piece of incidental political advertising but as a serious argument to be taken at face value and appraised as best we can via the perspectives and methods that are our stock in trade. Accordingly we identify four questions:

1. Do our models of national political process adequately account for war as a feature of international political interaction?

2. Does our account of war as a political phenomenon suggest that some form of supranational federation from the bottom up is likely to contribute to a solution to the problem?

3. If political amalgamation is a plausible solution to European conflict, what are the implications for the more detailed institutional structure of the European Union?

4. Is there a risk that the shift to confederation will create corresponding difficulties in international relations between Europe and other powers?

In this chapter, we engage these questions, and do so in defiance of principles of intellectual comparative advantage. These are matters on which economists have had relatively little to say. Perhaps such questions should be left to historians and international relations experts. But if so, so should much of the exercise of European constitution-making if the object of peace-building is to be a primary guiding principle of European institutional design.

1.2 War as Politics

In this section we first sketch three approaches to the analysis of war that might be taken up within the broadly rational actor tradition: one based on redistribution, one based on strategic interaction between nations, and one based on political failure. It should be no surprise that we argue that the third approach is the most promising. The remainder of the section is devoted to a slightly more detailed discussion of the nature of a political failure that contributes to war.

Within the standard rational actor analysis of politics, one chief engine of action is redistribution of one sort or another. Typically, within public choice analysis, politics is viewed as a scramble among competing interests, and policy decisions are often explained in terms of the "efficient" redistribution from minorities to decisive majorities, or from supine and ill-informed majorities to well-organized and politically influential minorities. Which direction of transfer predominates depends, roughly, on whether majoritarian electoral process or special interest lobbying is the more significant mechanism in play in policy determination.

The immediate question that comes to mind in a public choice context in attempting to explain war is, What redistributions are at stake? There are certainly stories one might tell here. Some people do benefit from war: suppliers of armaments and military inputs, perhaps the senior military establishment (those who survive), and individual politicians with a comparative advantage in war government. But the benefiting groups are too small and too unpredictable ex ante to explain wars either individually or generally. The fact that ex post some (remarkably few) people did better as a result of the great world wars than they would otherwise have done does not in itself constitute a promising route to an explanation of what happened.

Our view of the matter is that wars, at least large-scale modern wars but almost certainly more minor wars as well, impose very substantial net costs on even victorious combatant nations. The gross costs are typically very large and widespread, and the gross benefits are generally small, and focused on a small fraction of the population. Under these circumstances a general explanation of war based on the redistributive forces of political processes seems implausible.

An alternative account of war might focus on nations rather than individuals as the relevant actors and see war as one possible outcome of a game played between nations: perhaps a Prisoner's Dilemma Game in which a peaceful outcome Pareto dominates war, but where war is the dominant strategy for individual nations; or an Assurance Game in which it pays to play "peace" only as long as everyone else plays "peace"; or a Chicken Game in which players occasionally fail to "pull out."[4] However, we should make two points about all such attempts. First, any such attempt must be based on identifying expected net gains from war for at least some nations. Second, in focusing on the nation as the effective actor, all these formulations deny the more disaggregated mode of analysis that is a characteristic of public choice analysis and economics more generally: individual conduct is subsumed under the presumed common interest of the nation-state players. Rational actor analysis has nothing further to contribute. We think this approach is not helpful, in general, although there may be specific circumstances where war is closely identified with an individual—as in a dictatorship.

In more democratic settings Kant's famous conjecture that democracy would be conducive to a reign of "perpetual peace" arises. Once the political decision-makers and the affected potential combatants are one and the same group, individual rationality should dictate that war is rarely the preferred alternative. While dictators may make wars on democracies, and democracies may be forced to enter the field, the expected losses will effectively restrain bellicose action by well-functioning democracies.

Despite the empirical evidence that war is rare between democracies,[5] we think that this conclusion is too optimistic about democracies. It too easily assumes that democracies work well, that they provide a direct connection between the interests of the citizenry and the actions of the state. On the contrary, we think that collective decision-making is prone to certain kinds of failures—one symptom being the excessive propensity to make war. By "excessive" we do not mean "large", however. We fully accept the empirical evidence that democracies are less likely to engage in wars than nondemocracies, and that the absolute frequency of war between democracies is low. Nevertheless, since the costs of war can be extremely high, even a small reduction in the probability of war may represent a valuable prize.

If circumstances arise where national leaders are engaged in an international diplomatic game in which war is one possible outcome, we think that they will generally be encouraged by features of the democratic political system to use strategies that involve an excessive risk of war. Indeed, we suspect that democratic public opinion, rather than always playing the role of a brake on the war-like ambitions of a leader, will sometimes oblige relatively pacific leaders to adopt more bellicose strategies.

There are, no doubt, many possible ways to model this political failure. Hess and Orphanides (1995, 2001), for example, build on the principal-agent model of political leadership, where incumbent leaders need to build a reputation if they are to secure re-election and where, for some leaders (those with modest economic management skills), participating in an avoidable war may be the best means to that end. This issue arises because voters cannot observe, ex ante, all the detailed characteristics of candidates for political leadership. War sometimes becomes a means by which leaders can signal certain desirable qualities of character to the electorate.

In a slightly different but parallel view, Bueno de Mesquita and Siverson (1995) and Bueno de Mesquita et al. (1999) provide a model of the link between domestic politics and war that emphasizes the need of political leaders to compete for office. The results suggest that democracies will choose war in some circumstances and, conditional on being at war, will devote more resources to war than would an otherwise similar autocracy. This reflects the fact that a democratic leader has more to lose politically in the event of losing a war and so will be both more wary of entering a war, and more determined to win once it has commenced.

These models focus on political failures that relate to political leaders. While we agree that such models may be important, we wish to explore a different form of political failure that locates the failure within the logic of popular voting in a large electorate. The central theoretical point that we stress relates directly to the nondecisiveness of individual action in large-scale collective action contexts. In a large electorate setting each individual voter is asymptotically irrelevant to the final outcome. By this fact, the relative payoffs to different elements in the agent's utility function are radically altered. The voter can express her views without the discipline of having to take responsibility for the consequences that her actions (together with the actions of others) bring about. Her posture toward the objects of collective choice becomes symbolic or expressive, rather than instrumental. The general logic of this claim has been developed at some length in other places (Brennan and Lomasky 1993; Brennan and Hamlin 1998, 1999, 2000a, b) and will not be repeated in detail here. The general point is one that should be familiar to economists, who generally mistrust opinion poll data and the results of experiments in which subjects are not faced with the full incentives that would apply in real world settings.[6]

Individuals at the ballot box are more like people cheering at a football match than shoppers in a supermarket. Voters express an opinion but they are not individual choosers. The opinions they express are likely to be conditioned more by issues such as the individual voter's self-image and the identification with the public image of a candidate, than by direct considerations of the individual's interests and how they would be affected by the candidate's policies. We believe this fact is central in understanding one important source of political failure. An important feature of democratic politics is that electoral competition brings to the fore issues for which individuals are likely to cheer—matters of high moral value, or significant symbolic resonance—and settles them on the basis of the volume of cheering. This feature sometimes has the effect of producing political outcomes that few, if any, of the individual voters would actually choose if they were given the responsibility of individual choice. The instrumental costs and benefits of alternative courses of action are salient in a setting where the individual is decisive. Those instrumental considerations are backgrounded in a context where the individual is only able to cheer.[7] The contexts in which symbolic/expressive considerations are likely to diverge greatly from instrumental considerations are those where the prospect of this form of political failure is most pressing.[8]

One such prominent context is that of military conflict. Nationalism, military pride, and patriotism are matters that engage a populace's emotional and expressive energy. It is indeed an alarming feature of a democratic system that political leaders are able to mobilize enormous popular support by a careful timing of military adventures. Margaret Thatcher at the time of the Falklands war, George Bush Sr. at the time of the first war against Iraq, and George Bush Jr. in the second war against Iraq are recent examples. But we should be clear as to what exactly we take these cases to be examples of. On face value, they indicate a positive relationship between the electoral popularity of incumbent leaders and war, and not necessarily the leaders' manipulation of that relationship. We provided no evidence of the leaders' motives in the cases cited, and draw no inferences. However, the general proposition that leaders desire to retain office, together with the empirical evidence that manipulation of external affairs is a possible mechanism toward this end, should be enough to make one at least mildly anxious. Of course, we do not need these recent examples to make the point. It is a commonplace that the best mechanism for the creation of national unity is a common enemy, invented or otherwise.

An exaggerated impulse toward war then is, we think, an outcome of political failure. It is not a sort of political failure that the intellectual habits of orthodox public choice theory are likely to focus on, however. This is because the way in which the "free-rider problem" becomes evident is less a matter of the undersupply of defense (a euphemism for military expenditure) than of oversupply. It is nevertheless an instance of "free-rider" reasoning in two senses. First, an individual voter is effectively free-riding on the collective expression of enthusiasm for the military enterprise. The logic of interaction that characterizes this voter's dilemma is very close to the logic of the n-person Prisoner's Dilemma, though we concede that the application is somewhat different.

Second, the action of each domestic electorate imposes a substantial external cost on neighboring constituencies. It would not be in the interests of any country to seek to solve a domestic problem of excessive bellicosity unilaterally. For a nation surrounded by a sea of bellicose neighbors, it would be a dubious strategy to be pacific.

Now it should be apparent that the latter consideration is a central informing proposition on which the European project is constructed. Forming a larger political entity seems to offer a means by which the relevant political externality can be internalized. If the diagnosis that we have offered is at all plausible, then a battery of questions arises. Is the larger political entity itself feasible? How large should it be, and how should it be structured? Would the creation of a Union of nations not simply shift the problem from one location to another—from the national level to the level of relations among Unions of nations?

Some of these questions remain salient, even if our particular diagnosis of political failure is mistaken. Consider the relationships among Unions of nations, for example. If creating an inclusive political entity is a solution to the forces that make for war within a specific region, it is proper to worry about the prospect of war between that larger entity and those entities and countries left outside. Put more pointedly, the impulse for a confederated Europe already draws part of its energy from a desire to be a big player, and specifically one on the same scale as the United States. There are further suggestions that European countries ought to be coordinating their aid policies in such a way as to defend and promote united political interests—much as the US government does. And what goes for aid policies goes no less for bargaining strategies on intellectual property, trade arrangements, and the whole range of issues on which power at the international negotiating table is important. Is it totally implausible that fifty years from now, tensions may develop among the United States, Europe, and an Asian bloc to the point of war? History is full of alliances and wars that seemed implausible fifty years earlier. One thing that public choice theory teaches us is that coalitions of interests are unlikely to be stable. It may simply be a failure of the imagination to conceive of the possibility of a future war between Europe and the United States, especially if we believe the causes of war to be related to fundamental properties of politico-social organization. A danger with the European Union may well be that it is a solution to yesterday's problem. And, more to the point, to the extent that it is a solution to yesterday's problem, it may foment tomorrow's problem. To see this, we need to examine the grounds for thinking that a federation will reduce risk of war among the parties to the federation. We then need to examine the implications of that line of reasoning for the external relations of the more inclusive polity.

1.3 Federation as Support for Peace

What reason do we have to believe that confederation will reduce the likelihood of war between the confederating states? Clearly, there is nothing axiomatic about such effects. Civil wars are not unknown, even within federations. And sometimes the reconciliation of a conflict may take the form of creating separate and distinct political units (as in the partitioning of Yugoslavia). Where there are significant ethnic, tribal, linguistic, and/or religious differences among subpopulations, keeping a certain political distance might be thought be more conducive to peace than political cohabitation. The history of the partition of India and Pakistan, or of Ireland, makes it abundantly clear that there are no simple general rules here. Indeed, federalism is sometimes discussed as one mechanism for building institutional fences between different communities, rather than as a means of bringing different communities together. So we must first be clear as to our meaning of federation in this context. Throughout this chapter—precisely because of our focus on the case of the European Union—we regard federation and confederation as the bringing together of previously distinct political entities—federalism from the bottom up, as it were. Of course, there is also the possibility of the creation of a federal structure from the top down—by partition, separation, or some other loosening of links relative to a unitary structure. We have no desire to argue that all forms of federal structure, whatever their history, are always and everywhere a force for peace, but we do believe that there is a systematic argument to be made for the view that the creation of a larger, more inclusive polity with the relatively complex internal structure that is typical of federal systems may be the more effective means to maintain peace than a divided set of independent polities.

Before sketching the argument, it is worth mentioning two parallel lines of thought, both relevant to the European case, that do not depend of any particular political confederation: one is concerned with economic integration, and the other with military alliances. The economic argument is simply that anything that encourages genuine interdependence, though not necessarily political integration, among countries will tend to reduce the probability of war between those countries. Thus purely economic integration of the type that reduces the ability of country A to operate without cooperating with country B may be expected to reduce the probability of war between A and B by raising the cost of such war. We take this point but do not rely on it too heavily, since our diagnosis of the expressive nature of the issue underlying the politics of war is such that the true costs of war may be expected to have relatively little impact on the probability of war. Of course, economic interdependence can sometimes be interpreted as economic dependence, which can in turn fuel political antipathy. Nevertheless, if political structures can be found that address the basic issue we identify, we would expect those political effects to be reinforced by the effects of the more general economic integration that can be expected to go alongside political confederation. Similarly, while military alliances can in some cases support peace, there is plentiful evidence that unless the military alliance is firmly grounded in a broader political understanding, it is unlikely to have significant or long-term impact.

In what follows we focus on political integration or confederation rather than on purely economic or military cooperation. We should acknowledge that there exists a considerable literature on the relationships between democracy, federalism, and war. This literature draws on a number of theoretical traditions and provides considerable empirical analyses. In particular, the "correlates of war" program of research represents a major contribution to any understanding of war (for an excellent introduction and survey, see Geller and Singer 1998). Our purpose here is to add a further argument to this literature based on the idea of expressive political behavior.

In developing the idea of political confederation as a means toward peace, the first key issue is one of separating, as far as possible, political decision-making from structures of symbolic or expressive significance. This is what we mean by "taking the heat out of politics." It is hard to imagine a form of national political competition that does not excite nationalism. If decision-making, however, is shifted to a different level, and particularly one that cuts across national lines, it may be possible to uncouple the practical from the symbolic. For this to be possible, there have to be different levels, and these levels have to be as orthogonal as possible to existing "fault lines" between symbolically significant groups.[9] This idea has two aspects that we should stress: one directly concerns the constitutional design of the structure of government and the principle for allocating decision-making powers to levels of government, and the other concerns the value of civic engagement in the political process. We will discuss each in turn.

In standard public economics there is a clear approach to the design of federal systems and the allocation of responsibilities to levels of government in a federal structure. The argument is broadly in line with the idea of subsidiarity as developed in the European Union, which indicates that any decision should be made at the lowest level consistent with competence and efficiency. We would suggest that the issue of the institutionalization of peace provides a countervailing argument. One aspect of the standard approach is that decisions should be made by the groups most directly concerned, and that the levels of decision-making should therefore be designed to match natural constituencies of concern. The logic of this recommendation rests heavily on the assumption of instrumental decision-making at each level so that all relevant externalities are internalized. But, as we have already suggested, we do not believe that this assumption is appropriate. Further, if we consider the question from the more expressive/symbolic perspective, we gain a very different view. It is exactly the identification of natural constituencies that raises the problem from this perspective.

At the same time we might question, from the expressive/symbolic perspective, whether the orthodox pattern of decentralization does internalize relevant externalities. If voting is not instrumental by nature, it is not plausible to expect the outcomes of voting to be efficient relative to the underlying interests of the enfranchised citizens. Expressive voting may even introduce additional political externalities of the type already discussed. So the design of a federal system on the basis of recognition of the symbolic/expressive nature of democratic voting may depart sharply from the design that appears optimal under the assumption of instrumental voting.

More specifically, issues that have the potential for exciting symbolic/expressive passions—issues that are "hot"—should be allocated to levels of government, and styles of decision-making, that tend to "cool" such passions. There are a number of possibilities along these lines. The first and most obvious is in the definition of the relevant electorate, but equally we would point to possibilities associated with what might seem at first glance to be less democratically accountable decision methods. The operation of the European Commission, for example, is often criticized for being relatively remote from democratic pressures, but this might be read as an advantage if it serves to insulate decision-making on particularly sensitive issues from the hurly-burly of politics as usual. In short, a democratic deficit of the type often identified with the operation of European institutions may not be all bad—it may indeed provide a counterweight and offset any overheated democratic enthusiasms at the national level. Equally, indirect forms of election and representation might be used.[10]

Of course, taking the heat out of politics is likely to make politics less engaging. Here we encounter a tension between the idea that politics should be structured to filter out the symbolic/expressive, and the idea that politics should be structured so as to encourage wide and active participation. Our point is simply that participation should not be viewed as an end in itself, and should be a matter of type and quality of participation as well as a matter of sheer volume. The most attractive model of fully participative democracy is that normally discussed under the heading of "deliberative democracy," where the understanding of democracy is that of a popular debate in which ideas and ideals are openly and impartially examined with the aim of reaching consensus by argument and persuasion. This conception of democratic politics is far removed from the extreme economic model in which individual citizens' views are taken as fixed, and the object of the political process is to aggregate these views by voting. If political institutions are to play a role in encouraging more deliberative democratic politics, they must be designed with that end in mind. And there is likely to be a trade-off between the quantity of participation and the quality of that participation—not least since in any system of mass participation the incentives to engage seriously with the process will be diluted and rational ignorance will tend to undermine the quality of the participation.

A second key point in support of confederation as a support for peace relates to complexity and the division of sovereignty. This may seem odd since complexity and the division of sovereignty have often been identified as among the chief problems of federalism. For example, Tocqueville famously wrote that: "The most prominent evil of all federal systems is the complicated nature of the means they employ. Two sovereignties are necessarily in presence of each other" (de Tocqueville [1835] 1945, p. 172). He went on to write, "The second and most fatal of all defects, and that which I believe to be inherent in the federal system, is the relative weakness of the government of the union ... a divided sovereignty must always be weaker than an entire one" (p. 173). And further, "I cannot believe that any confederate people could maintain a long or equal struggle with a nation of similar strength in which the government is centralised" (p. 178).

Note that as Tocqueville was arguing that federal unions might be expected to be relatively weak in military terms, he took "strength" and "weakness" to have a clear military dimension. But note further that he was concerned with the external military strength or weakness of a federal union, and not with its internal properties. By contrast, we are concerned primarily with the question of internal peace—and here the complexity and division of sovereignty seems to be an advantage of federalism, rather than an "evil." The most direct point here is that any division in sovereignty, and hence in political loyalties, will generally render the idea of military conflict between parts of the federal whole less likely. By definition, there will be areas in which the two potentially conflicting parts actually identify themselves as united, and there will, again by definition, exist political institutions that tie the two parts together and so form natural routes of communication. At the same time the government of each part of the federation will lack the required ultimate political authority or sovereignty. Of course, these results will only be true in a moderately well-functioning federation. It is not difficult to imagine a situation where disputes between parts of a federation reach the point of military conflict and signal the end of the federation. To say that federation cannot prevent all wars is not to say that federation cannot reduce the incidence of wars.

Complexity and the division of sovereignty, and the separation of political decision-making from symbolic fault lines are, then, our two themes. These are the two basic mechanisms by which confederation may hope to achieve a more peaceful outcome for its members. So far we have sketched these ideas in very broad terms, but before going into slightly more detail it is worth re-emphasizing that these ideas should be seen as constitutional principles rather than as principles of policy-making, and that, as constitutional principles, they pull in rather different directions than the more standard set of constitutional principles that informs economic discussions of constitutional and institutional design.

1.4 Institutional Implications for Europe

In the context of designing the European constitution we want to speculate on the implications of taking seriously our arguments on both the political failure that leads to an exaggerated risk of war and the broad nature of a confederal institutional structure that might mitigate this failure. In so doing, we adopt the method of outlining some institutional arrangements that seem to us to institutionalize peace. We make no claim that institutionalizing peace is the only purpose of the European Union that should be recognized, and therefore we make no claim that the institutional arrangements that we outline are even close to optimal once all things are considered. But we make no apology for this. Most of the debate on the European constitution proceeds without reference to peace as an objective, and therefore runs the risk of completely ignoring the institutional requirements of peace. In erring in the opposite direction, we aim to slightly redress the balance.[11]

Given the emphasis on peace it is worthwhile to consider aspects of the European constitution that bear directly on matters of defense and security, before considering more general aspects. And here it is particularly useful to begin with the final report on defense from Working Group VIII of the European Convention, 2002. This document sets out recent developments in defense matters at the European level, and makes a number of recommendations to the constitutional convention in relation to defense and security issues. At the Cologne and Helsinki European Council meetings (June and December 1999) the decision was taken to provide the European Union with the capacity for autonomous action, backed by credible military forces, and independently of NATO, so that the European Union could launch and conduct military operations internationally. The European Council also established the post of High Representative to lead EU policy in areas of "flashpoint diplomacy" and European Security and Defense Policy (ESDP). It is particularly notable that all matters relating to the ESDP are ruled out from the possibility of applying qualified majority voting so that all member states retain a veto. The broad thrust of the new recommendations is to further enhance the European role in matters of defense and security, in particular, by expanding the set of "Petersburg tasks" (the set of tasks that may require an EU military force), by extending the role of the High Representative so that he or she can initiate and direct action while reporting to the Council, and by encouraging the use of "constructive abstention" to ensure that the formal requirement of unanimity does not prevent significant groups of member states from acting even where some other member states may not approve.

By these recent developments and proposals, it can be foreseen that in military decision-making the European Union will play a larger role alongside the individual states and NATO.[12] Furthermore it is clear that the mechanism that will enhance the European Union role is relatively remote from popular voting. Indeed, the creation of the High

Representative moves a short distance in the direction of setting up an independent agent whose role might be analogous to that of an independent central banker. By analogy, then, the primary idea is that of setting up an agent who is not directly accountable to an electorate but is instead accountable for the delivery of a specific policy. This independence insulates the agent from political pressures.

All these considerations seem to us to be in line with our general argument in that they shift the debate on military matters away from the natural constituencies, thereby reducing the heat of the political debate. At the same time the complexity of decision-making in the area of defense is increased by ensuring that negotiations at NATO and EU levels are a counterweight to any internal populist pressure within any national government contemplating military action.

Other considerations in this direction can be imagined. Most obvious is the formation of a European military force that stands alongside national military forces and permits the military capacity of individual nations to be reduced. Of course, the tension here is that in creating a strong integrated European military power, one might lessen the probability of war within Europe but risk increasing the probability of war between Europe and an external power. To minimize the probability of war overall, one needs to divide and share the responsibility for military matters in ways that limit national risks without creating a military superstate. But there is yet another facet to this issue. Our diagnosis of the type of political failure that underlies the exaggerated probability of war operates because of the scale of expressive/symbolic commitment that is invested at the national level of political decision-making. A shift of military capacity from the national level to the European level would not necessarily replicate the same problem on a larger stage, unless there is also a shift in expressive/symbolic attachments. To put the point more plainly, an integrated European polity could only suffer from the identified political failure if the European Union comes to occupy a strong place in the expressive/symbolic landscape of its citizens.

Moving outside of the narrowly military area, what more general comments may be made about the design of constitutional structures to institutionalize peace? We identify a number of critical points:

1. To diffuse political pressures, stress the establishment of law, particularly law in relation to individual rights, rather than national or group rights, and the judicial process, rather than the creation of political competition at the European level.

2. To reduce the force of political competition and encourage debate in representative bodies that do not divide along national lines, rather than the empowerment of directly elected politicians.

3. To stabilize political outcomes and reduce the power of any specific group, and divide power across a variety of institutions, with different patterns of representation and different degrees of electoral accountability.

4. To protect smaller nations and minorities and provide an assurance of stability, and use supermajority voting.

5. To counterbalance expressive/symbolic identification at national level and build identification at the European level.[13]

These points all identify measures that either take the heat out of politics or exploit the complexity and divisions inherent in a federation. These points should also be familiar to any observer of the European Union as they are among the features of the European constitution that are most often criticized for limiting the democratic responsiveness of Europe, for institutionalizing a form of lowest common denominator bargaining among member states, and for rendering the European Union intrinsically conservative and bureaucratic. Our view, however, is that these features also promote the institutionalization of peace, which we take to be a vital part of the underlying purpose of the European Union. Any accompanying bureaucracy, conservatism and similar inefficiencies may be a price worth paying for an increased prospect of peace.

A further problem relates to the issue of whether practical measures that take the heat out of politics would be supported in the political arena. This may appear unlikely as politicians would have to give up "hot" issues. Why should national politicians be willing to give up issues that excite national passions? We argue that this may be attractive in the same way that "tying one's hands" in other policy areas may be attractive. Just as politicians have been willing to give up control of monetary policy to an independent central bank because the heat of politics is argued to distort monetary policy decisions, so we would expect other relocations of authority to be achievable. However, we stress that we do not believe that any relocation of authority is possible just because it is desirable. We take seriously the point that any relocation of authority has to be compatible with the incentives faced by the initial holders of political authority, and we recognize that this may affect the range of reforms achieved.

There is also a question of coordination among states. If national governments recognize the value of insulating a particular aspect of policy from the pressures of popular, national politics, why should the relevant institutional solution be European in nature? Why not a plethora of national solutions rather than a coordinated European solution? The answer derives from the explicit recognition that the aim in view—the reduction of the possibility of European war—is essentially inter-national. The payoff to any one member state engaging in the relevant institutional reform depends crucially on the reforms undertaken in other member states.

1.5 Concluding Comments

We developed our discussion from a rather different interpretation of the standard quote from Clausewitz on the relationship between war and politics.[14] Rather than treat war as a means by which states might pursue international political ends, we see a potential connection between the mechanics of domestic democratic politics and war. In our view, the nature of democratic political competition results in a political failure that implies an increased risk of war. We suggest that the establishment of the European Union can be understood, in large part, as an attempt to institutionalize peace. Conceptually the European Union is an enterprise that goes far beyond simple economic integration or military alliance. It is an attempt to construct a genuine political counterweight to political failure. The success of this enterprise depends, however, on the details of the European constitution. It is not the case that political integration of any sort will promote peace. The institutional reforms that we suggest are essentially reforms that both reduce the heat of politics and employ relatively complex structures that dissipate power and disassociate it from its natural constituencies. Such reforms will also carry costs. However, if overall costs and benefits are compared to reach a fully rounded evaluation, any institutional arrangement that can offer a small reduction in the probability of war will, in the end, be worthwhile.

We do not suggest that all wars that involve democracies derive from political failings within the democratic process, nor do we claim that the expressive nature of popular voting is the only relevant political failing. We rather want to show that there is good reason to be wary of this particular form of political failure and to take out some institutional insurance. In this sense our argument may be seen as belonging to the tradition of identifying checks and balances within a political structure. Just as the separation of powers might, under certain circumstances, provide valuable checks on the powers of individual political agents, so might a supranational European confederation of a type that is not too directly democratic provide a valuable check on the operation of democracy at the national level.

In drawing to a close, we want to return briefly to two issues. The first is the question of whether reduction of the probability of war within the Union might simply shift the threat to another level. We doubt this. Much of the work that is being done to institutionalize peace in the European Union is being done by dividing and separating powers, and in particular, by separating military authority from arenas where political competition excites certain expressive or symbolic passions. It is not simply that a militarily strong Europe will counterbalance the warring tendencies of individual European nations. If this were all that was going on, we would agree that there might be a increased threat of external wars. But even that would only be attempted if political processes at the European level generate the same expressive and symbolic pressures as they do at national levels. In other words, if both military decisions and expressive/symbolic identification are shifted to the European level, then we might expect to reduce the threat of internal wars but increase the threat of external wars. Now, if we can rub out the connection between military decision-making and expressive/symbolic identification, the risk of war might be reduced overall.

A final issue we raise relates to the popular desire for autonomy. It is a commonplace to observe that the first call of a self-identified group within a larger polity is often for autonomy or self-determination. At the extreme, this amounts to a claim of secession. Moves to autonomous substates might be seen as the opposite of the confederation process with which we have been concerned. The point is that the political appeal of autonomy may be another example of the expressive/symbolic nature of political behavior, but it does lead to a fragmentation of states by secession or partition that might be associated with the risk of war. However, autonomy is a quality that can be accommodated by an appropriate federal structure.[15] The peace-enhancing properties of bottom-up federalism that we have discussed in the European context might also be available to top-down federalism of the sort that might be applicable in circumstances such as those seen in the former Yugoslavia. However, the necessary institutional structures must be put in place. Federalism alone is not enough.

Notes

Our thanks to Marko Köthenbürger, CESifo conference participants, and two referees for helpful comments.

1. Many think it is a mercantilist myth that the case for freer trade depends on countries matching the efforts of each other. Most of the benefits of liberal trade policy accrue to the country that initiates the policy; hardly any go to that country's trading partners. Put another way, tariffs are essentially redistributions within a given polity, and not between that polity and others.

2. See *http://european-convention.eu.int*.

3. See CONV 528/03 Annex 1 Article 3, paragraph 1.

4. Bueno de Mesquita (1980, 1981) presents a model of this general type in which states act as if they are individually rational agents. Decision-making then hinges on attitudes toward risk rather than a particular game structure. For critical discussion, see Majeski and Sylvan (1984).

5. The evidence and a range of explanations are reviewed by Geller and Singer (1998).

6. To explore the opinion poll analogy a bit more, studies of behavior in certain circumstances imply nothing for behavior in other circumstances. We believe, however, that opinion polls are likely to yield quite accurate results precisely because voting and opinions are both essentially expressive activities. Questions about purchasing behavior or about changes in one's pattern of consumption if prices change are likely to produce less reliable results. Then there are questions that have some moral significance where the answers are likely to be downright misleading. The use of questionnaires to estimate alcohol consumption, or the extent of tax evasion, or domestic violence is unreliable for precisely this reason. Societal attitudes toward the activity intervene to give respondents an incentive to misrepresent their practices. Wherever practice and values part, questionnaire results are likely to reveal more about values than they do about practice, even though practice is the subject of the inquiry.

7. The tension between the expressive and instrumental voting also applies to the question of strategic voting. The standard argument supporting strategic voting is instrumental: it relies on the individual voter's ability to see through the structure of the game and take sophisticated decisions that influence the outcome. Persson and Tabellini (1992) argue that voters may vote strategically to ensure that an outcome reflects their preferences even when the policy process is somewhat independent of electoral pressures. However, this line of argument is less forceful in a setting where instrumental voting is not assumed to be the general rule.

8. Not all instances where symbolic and instrumental considerations diverge involve political failure. They may even be instances of emphatic political success. The veil of ignorance familiar from the work of Rawls and Buchanan often commends itself because the "preferences" to which it gives rise are less "distorted" by (excessive) self-interest. The veil of insignificance characteristic of large-number collective action has this same feature: the weight of rational self-interest is radically diminished, narrow selfishness is moderated, and voters are free to entertain great dreams. Not all of their desires will be disasters in the making. But nothing in the exercise of collective choice can ensure that we avoid the disasters in the making.

9. A similar point is made by Hechter (2000) who points to decentralized decision-making in multinational states as a means of reducing the demand for nationalism. He

suggests that too little decentralization tends to incite rebellion against the center and that too much decentralization tends to fragment the state.

10. As might other institutional arrangements. One possibility here is a functional overlapping competing jurisdictions (FOCJ) structure, as advocated by Bruno Frey and others (see Frey and Eichenberger 1999). Overlapping jurisdictions can reduce the correlation between jurisdictional boundaries and symbolic communities, while the functional nature of jurisdictions can "cool" politics by shifting attention to more practical issues.

11. For a somewhat related discussion of the institutional means of mitigating ethnic conflict, see Grofman and Stockwell (2000).

12. Eleven of the current European member states are also members of NATO. Among the set of EU candidate countries, four are members of NATO and others are in the process of joining.

13. Of course, it is a matter of balancing expressive identification at national and European levels. Too strong a European identity can also cause problems. At the moment, however, it appears to us that the appropriate balance is more Europeanism and less nationalism.

14. The full quote is "war is not merely a political act but a real political instrument, a continuation of political intercourse, a carrying out of the same by other means" (Clausewitz [1837] 2000, p. 280).

15. Increased pressure for secession may be one price paid for institutional reforms of the type advocated here. A type of equilibrium may emerge between the extremes of self-determining nations at high risk of war and a fully coordinated super state at high risk of civil war in support of claims of secession.

References

Alesina, A., I. Angeloni, and L. Schuknecht. 2001. What does the European Union do? Working paper 8647. NBER, Cambridge, MA.

Brennan, G., and A. Hamlin. 1998. Expressive voting and electoral equilibrium. *Public Choice* 95: 149–75.

Brennan, G., and A. Hamlin. 1999. On political representation. *British Journal of Political Science* 29: 109–27.

Brennan, G., and A. Hamlin. 2000a. Nationalism and Federalism: The Political Constitution of Peace. In G. Galeotti, P. Salmon, and R. Wintrobe (eds.): *Competition and Structure: The Political Economy of Collective Decisions*. Cambridge: Cambridge University Press.

Brennan, G., and A. Hamlin. 2000b. *Democratic Devices and Desires*. Cambridge: Cambridge University Press.

Brennan, G., and L. Lomasky. 1993. Democracy and Decision. Cambridge: Cambridge University Press.

Bueno de Mesquita, B. 1980. An expected utility theory of international conflict. *American Political Science Review* 74(4): 917–31.

Bueno de Mesquita, B. 1981. *The War Trap*. New Haven: Yale University Press.

Bueno de Mesquita, B., and R. M. Siverson. 1995. War and the survival of political leaders. *American Political Science Review* 89(4): 841–55.

Bueno de Mesquita, B., J. D. Morrow, R. M. Siverson, and A. Smith. 1999. An institutional explanation of the democratic peace. *American Political Science Review* 93(4): 791–807.

Clausewitz, K. von. [1837] 2000. *On War, Reprinted in The Book of War*. New York: Modern Library.

Frey, B. S., and R. Eichenberger. 1999. *The New Democratic Federalism for Europe*. Cheltenham: Edward Elgar.

Geller, D. S., and J. D. Singer. 1998. *Nations at War: A Scientific Study of International Conflict*. Cambridge: Cambridge University Press.

Grofman, B., and R. Stockwell. 2000. Institutional design in plural societies: Mitigating ethnic conflict and fostering stable democracy. Mimeo. University of California, Irvine.

Hechter, M. 2000. *Containing Nationalism*. Oxford: Oxford University Press.

Hess, G., and A. Orphanides. 1995. War politics: An economic rational-voter framework. *American Economic Review* 85(4): 828–46.

Hess, G., and A. Orphanides. 2001. War and democracy. *Journal of Political Economy* 109(4): 776–810.

Kant, I. 1939. *Perpetual Peace*. New York: Columbia University Press.

Majeski, S. J., and D. J. Sylvan. 1984. Simple choices and complex calculations: A critique of the war trap. *Journal of Conflict Resolution* 28: 316–40.

Mueller, D. 1996. Constitutional quandaries in Europe. *Constitutional Political Economy* 7(4): 293–302.

Persson, T., and G. Tabellini. 1992. The politics of 1992: Fiscal policy and European integration. *Review of Economic Studies* 59: 689–701.

Tabellini, G. 2002. Principles of policymaking in the European Union: An economic perspective. *CESifo Forum* 3(2): 16–22.

Tocqueville, A. de [1835] 1945. *Democracy in America*, transl. by H. Reeve. New York: Vintage Books.

Working Group VIII of the European Convention. 2002. *Final Report: Defence*. CONV 461/02. Brussels: Secretariat of the European Convention.

2 Competitive Federalism by Default

James M. Buchanan

2.1 Introduction

In February 1990, I presented a lecture at a Paris conference under the title "Europe's Constitutional Opportunity." I suggested that the time was ripe for the Europeanization that was already in progress to be directed toward the organization of a genuine competitive federalism, with a strong, but quite limited, central authority, and with the competing nation-state regulatory regimes all operating within an enforced open and integrated economy. I soon realized that my argument was quite naive; I had, simplistically, assumed that the unexpected demise of Marxist socialism, both in idea and in practice, would have substantially reduced the *dirigiste* thrust toward Europe-wide regularization-harmonization primarily stemming from the Brussels bureaucracy. The reaction, however, was such as to suggest that the events of 1989 had little if any effects on attitudes concerning the ultimate organization of Europe.

I was even more surprised, however, by the reaction from the right, as it were, from the vehement criticism from those who were unwilling to countenance any cession of national sovereignty at all, and who, literally, were angered at even so much as the word "federalism." These advocates, centered at that time in what was called the "Bruges group," later to be joined by Mrs. Thatcher, were dominated by spokespersons from the United Kingdom, although the membership was not exclusively British.

It soon became evident that there was little mileage, politically, in the idea of "competitive federalism," as such and that the discussion was reflective of ivory-tower theorizing about ideal types with little or no prospect of securing so much as passing reference in ongoing political discourse. Aside from some support by the European

Constitutional Group, itself staffed by academic economists, there was no attention to, and consequently no understanding of, competitive federalism as an organizational ideal for the structure of Europe that might be brought into reality.

There was no interest group, either in actual or potential existence, that could be brought to promote the organizational structure of competitive federalism as an objective for constitutional construction and change. And the observed strengths of the opposing forces in support of centralized European authority, on the one hand, and undiminished national autonomy, on the other, ensured that the academic-scientific ideal could scarcely get a respectable hearing, much less general acceptance.

The academicians who held up the idea of an effective competitive federalism, as that structure of European governance that would, indeed, be most conducive to the general prosperity of the peoples, along with the preservation of their liberties, seemed to be left outside any politically relevant dialogues. It is not surprising that the academicians, myself included among them, were frustrated.

2.2 The Constitution as an Emergent Structure

Our frustration should have been tempered, however, had we recognized that outcomes in politics, as in markets, *emerge* from a configuration of interdependent forces, rather than from a definitive selection from a choice set confronted by a unitary decision-taker. And, importantly, this emergent character is descriptive of the generation of outcomes defined in terms of structural-organizational parameters as well as the more familiar policy outcomes generated within the limits of established institutions. We can, with benefit, take a leaf from the Hayekian gospel here, and apply an evolutionary perspective, of a sort, to the European setting. We can, however, go beyond the Hayekian stance of acquiescence and make an effort to understand and to predict the pattern of emergent results, at least within broad limits.

This approach is helpful in evaluating the European constitution, both in retrospect and prospect, from our vantage point in 2003. For more than two decades, we have observed the activities of the conflicting interests in the establishment and operation of the European community. It seems evident that the ultimate constitution for Europe has not been and will not be "constructed" from design, nor even from some explicit multidimensional compromise among competing designs. The set of institutions, organizational forms, rules, practices, and conventions that may eventually come to be called constitutional will, instead, emerge from the ongoing processes of interaction among quite separate forces, each one of which possesses some independent authority to influence the pattern of development. The necessarily emergent character or attribute stems from the elementary fact of interdependence among the actions taken by the separate forces, each one of which may, in itself, reflect some amalgam of subsidiary, and related, interests. None of the elements in the whole nexus of interaction here can be properly modeled as if choices are made among stylized constitutional structures that are simply not within the relevant choice sets of anyone.

Note, in particular, that the emergent property of that which will become the effective constitution may, but need not be, referenced in evolutionary terminology. There is considerable confusion in some of the discussion on this score. Institutions may, of course, evolve over the course of history, and survivability may be a possible test of functional efficacy. But it is misleading to conflate evolution and interdependence as causal sources of emergence.

I have referred to separate but interdependent "forces," each of which may somehow be modeled as if it chooses among its separately confronted options and, in consequence, generating results that are derivative from the intersection of choices severally made rather than from any monolithic decision structure or rule. To model these forces as choosers is questionable (more on this point below), and even at the level of abstraction in this chapter, to stylize the analysis by reducing the number of forces to two is open to challenge. Nonetheless, I shall proceed.

2.3 The Emergent Constitution as the Outcome of a Dynamic Two-Player Game

Consider only two sets of forces, each one of which does have some influence in shaping the structure of the European constitution. First, there are the forces of centralization, associated with Brussels-led bureaucratic *dirigisme*, along with intra-Europe pressures toward centralization. These forces act as if the aim is to regularize and harmonize the historically separated national economies into a wholly integrated European nexus, with little or no national differentiation, as such. If this set of forces should secure monolithic dominance, any effective competitiveness among the several nation-states along relevant collectively determined dimensions would be eliminated. Such a scenario does not seem to be descriptive, however, despite the apparent success of these forces in the Maastricht Treaty.

Second, and in opposition, is that set of forces reflecting residual nationalisms. The aim seems to be the maintenance of full political sovereignty in the existing pre-community nation-states, with only voluntary submission to Europe-wide regulatory norms. In the unlikely event that this set of forces should secure dominance, the European constitution would embody relatively little predictability as regards permanent structures for integration. An upside scenario would describe genuine competition among national regimes in an open free-trade area, with predicted efficiency-enhancing results. The downside scenario would describe economic nationalism at its worst, with the 1930s offering the historical parallel.

My point of emphasis here is that *both* sets of forces possess, and will continue to possess, independent authority to influence the course of events from which the European political-regulatory structure of the new century will emerge. Neither of the two opposing forces will be sovereign in the sense that their influence will exclusively determine the pattern of institutions that will be generated. This pattern will reflect characteristic features of the interdependence in the dynamic historical setting.[1]

It is difficult to use familiar analytical metaphors in discussing the reality of the emergent European constitution, inclusively defined as the whole set of operative institutional arrangements that will develop. The two opposing forces or pressures noted, those of centralization and national autonomy, suggest that a two-party game setting might be useful—a setting within which each party or player pursues its own objective in partial conflict with that of the other but in which both parties find it advantageous to remain in the game. Neither party chooses to exercise an exit option.

This metaphor may yield some insight here, but it remains flawed by the absence of monolithic "players" on either side of the interaction—players whose choices among options might be modeled by familiar precepts of rationality. In fact there is no "chooser," as such, on either side of the account here. Nor is there even a team in any meaningful sense. The strategic choice, or so it might be described, will be emergent from an interplay of separated subinterests, all of which may, for present purposes, be subsumed under or incorporated into the single "player." It is as if we need a multi-level game setting, in which pico-players interact so as to generate an emergent strategy choice, which then becomes an input into the more inclusive game from which a final result emerges.

This conceptualization, in turn, has implications for prospects for any shift from the emergent Nash-like equilibrium, even should this position exhibit properties that indicate its relative inefficiency when assessed against criteria defined for either "player" or even by outside observers. There is no institutional means through which binding agreements might be made because there is neither unity nor permanence on the part of either "player."

2.4 A Competitive Federalism

The emergent constitution of Europe will be described neither as a unitary state nor as a set of autonomous national polities linked in a free-trade nexus. The structure will necessarily be federal in nature, with a division of political authority between a central Europe-wide set of institutions and the nation-states. And, to the extent that this structure is genuinely federal, it becomes almost redundant to append the word "competitive" as a descriptive adjective. The dimensions along which the nation-states will effectively compete, one with another, will depend on the emergent institutional structure as well as upon the more or less "natural" extent of socioeconomic interaction, with the latter in part determined by technological developments. The shoe-shines offered for sale in Turkey (as a potential member state) would scarcely be competitive with those in Finland, even in the total absence of any Europe-wide regulation. On the other hand, modern access to television does allow potential customers in Finland to see, and therefore to wonder at, the shoe-shine stands in Istanbul. If, perchance, differing localized regulatory regimes in the separate nation-states should create obvious differences in comparative inefficiencies, the strictly localized nature of the activities involved need not remove the influence of among-state competition.

In the ordinary working of markets, as analyzed by economists, competition is an efficiency-enhancing feature. Effective competition implies that potential freedom of entry into economic activity will forestall, or at least limit severely, the possible exploitation of buyers by monopoly producers-sellers or of sellers by monopsony buyers-users. Buyers and sellers are confronted by multiple options among which they choose. It is clear that the "competition" among separated nation-states in a federal structure is of a different sort from that idealized by economists in application to ordinary markets. The "sellers" of regulatory services are the collective agencies of the national polities. And it is not easy to think about prospects for shifting among sellers, in part at least because of the publicness features of the services. We could scarcely think of the users-consumers of educational services in Denmark being able to shift their "purchases" to suppliers from Norway, even should they feel exploited.

The competition must be less direct than that modeled in idealized market structures. If a member state should, for example, impose efficiency-reducing regulations on a market or provide collective services in a resource-wasting manner, the results will show up, first of all, in the comparisons reported in the league tables—comparisons that have become much more sophisticated and more widely disseminated with modern technological improvements. Second, the analogue to the market will emerge through the reduction in investment by foreigners in the local economy and by the shift of local investments to other economies. Further shifts will involve outmigration of some parts of the labor force. Working through these indirect means, competition among the separate units in an integrated federal structure will ensure that collectively imposed regulations at the local level will be forced to remain tolerably efficient, and further that the services collectively provided at this level will be organized efficiently, again within limits.

The indirect competition among the member states *within* the federal structure along the dimensions of adjustment under member-state authority will protect citizens in two different respects. First, the openness of the Europe-wide economy in terms of flows of both goods and resources will ensure against major efficiency-reducing policies in any member state. Citizens will be more fully protected against the excesses of their own dominant political coalitions. Much of the discussion fails to incorporate the recognition that the interests of citizens within any state are not monolithic. Second, citizens throughout Europe will be protected against exploitation by dominant coalitions among member states that, under a unitary authority, would impose Europe-wide regulations designed to benefit some national interests differentially at the expense of Europeans generally.

In a careful and otherwise well-balanced analysis of some of the issues here, Guido Tabellini (2002) seems to neglect the possible efficacy of competition among the separate political units within the single-market nexus. He stresses the danger that these separate units might embark on discriminatory protectionist policies if they are allowed too much independent regulatory authority. My own sense is that while localized interest groups will continue to exert pressures for such actions, these will be countered to an extent by the constraints of the single market itself, including, as noted, the availability of information on comparative national performance.

2.5 Dr. Pangloss, I Presume

A secondary purpose of this chapter is to suggest that the European constitution that will emerge, warts and all, need not be evaluated primarily in the negative. Despite its failure to meet the standards of either the Brussels bureaucracy, the Europe-wide cartelizers, the little Englanders, or the academicians, the structure that seems most likely to emerge may satisfy the minimax criterion that can be usefully borrowed from game theory. The worst possible scenarios, from the perspectives of either of the two opposing forces, will be avoided. Europe-wide domination by a powerful central authority with little residual localized controls—this worst case result as feared by the nationalists is highly improbable, if for no other reason than the influence of the separate historical traditions of the member units. It is perhaps equally improbable that the emergent structure will describe a Europe of nation-states with separate powers akin to those available prior to World War II. For this worst case scenario as feared by the pan-Europeans to occur, the whole half-century shift in public attitudes toward Europe as a meaningful unity would have somehow to be erased.

To suggest that the emergent structure may satisfy the maximin criterion for parties on both sides of the constitutional game is persuasive. But to go further and suggest that the structure may also meet the criteria for efficiency in some broad Paretian sense may, at first glance, seem more controversial. This additional attribute of the emergent structure, however, simply stems from the recognition that, as modeled here, the two "players" in the game are strictly opposed, one to another, in their interests. It is as if the game is necessarily zero-sum, or, geometrically, that there is only one dimension of adjustment. In this setting any outcome meets the Paretian criterion for efficiency.

Note that the position outlined here is not subject to the charge that the claim for efficiency is necessarily circular in that I am defining that which emerges as being efficient simply because it emerges. It is the opposition of the two conflicting forces in the game as herein modeled that allows me to advance the efficiency claim. By contrast, in a setting where there exist both conflictual and cooperative elements, that which emerges from separated actions need not be efficient. Witness the familiar PD as the classic example.

Although somewhat peripheral to the specific discussion of the European constitution, the analytical point here is of some significance. If the abstract model includes possible adjustments only along a unidimensional spectrum (centralization versus decentralization of regulatory authority), *any* emergent solution is, by definition, Pareto efficient, given the presupposition that the two interacting "parties" are both within the limits of their bliss positions. The Pareto criterion for efficiency is almost meaningless in this setting, which is analogous to a purely distributional game. If, however, a second dimension of possible adjustment is somehow introduced, and if preference orderings of the two "parties" are interdependent at all over the two dimensions, explicit efficiency-enhancing changes may be identified by external observers, even if the latter remain unwilling to impose their own evaluations.

More or less as a side point, note that the attribution of "efficiency" (or "fairness" or "justice") to that which emerges in an interdependent interaction is conceptually different from that which is explicitly agreed upon, as normally analyzed in constructions in contractarian political philosophy. In the latter, explicit agreement on a rule or institution becomes itself the criterion for labeling the rule, so chosen, to be "efficient" (or "fair" or "just"). In the setting under examination here the two parties, as modeled, do not agree on any element of the structure or on its totality. Instead, this structure emerges because each of the parties, or forces, has independent ability to influence the solution. It is therefore possible (as in the classic PD) that if the separated choice setting could be explicitly changed into a collective or joint decision exercise (via a genuine constitutional convention) with binding enforceability, agreement could be reached to modify adjustments along the several relevant dimensions and to attain a solution more desirable for all parties (the criterion for Pareto superiority).[2]

In the European political environment, as noted, there are two barriers to this avenue for reform. First, the basic interaction seems uni- rather than multidimensional, and, second, there is no prospect for ensuring binding enforcement of agreements once made.

My argument is, of course and as noted, subject to the more general methodological criticism that my ultimate definition of efficiency rests on the evaluations, as revealed in actions, of the interacting parties rather than on those of some external and presumably omniscient observer. But where is the analyst-observer who can assign objective trade-offs between the acknowledged values of markets uniformly regulated under generally motivated authority and the protection against differentially motivated but nominally uniform regulation? How can objective values be assigned to the limits on exploitation that only competition can ensure? And how can these values be offset against the discriminatory actions that competition itself will allow? Until and unless such questions as these and others can be answered, there seems to be simply no basis for resorting to efficiency criteria other than those revealed by interactive behavior.

I should stress that the "efficiency" referenced here is that which applies to the structure of institutions that will emerge dynamically from the ongoing "game" between the two opposing forces. Regardless of the demarcation lines between the authority of the central government and the separate member states, the particularized pattern of results will be predicted to include instances of gross departures from allocative efficiency norms of the more familiar sort. The central authority will surely extend its regulatory umbrella beyond efficiency limits in the interest of dominant coalitions in the decision-making process, thereby choking off avenues for economic growth. And the separate national units will, within the limits of their assigned and evolved regulatory jurisdictions, impose discriminatory protectionist policies that destroy potential value. Economists, in their properly functioning roles, can point out such departures from the standard norms for allocative efficiency, no doubt with some, if restricted, success in securing changes. But the presence of such inefficiencies, as generated through both the central government and the separate member units, need not be indicative of any "inefficiency" of the constitutional structure itself. At issue here is the question as to what constitutional structure will *minimize*, not eliminate, aggregate allocational distortions. Neither the central political unit, or units, nor the separated members can be predicted to meet allocative norms as laid down by economists; each political unit will act as interest group pressures are reconciled within its own decision structure.

There are, of course, feedbacks between departures from allocative efficiency norms and the efficiency of the constitutional structure.

Mistakes can be made at all levels of consideration and policy implementation. For example, an overcentralization of authority that might produce excessive regularization over all of the market territory would soon feed back on public consciousness through observed reductions in rates of growth. Or, contrariwise, devolution-retention of too much authority in member states might threaten the values of market integration through observed retrogression. My argument is that such mistakes in constitutional assignments will tend to be corrected by the ongoing interplay of the opposing forces that will describe the Europe of this century.

2.6 Conclusion

More than a century ago Knut Wicksell (1896) warned his fellow economists against discussing policy reforms as if they were proffering advice to a benevolent despot, an entity that is both able to implement changes and willing to base those changes on the advice so proffered. Those of us who have, in past decades, advanced arguments in support of an idealized competitive federal structure for Europe might be properly chastised on similar grounds. We have not faced up to the question as to whom is to be expected to put in place the structure that we recommend. The effective constitution for the Europe of this century will not be "laid on" by any monolithic decision maker, or even by some explicitly constructed special assembly operating under well-defined rules. As has often been noted, there will be nothing analogous to the America of 1787, and there is no European James Madison waiting in the wings.

In contrast with the within-Sweden setting that Wicksell confronted, where he could, indeed, predict how changes in parliamentary decision rules might generate patterns of results favorable to all parties, it does not seem possible to change the metaconstitution from that which the effective constitution for Europe must finally emerge. The conflicting forces, those that exert continuing pressures toward centralization of authority, on the one hand, and those that exert pressures toward decentralization and localized autonomy, on the other, cannot be reconciled in some all-inclusive constitutional "bargain" that would be binding. There is, first of all, no second dimension that might make compromise possible. Second, even were such a dimension present, neither "player" is in itself sufficiently organized to allow commitments to be made. Who could possibly represent the ongoing generations of Brussels bureaucrats and their cartelizing fellow travelers so as to guarantee their continued adherence to constraints that counter their own current interests? And who could represent the ongoing generations of national politicians and guarantee prevention of their response to local exigencies, regardless of a larger European purpose?

The secondary aim of this chapter is to suggest that those of us who have argued in support of an effective competitive federal structure for the European polity should not despair. We should recognize that political organization—the constitution as it were—that must emerge from the processes of dynamic interaction between the two forces noted will have at least some of the properties of the idealized structure. The separated nation-states of Europe are not likely to shed off their histories of national autonomy and jump in, naked as it were, into a unitary monolith that remains in the process of being created. A new structure, Europe as an entity, has already come to have an independent existence that involves the command of personal loyalties. Over a long period, of course, the European Leviathan may well become a dominant and dangerous force.

The century promises to be analytically as well as practically interesting, and perhaps not nearly so chaotic, politically, as might have been feared. And, finally, the integrated European economy may well prove to be more efficient than some naysayers have predicted.

Notes

1. For a comprehensive argument to the effect that constitutions generally emerge from game-like interactions among competitive forces, see Voigt (1999).

2. Given its membership structure, it seems highly unlikely that the d'Estaing council in being (2003) can serve this purpose.

References

Buchanan, J. M. 1990. Europe's constitutional opportunity. In *Europe's Constitutional Future*. London: Institute of Economic Affairs, pp. 1–20.

Tabellini, G. 2002. Principles of policymaking in the European Union: An economic perspective. In H.-W. Sinn (ed.), *Europe after Enlargement*. Munich: CESifo Forum, pp. 16–22.

Voigt, S. 1999. *Explaining Constitutional Change: A Positive Economics Approach*. Cheltenham, UK: Edward Elgar.

Wicksell, K. 1896. *Finanztheoretische Untersuchungen*. Jena: Gustav Fischer.

3 The Assignment of Powers in an Open-Ended European Union

Pierre Salmon

3.1 Introduction

A major characteristic of the European Union is its evolving or transitional nature. This can be observed along at least three dimensions: in the way European institutions make decisions, in the size of the membership, and in the role played by the EU institutions within the overall governmental system of the part of Europe they cover. To the public, the last dimension is certainly the main one. EU institutions have progressively become central in an increased number of policy domains. In addition to international trade and agriculture, they have acquired a dominant influence over regulation, competition, and money. Other domains, such as internal security and immigration, may follow in the near future. Growth in the role and importance of Brussels (understood broadly so as to include Frankfurt, Luxembourg, and Strasbourg) is certainly the main perceived factor underlying the widespread perception that European integration is an ongoing process rather than a state, or the European Union is under construction rather than merely incomplete or unachieved.

Of course, if one turns to the question "transition to—or construction of—what?" things become more controversial. There is no agreed or even, perhaps, lucidly firm answer to that question. The European Union may well become a sovereign state—and, if so, of a federal type—but it may also stabilize as some completely unprecedented (e.g., postnational) form of political organization. Many interrelated things or events can deviate the process in the one or the other direction, or, for that matter, directions currently unforeseen, such as collapse. In the language of modern theory, European integration, like some other institutional transformations or transitions of comparable magnitude, is subject to strong "aggregate uncertainty" (Roland 2000).

This, together with the absence of consensus on ultimate objectives, gives its evolving or evolutionary nature the specific characteristic of being very open-ended.

To what extent is the apparently ambitious idea of "a constitution for Europe" compatible with the perspective just recalled? Much depends on what is expected from that "constitution"—on the extent to which it is seen as qualitatively different from the constitutional or quasi-constitutional rules that already govern EU institutions. In the next section, I will consider some of these expectations and argue that the ideas of the transitional and open-ended nature of the European Union, on the one hand, and of "a constitution for Europe" to be agreed on in an explicit way, on the other hand, are neither contradictory nor immediately harmonious or consonant.

A way to make them work together is to focus on the aspects of constitutional or quasi-constitutional provisions responsible for shaping or constraining evolution. If the question is what change in the constitutional setup may be brought about by an explicit constitution for the European Union, the particular perspective stressed above suggests that we should pay some attention to the question of how any contemplated constitutional changes (e.g., an increase in the role of the European Parliament, or of majority-voting in the Council of Ministers) might affect the said shaping or constraining. This chapter does not directly address that question, but it purports to contribute to it in a preparatory way by analyzing some important consequences of present arrangements on the shape of the integration process. The most crucial consequence, probably, is monotonocity or irreversibility: the present setup makes the integration process run in a monotonous direction—allowing it, or often causing it, to stall, but only with great difficulty to be reversed.

The elements of the present constitution that produce that result are considered, under somewhat extreme assumptions, in section 3.3, which shows the crucial importance of reversals. Section 3.4, focused on position-trading, offers a more balanced or realistic view of constitutional constraints on reversals. It is argued in that section that even under these more realistic assumptions, the existing constitutional arrangements do make reversals very difficult, and in that sense favor the status quo. By favoring the status quo, however, they also constrain the possibility of moving ahead, as analysed in section 3.5. The integration process thus appears as an instance of the gradualist approach to large changes or transitions, an emerging theoretical domain whose importance is well illustrated by Roland (2000). But it is a very particular form of gradualism, as argued in section 3.6.[1]

My analysis does not reflect personal preferences with regard to the pace of integration or lead to a particular normative or prescriptive position with regard to constitution-making at the EU level. As explained in the concluding section, this does not mean, however, that it is devoid of any operational significance. The analysis suggests a relatively precise criterion—angle, indicator, perspective, dimension, and so on—to be selected, together with other considerations, and whatever one's preferences or opinions about integration, for the purpose of judging or, simply, reading proposed constitutional or quasi-constitutional innovations.

3.2 Constitution-Making and the Evolving Nature of the European Union

What is expected from the present and forthcoming phases of constitutional activity? At the pro-European end of the spectrum of positions about European integration, many traditional federalists think or hope that such phases signal that the time has come for the constitutional creation of a federal state. Federal systems are compatible with many kinds of arrangements, in particular a high degree of decentralization, and the experience of existing decentralized federations is important when thinking about the European Union (Kirchgässner and Pommerehne 1996; Schneider 1996; McKay 2000; Salmon 2002). Also, as experience shows, the degree of centralization typically evolves or fluctuates quite a bit in the course of time (Breton 1996; Winer 2000).[2] Thus a federal constitution for Europe would certainly allow some kind of subsequent evolution. Still this would take place within the limits of the defining characteristics of federal states, and this requirement is not innocuous. Two features of federations may prove particularly constraining. Even if very decentralized, the new federation would become a state. It seems difficult that such characteristic does not imply acting in a unitary way in domains such as defense and foreign affairs. Even more significantly perhaps, by the way of their participation in federal elections and referenda, voters making up a majority of the population of the federation would be entitled to impose their views unilaterally against unwilling minorities in some important areas (e.g., taxation) and the minorities would have to acquiesce. As many federalists are well aware, given the present array of opinions in Europe a constitutional outcome of that kind is plausible only under an increased fragmentation of the EU membership, with the United Kingdom and some other member countries keeping out of federal ties for an undetermined period.

Now fragmentation may be interpreted in such a way that it provides a second means (the first, mentioned above, being evolution within the limits of federalism) to reconcile the immediate establishment of a federal state with the evolutionary and open-ended nature of the European Union. For that purpose a new constitution allowing deeper integration among a subset of countries could be interpreted as a way to deal with aggregate uncertainty, along a line similar (but not identical) to that suggested by Dewatripont et al. (1995).[3] Federal arrangements would be tried by some and, if successful, others could join (or secede completely). It seems natural also (although deceptively so, as we will see) that if the arrangements were deemed unsuccessful, a reversal could take place with a return to something like the status quo, entailing restored homogeneity. One must admit, however, that joining a federation or seceding from it are moves that suggest discontinuity rather than gradualism. Also, giving a crucial role to the possibility of reversals seems quite foreign, as we will see, to the particular form that evolution takes in the European Union. For these reasons as well for others familiar to the historians of ideas about European integration, the evolutionist and the federalist perspectives are mutually compatible only to some point.

Situated on the other side of the spectrum, a second view is that of the relatively moderate eurosceptics who see in a constitution for Europe above all a way to block further integration, or even, perhaps, to obtain reversals in some areas.[4] Many politicians and probably voters, not only in Britain, fall into that category. It seems a logical implication of that position that the constitutional and the evolutionary perspectives are essentially incompatible.

There are many economists and especially public choice economists whose writings make them seem close to euroscepticism. In reality their position is generally different. It can be broken up into three views. First, they do not mind, or even they favor the process of integration accelerating in noneconomic areas. In this, their position is not so far from that of the federalists. Second, they fully support the integration of markets, including the elimination of all impediments to trade and distortions of competition. Third, they would like the constitution to block centralizing tendencies with regard to public finance and to economic and social policies other than those required for the implementation of the single market. This three-pronged position leads to a view of "a constitution for Europe" that makes it also largely incompatible with the transition interpretation of the European Union. According to these economists' views, the main responsibility in domains such as foreign affairs, defense, and market integration could or should be assigned to the EU level.[5] The trend toward an ever-increased involvement of the EU level with the other policies, and its consequences with regard to finance and personnel, should be suppressed. This tends to give the recommendations a connotation of static equilibrium that renders them, if not incompatible, at least dissonant with that attached to institutional evolution.

In the middle (to speak loosely), whatever their own preferences, most actors and commentators expect a constitution for Europe to embody a compromise that will remain valid for some limited period of time and will change a little but not radically the hybrid nature of the European Union. This view is quite realistic. More important for our purpose, it implies no denial of the evolutionary nature of the European Union. The future constitution, if it comes into existence, is widely perceived as one step, important perhaps but not final. The other feature, open-endedness, is another matter, however. Analyses fully conscious of the evolving and transitional character of the institutional setup suggest nonetheless relatively precise or detailed types of constitutional arrangements. This is a perfectly natural and even fruitful attitude, especially in the context of ongoing constitutional debates. However, inasmuch as it leads to suggestions that do constrain or shape future solutions in an identified way, it does signal some departure from perspectives that have the characteristic of putting open-endedness at center stage.[6]

3.3 The Constitutional Entrenchment of a Goal-Oriented Evolution

How do the current arrangements support the evolutionary nature of the European Union? In this section, I assume that the issues are dealt with separately, without any attempt to link them for the purpose of bargaining. The three main ingredients of entrenchment are the definition of the goal or European integration as "ever-closer union," the *acquis communautaire* principle, and unanimous decision-making in the Councils.

The Objective of an Ever-closer Union

All the member states have solemnly pledged to "construct Europe." In the preamble of the Treaty of Rome, they express this commitment by asserting that they are "determined to lay the foundations of an ever-closer union among the peoples of Europe." Thirty-six years later, in the preamble of the Treaty of Maastricht, the member states, including this time the United Kingdom, declare themselves to be "resolved to continue the process of creating an ever closer union among the peoples of Europe." The fact that this is immediately followed by the phrase "in which decisions are taken as closely as possible to the citizen in accordance with the principle of subsidiarity" is a welcome but minor qualification.

Different interpretations of this commitment have been proposed. One of them reduces it to little more than an obligation to support exchanges of ideas or persons across Europe. It can also be claimed that since ideas, circumstances, and majorities change over time, this type of government commitments can only be weak (even if ratified in the name of the people). All this may be true, but it remains that those who pretend to adopt a diminishing interpretation seem nonetheless upset by the formulation used in the treaties and fight for its elimination from the future documents. This suggests that the minimalist interpretation lacks empirical support. The more generally agreed view is that by the pledge to foster an ever closer union, the member states have committed to reinforce over the years the decision-making capacity of the European institutions.[7]

The centralizing tendencies of the Commission, of the European Court of Justice and of the European Parliament have been noted by a number of authors, typically critical of the phenomenon observed (Vaubel 1994). It is difficult to deny the existence of these tendencies, nor that they are generated by imperialistic motivations typical of most organizations. However, given their commitment to pursue the project of "constructing Europe," and the indirect way they thought this was to be done (I turn to that below), the creators or shapers of the European institutions necessarily had to entrust to these institutions a major role toward the realization of the project. As a rule, thus, the centralizing tendencies do not reflect an unwanted and unforeseen phenomenon of bureaucratic drift, nor consequences of institutional decisions made for completely different purposes. More plausibly they constitute an instrument designed or contrived to serve the member states' common project (Salmon 2003a).[8] Even if, as seems clear, some governments would have preferred otherwise, that is, no centralizing tendency to operate, the logic of their acquiescence to the project undermined their capacity to bring about the emergence of alternative structures generating no such tendency. This brings us to the second ingredient mentioned above.

Acquis communautaire

To borrow from Knud Erik Jørgensen the title of his very interesting article (1999), the *acquis communautaire* principle is "a cornerstone of the European edifice." It refers to all the obligations accumulated since the predecessors of the European Union (the European Community, of course, but also in some respects the European Coal and Steal Community of the early 1950s). There are two interpretations of the way in which the *acquis* operates. The less extensive one is related to the accession of new members. Applicant countries must accept to fulfill all of the obligations constituting the *acquis communautaire*. This is nonnegotiable. A delay for implementing some obligations is usually conceded, but besides that, there are only minor exceptions to the principle.

The *acquis communautaire* principle, endowed with a more extensive interpretation, is now endorsed by the Treaties, notably those of Maastricht and Amsterdam. The formulation implies that it is an objective of the European Union to integrally maintain the *acquis communautaire*.[9] I do not think that this is an enforceable commitment, and thus I stick to the less extensive status related to the accession of new members, which is enough for my purpose. As many other constitutional rules of the European Union, the *acquis* started in a somewhat inconspicuous fashion. It took the form of a contextual negotiation attitude adopted by the Commission and the six original members of the European Community to deal with the first candidacy of the United Kingdom—which would have much preferred to negotiate the rules and decisions it had to adapt to. That candidacy failed perhaps because of the condition. In 1969, on the initiative of the Commission, the principle was officially adopted by the six member countries as a condition imposed on the four applicants, Denmark, Ireland, Norway, and again, the United Kingdom. The condition remained in force in the following enlargements.

The accumulation of rules and decisions over several decades has led the size of the *acquis communautaire* to become really enormous.

But particularly interesting is the way the domain it covers has been enlarged. The "political objective of the Treaties" was in from the beginning. The main doctrines of European Law (direct effect, supremacy, etc.), as framed by the European Court of Justice, was imposed (albeit not completely formally then) at the last minute before the final step of the first enlargement. Democratic principles and human rights were included for the negotiation with Greece, Portugal, and Spain. Neutral countries such as Austria, Finland, and Sweden had to accept the Common Foreign and Security Policy, including its (admittedly somewhat abstract) implications on defense, because they were part of the Treaty of the European Union already in force when they applied. The *acquis communautaire* imposed in the accession treaties of 2003 includes "the principle of open market economy with free competition."[10]

Each accession treaty is a kind of contract, which means that new members have the legal and moral obligation to take on board a number of explicit principles, many of which started as much more informal and even tentative propositions and only later evolved to take their present form. In this process, what was initially meant to be a tentative constitutional interpretation may become the object of a formal recognition in an accession treaty and, as such, given an enhanced status by the European Court of Justice. Of course, once they are full members, the former applicants have the same rights as those enjoyed by older members. Consequently they can question or challenge what they want in existing arrangements—that is, in the *acquis communautaire*. The problem faced at this point, however, is the rule that would have to be used to decide a change.

Unanimous Decision-Making in the European Councils

The formal procedure to revise the EU constitution is unanimous agreement by the governments of the member countries followed by ratification in each country either by a vote in parliament or by a referendum. There are at least three reasons why we can neglect the ratification procedure and concentrate on the unanimous agreement between the governments. The main reason is that even if the need to get ratification is certainly an important concern in the minds of negotiators, it is normally fully integrated, together with other concerns, in their position, attitude, or strategy. The politicians involved here have been democratically chosen; they are supposed to represent the views of their constituents, and thus ratification is only a kind of confirmation that this supposition is correct. A ratification that fails reveals a mistake or is a small-probability event, in both cases not something very significant. Second, there are cases where ratification does take a particular importance, but this introduces considerations that, although interesting, are not our main concern here. Bruce Ackerman (1997) argues that there is something like a founding act in the narrowly positive referendum that served in France for the ratification of the Maastricht Treaty. Negative referenda, that is voters refusing to approve a Treaty signed by their representatives, as in the case of Norway, Denmark, and Ireland, also make up intriguing subjects, but their occurrence remains exceptional. Third, a very large number of decisions and rules can be changed only by unanimous consent of the member countries, even though the changes do not have to be ratified by the national parliaments or by the way or referendum. A large subset of these rules can be considered as constitutional or quasi-constitutional nonetheless.

In the next section I qualify the stringency ascribed to the effects of the rule of unanimity. But, for the moment, let us assume that the rule is applied in a way that makes it practically stringent, and neglect also large constitutional changes brought about by the major treaties. This allows the following story: clause A corresponds to the preferences of the founding six member countries. It is imposed on the next three member countries on the occasion of the first enlargement, on three more members on the occasion of the second and third enlargements, and again, on three new members on the occasion of the fourth enlargement. Let us stop here. The six founding members liked the clause and, we assume, still like it. The nine other members dislike it but have agreed to abide by it as long as it is not changed, thus in a weak sense have acquiesced to it (they did not dislike it to the point of giving up their application). In any case, they have to bear with it because changing would require also the consent of the six founding member countries, which, under the present assumptions, have no reason to award it. This story is not fully acceptable for reasons examined in the next section, but the path dependency it suggests is an important feature of reality. The organization of the European Union still reflects to some extent the arrangements agreed by the six in the 1950s and is thus still influenced by the goals and beliefs that they shared.

3.4 A More Realistic View of Constitutional Constraints on Reversal

The conditions under which decisions are made in the European Union, especially the decisions that have a constitutional or quasi-constitutional character, create a propitious ground for what Robert Cooter (2000) calls the "splicing of issues," that is, a mechanism that brings issues together so that positions over them can be exchanged. By analogy with vote-trading (also often called log-rolling), but to take into account a more general context, I will refer to that mechanism as "position-trading." The pervasiveness of recourse to that mechanism certainly qualifies the stringent effect of unanimity rule assumed in the previous section. But does it completely prevent constitutional rules to protect the *acquis communautaire* (and with it the "ever-closer union" stipulation)? I think not, as I will try to show after some remarks on the said "issue-splitting" or "position-trading" mechanism.

Bargaining under a Rule of Unanimity

On the occasion of large multidimensional negotiations leading to new treaties, such as those that led to the Single European Act or to the Treaty of Maastricht, many issues can be brought together that allow a lot of side-payments, exchanges, and compensations. As a consequence the attachment of a country to a particular element of the status quo can be overcome despite the veto power that the rule of unanimity awards that country on that issue. For its opposition to be overcome, the other participants in the negotiation must pay something. In a large negotiation most if not all countries, despite their veto power, will loose something on some issue, that is, will turn out to have made some concession.

Important decisions requiring unanimous consent of the member states are also made in settings other than multilateral negotiations. They are usually embedded in an ongoing process of bargaining among the states. The forum used for such bargaining can be ordinary diplomatic channels, bilateral summit meetings among heads of state or government, the Council of Ministers, or the European Council.[11] The government of the country chairing the two councils for the current semester usually serves as facilitator of bargains or compromise. To simplify, we can assume that bargaining takes place in the latter forum. Many issues are considered at each of the meetings of the European Council and these meetings take place twice a year. This means that decision-making can be multidimensional and/or sequential in time, each individual decision being made with due consideration of the others made or to be made contemporaneously, or situated in a slightly more distant past or future but always under a perspective of repeat business. This provides ample room for mutually beneficial reciprocation of positions over issues and characteristics of solutions. It must be noted that the items exchanged are not exclusively constitutional or quasi-constitutional characteristics but include also policies that address purely material concerns or, at the limit, include cash (under Margaret Thatcher, concessions about the refund to the United Kingdom was part of the compromise that led to the Single European Act).

There is a widespread claim that the outcome of decision-making under a rule of unanimity will typically correspond to a so-called lowest common denominator.[12] One implication of the foregoing discussion is that the idea cannot be correct. Indeed, pure empirical observation should be enough to show that. New policies are often adopted that are known by all observers to be disliked by many if not most of the member states who nonetheless unanimously give their assent to them. The elementary reasoning above explains how these policies are supported as elements of a larger position-trading compromise. What observation also tells us is that sometimes unanimous decision-making does lead to the lowest common denominator but only in its simplest form, which is inaction. The explanation is also fairly straightforward: compared to what a result more to their taste would bring to members X, the bribes they would have to pay to get that result are too high.

Bargaining and position-trading over several issues also take place under majority-voting, as the literature on log-rolling has long demonstrated. One implication, which is well known, is that the median voter may not be decisive. Another is the blurring of the dividing line between issues that are decidable by majority-voting and issues that require unanimity. What will count now, whether or not the rule is unanimity or majority-voting, is the intensity of the preferences of all the members on all the issues presented for negotiation. The difference between the two forms of rule remains important but in a more complex way than it would be in the absence of position-trading. Say a member X is opposed to a proposal whereas a majority of members are in favor of it. Under the rule of unanimity, X would have to be compensated to accept the proposal, and possibly the required compensation could be infinitely high. Under majority rule, if X obtains that the majority does not impose its adoption even though it could, X incurs a cost: subscribes to a debt that will have to be repaid in the form of a concession in another area or on another occasion.

What Does This Mean for the Entrenchment of the Acquis communautaire?

The main idea that we should keep in mind is that a unanimous reform is always Pareto improving. The new situation must be at least as good as the old one from the standpoint of each member. Whereas, under majority-voting, in the end the question is whether a majority considers the new package (including all the compensations and side-payments) as better than the status quo, under unanimity it is each member who must judge the package better or not worse than the status quo.[13]

The *acquis communautaire* is more or less what we mean here by status quo. Suppose that the main thing to be changed in that status quo is the elimination of the clause A mentioned in the previous section and that this clause is a constitutional characteristic that has the dimension of a public good. Suppose that A provides utility to some members. To accept the elimination of A, these members will have to be compensated and if their preferences for A are intense, the required compensation will be costly. Suppose in addition that the compensation can only marginally take the form of something akin to cash but must take above all the form of changes in some policies that also have the nature of public goods. Then finding a package that will satisfy the Pareto criterion referred to above will certainly not be easy. It will require much energy and creativity.

If it were available for that purpose, the power of initiative and leadership of the Commission would be most helpful, but the Commission is "a guardian of the treaties" and thus also, together with the European Court of Justice, a guardian of the *acquis communautaire*. More important, as noted, the logic of its situation (as contrived by the "founding fathers" of European integration) leads it to be biased in favor of integration. Thus the Commission is most likely to play against the elimination of A, except if it also receives some sufficient compensation in the form of a pro-integration move in some other area.

Because of the assumption in this section that under unanimity rule, it is possible to overcome a veto by the award of a compensation, the capacity of constitutional rules to maintain the status quo, and thus the *acquis communautaire*, is no more a matter of logic but an empirical question. Our discussion can only *argue* or *suggest* that the status quo will normally be quite resistant to attempts at changing it in the direction of a reversal, even assuming that a majority wishes such reversal. And the history of European integration readily confirms that significant reversals have been infrequent.

Does the argument, however, also apply to large-scale negotiations of the kind that led to a new treaty such as the Treaty of the European Union (Maastricht) or the one that may be agreed on in 2004? I think that the argument does apply. The important point is that the existing treaty remains in force as long as a unanimous agreement on a new treaty has not been reached. This puts those who do not object too much to the existing treaty at an advantage in their negotiation with those who want to change it a lot—another way to say that the status quo is resistant. At this point a question arises that could also constitute an objection to the thesis that existing constitutional constraints favor a goal-oriented evolution of the European Union. If the constitutional rules favor the status quo, how is it possible that they do not also hamper the evolution itself?

3.5 Constitutional Constraints on Moving Ahead

The answer to the question raised at the end of the last section is straightforward: the constitutional rule of unanimity for the most important decisions (and some others as well) favors the status quo, and thus (at least with regard to direct effects) does slow down the process of integration. It does not block it completely or definitely though. *Pace* the unproven theory of the bicycle, once popular in circles close to Brussels, the process can stall for a relatively long period of time and then accelerate again. Its main property is thus monotonicity or irreversibility: either no movement at all or positive movement along one direction, no reversal. Hence the feeling of inexorability typically shared by eurosceptics.

Let me again reason in two stages. Assume first that there is no bargaining over issues among the member states. Given the rule of unanimity, every step forward must be Pareto improving on its own merits. This, however, does not preclude each member deciding on the basis of several criteria. Some members (the *pragmatists*) have only one concern: the expected net effectiveness of the proposal with regard to meeting the concrete need(s) in discussion. Other members (the *ideologues*) are concerned in addition about how the project fits into the overall evolution of the European Union. Among the latter, some (the eurosceptics or, perhaps less ambiguously, the *europhobes*) consider as negative the fact that the proposal constitutes one step forward in the integration process, whereas others (the *europhiles*) consider this as positive.

Officially nobody is europhobe (in the sense used here) in the Council of Ministers or the European Council. Let us assume for a moment that this is true. We need then consider only the pragmatists and the europhiles. For a project to be (here, unanimously) approved, a first condition is that it must thus be sufficiently attractive concretely to convince all the pragmatists. A second condition is that, for each europhile, the algebraic sum of what they perceive as the net concrete benefit of the project and what they see as its contribution to the integration process must be positive. For a europhile, a project may have a negative net benefit in concrete terms, or more generally be judged ill-advised in the light of concerns independent of the integration issue, and nonetheless be acceptable because of its contribution to the construction of Europe. If we reintroduce the europhobes, for each of them the progress that the project induces in the integration process, now valued negatively, must be compensated by a positive net concrete benefit of sufficient magnitude. Considering all the ideologues together, what counts is the algebraic sum of this net concrete benefit and the benefit or cost derived from a step toward increased integration. For a project to be adopted, this sum must be positive for each member.

Whether there are many or few integrative projects that meet this condition is an empirical matter. It is enough for the monotonicity property mentioned above that there are some. It may be the case that over some periods of time, no such project will make it, so to say, and integration will stall—or seem to stall.[14] Sometimes there will be a congestion of projects coming up at the same time, each apparently meeting the conditions. This may cause a reassessment of the net value put by some members on the projects (e.g., whereas each project, individually, would have been acceptable to the europhobes, the sum may be unpalatable). Limited capacity of attention, deliberation, or implementation will also impose a choice among acceptable projects.

Bargaining complicates somewhat the exposition without changing very much the substance. Necessary conditions can no more be singled out but the main ingredients in the overall result remain the same. To have a chance of being accepted, a proposal will now typically include various side-payments and compensations. To unanimously approve a proposal, each member will have had considered it an improvement on the status quo. In addition to the benefits and costs of the side-payments and compensations, the determinants of the final position of each member, however will be exactly those previously identified: the net benefit of the project with regard to the concrete need it constitutes a response of, and the positive or negative value assigned to its contribution to the process of integration. Certainly more proposals succeed than if there were no bargaining, but the overall result is qualitatively the same. Under the assumptions, integration progresses only when a project does pass the test, full stop.

To say a little more, empirical assumptions or speculations are needed. First, it is likely that the strength of europhily is stronger than that of europhobia. The ever-closer union objective is not only, so to say, wired in the instincts of the Commission, as noted, but it is also an important consideration among influential minorities (of citizens, elites, opinion, etc.), and possibly even majorities, in a large majority of the member countries. Supporters of integration will tend to welcome occasions to transfer new responsibilities to the Brussels level. This is reflected in the attitude of most member states. Opposition to integration is strong also in several countries, but at the level of government, it takes much more moderate forms. It is actually not clear that europhobia characterizes the preferences of any of the governments currently in office among the member states. After all, as noted, the expression "ever-closer union" is included in the official documents agreed on by all the member countries.

That europhily is stronger than europhoby is conjectural, especially when meant to cover also the future. What is more certain is that both europhily or europhobia, at the level of each member country, are variables that are not independent of the size of the integrative step considered. For instance, the same member state's government that would give a positive value to a small step toward integration might judge negatively a larger step. And even if there is probably not much europhobia that is relevant in any of the member states' governments with regard to small steps, this would obviously change completely with regard to a step such as establishing a federation or a superstate. This remark raises the question of gradualism, to which I will return.

Recent history provides many illustrations of agreements between europhiles and pragmatists or (perhaps) europhobes. The most striking is the negotiation which led in 1985-86 to the Single European Act. That agreement launched the "1992" single market project and for that purpose increased the role of majority-voting within the Council of Ministers. Among the political parties or coalitions in office at the time, the unanimous agreement involved the French Socialists, led by François Mitterrand, and the British Conservatives, led by Margaret Thatcher. Even in retrospect, the motivations of these two politicians, who played a large role in the negotiation, are not perfectly clear. It seems safe, though, to say that the fact that the former was a devoted europhile was decisive in the position he adopted, whereas both the budgetary rebate conceded to the United Kingdom and the freeing of markets played the main role in the assent given by the latter.

The commitments embodied in the Single European Act have turned out to have implications devastating for the feasibility of ideas that seemed at the time central to the doctrines of the two parties: still strong interventionism (industrial, in particular), in the case of the French Socialists, and resolute hostility to centralization at the EU level, in the case of the British Conservatives.[15] This raises a question not discussed so far, which is that of the indirect consequences and spillover effects of each step in the integration process. Before addressing it, let me mention a second illustration of assent to integrative steps by pragmatists or europhobes. During the negotiations that led to the Treaty of Maastricht—that is, a few years after the Single European Act and thus at a time when the centralizing implications of the Act could escape the attention of no one—the British Conservative Government proposed that the powers of the European Court of Justice be substantially increased and in particular that it should be given the right to impose fines, a proposal that was duly integrated in the new Treaty.

3.6 Constraints on the Form of Gradualism in the Integration Process

Associated with the name of Jean Monnet, the method adopted by the member states to integrate Europe is based on the famous *engrenage* or spillover principle. An integrative step decided in $t + 1$ raises problems that are typically solved or mitigated by agreeing in $t+2$ on a new integrative step, which in turn will generate problems calling for a solution in $t+3$, and so on. The underlying reason for that is the existence of complementarities (e.g., as noted by Persson, Rolland, and Tabellini 1997). The argument developed in the foregoing sections purports to show that the constitutional setup of the European Union favors this particular form of gradualism.

But this raises a number of questions. Why don't the governments choose an alternative process, akin to a big bang strategy, consisting in tackling all the necessary transformations simultaneously and establishing, say, a federation? Why aren't, in $t+1$, all of the integrative steps anticipated and taken into account when deciding the first step? In particular, why do the members who are the most lukewarm vis-à-vis integration act as if they are unaware of the distant implications of their decisions? One very strong argument for gradualism (central also to Roland 2000) is the one used by Popper to justify piecemeal engineering: if the conjecture that inspires the reform proves wrong, that reform can be withdrawn, so to say, at not too high a cost. But is this compatible with the obstacles put by the present system to any kind of reversal?

The Choice of Gradualism

Many generally convergent explanations are available. The foregoing discussion, based in particular on the heterogeneity of preferences across the governments or the political majorities of the member countries, points to a type of explanation that is relatively straightforward, even though it remains to be elaborated. I have proposed elsewhere (Salmon 1995) an interpretation of European integration that is much more unconventional, especially from the perspective of economics. I do not claim that this interpretation is the best one or the only one possible, but I summarize it here because I happen subjectively to find it more plausible than several others. It purports to account not only for the characteristic of gradualism but also for other features such as the process's roundabout and somewhat conspiratorial appearance. It does not mention *engrenage* but is largely compatible with it. Contrary to some interpretations of European integration, the story I suggested in the 1995 essay does not rely on a distinction between elites and the rest of the population; contrary to most interpretations, it does not suppose that integration is generally useful or justified in economic terms.

The basic assumption of European integration is that the ultimate aim, shared by citizens, is to create strong and shock-resistant ties between the populations of the member countries. This has a psychological dimension that cannot but be central. It implies a partial transfer in citizens (or in a sufficient number of citizens) of their attachment to—or identification with—one type of collective, their nation states, toward another, the new European entity.[16] This transfer is a gradual process that needs time. Citizens acquiesce to it, in principle, but for various reasons they suffer some discomfort from the prospect, and thus prefer not to think too much about it. Elected office-holders serve the interests of citizens by, first, proceeding with integration and, second, giving it a form that makes it not too conspicuous. My 1995 essay included two simple models. In both (with the exception of the variant summarized below), each individual transfer of power is temporarily costly in terms of citizen utility and/or productive efficiency.[17] It is consequently also costly, this time for office-holders, in electoral terms. But once citizens have adapted to the new division of powers, the cost becomes insignificant as benefits accrue from the transfer having strengthened ties. To decide each step, incumbent politicians, submitted to electoral competition, must enjoy some discretionary margin. The size of the margin constrains the size of the step—which explains why large steps are politically infeasible as a rule.

A variant is based on an idea often expressed in the context of integration. In this variant the process of market integration (so-called negative integration) generates in the people a gradual psychological process that allows, without this time any kind of temporary cost, a gradual transfer of powers (so-called positive integration). Any attempts to move ahead faster with positive integration than the psychological effects of negative integration will allow has ill-effects in terms of productive efficiency, and therefore in electoral terms.[18]

Apparent Unforeseen Implications

An obvious objection to the preceding reasoning would be why the implications of more integration are not foreseen by all those who participate in the decision. If a sequence of steps is expected by all, what difference would it make in the first step to decide on the whole sequence? The immediate response is simple: members often do predict correctly many indirect consequences of their decisions and they do take into account these effects when they adopt a position. But, if a member does not value positively the overall sequence that may follow from a proposed step in the absence of sufficient compensation on other matters, this will make that member adopt a negative position toward that step and thus, under the rule of unanimity, decide to block it. This constitutes another reason why many integrative projects are not adopted by member states, which does not add anything, qualitatively, to the previous reasoning.

A second response relates to the time horizon or discount rate of elected politicians. Ill-effects that are certain to follow from a decision a few years hence may not weigh much when balanced against reasons to take that decision due to political pressure at the current moment. A big consideration is that the decision-maker may expect not to be in office when the full effects become explicit. Another is that the pressure groups may also have a high discount rate. Such high discount rates are revealed, for instance, by the way the European Union typically overcomes a deadlock by adopting reforms on condition that their implementation be postponed.

The third response is the aggregate uncertainty already mentioned. Interactions are complex. Equilibria are multiple. External factors and shocks have major effects but are largely unpredictable. More generally, knowledge about unprecedented transformations is necessarily fragile and limited. All of this explains that the consequences of large-scale decisions are uncertain in a pretty radical sense of the word. Roland (2000) provides compelling theoretical and empirical arguments on this point. However, he derives from his analysis a major role for decision reversals. How does this fit with an interpretation of European integration in which reversals do not play such a role?

Gradualism without Reversals

As I argued earlier, reversals of policy decisions or assignments of powers are not completely precluded by the present rules, nor are they rendered completely impossible by the way the European Union works in practice. However, reversals certainly meet strong obstacles and are infrequent. When a problem calls for a decision reversing the integration process—a "disintegration" (or "repatriation") solution—or a new step in the integration, the first alternative will rarely be discussed and in reality the choice will be between inaction, letting the problem stand, and an integration-friendly solution.

This bias has several consequences. First, it can generate serious inefficiencies and difficulties. Second, the mechanism and its possible consequences are perfectly understood and anticipated by members. This awareness not only strengthens the reluctance to adopt policies of those who were already reluctant, but it may cool down the enthusiasm for moving ahead of all members. So it will be harder for the proposals to be adopted. Third, prudence will suggest limiting the size of each step forward—another reason for gradualism.

However, there are often several solutions to a problem. Each solution can generate in turn other problems that have themselves several solutions, and this means that, in the context of a given issue, excluding reversals will seldom seem catastrophic. As noted, transitions in general are characterized by multiple equilibria, which opens up the possibility of very different paths—feasibility not to be confused with optimality, of course. This explains that all institutional arrangements are highly path-dependent and vary considerably across countries and systems. The fact that reversals are difficult to make has a significant effect on the form and content of integration, but this does not necessarily entail a serious weakness. Because it does sometimes, however, the question arises of whether the rules should be improved. As indicated at the outset, this question is not addressed directly in this chapter, which only suggests adding an indicator to the set of indicators or criteria already in use to evaluate reform proposals.

3.7 Concluding Remarks

Several aspects of present arrangements claimed to be essential in the foregoing sections are seriously questioned currently in the context of the ongoing constitutional discussions. This is true in particular of the *acquis communautaire* principle, of the status given to the "ever-closer-union" objective, and of the application of the rule of unanimity to the assignment of powers and other constitutional or quasi-constitutional issues. Without trying to predict the outcome of negotiations or promote personal preferences, what can be said about possible reforms? The argument developed in the chapter provides a benchmark for assessing the effects of constitutional proposals. What are the effects of a proposal on what I have called monotonicity—that is, the monotonous character of the integration process or, in more dramatic words, its inexorability? The said process has often stalled or slowed down but seldom has it regressed. To produce monotonocity, the main factor is the difficulty of reversals. The easiness or difficulty of positive integrative steps is irrelevant. Thus, from the standpoint of monotonocity, the crucial point to examine in any proposal is its bearing on reversals, not on new steps.

Other criteria, more traditional or familiar than monotonocity, are likely to come to the mind more readily. Focusing on these other concerns is likely to be more natural. As a consequence the effects of new constitutional clauses on reversals and on monotonocity may be overlooked. This is particularly likely to be the case of proposals purporting to accelerate integration or to make it more democratic. Such proposals are often based on a negative assessment of the rule of unanimity—both per se and as a major obstacle to pro-integrative moves. To foster integration, the proposals generally purport to reduce reliance on decision-making by unanimous consent of member states. For that purpose, they typically include not only an increase in the role of qualified majority-voting but also enhanced power for the European Parliament, and, beyond that, for the voters themselves. It is easy to forget that at the same time as the transfer of new powers to the European institutions is facilitated by these mechanisms, inverse transfers, that is, reversals, also become easier to achieve, and thus that the monotonocity of the integration process may be undermined.

It is not claimed in this chapter that monotonocity is more important than the other criteria used to assess constitutional change. These criteria fully deserve the attention they get. Also monotonocity has effects whose relative weight will vary according to one's preferences. To mention two other than the main effect that defines the phenomenon (monotonous integration), it probably precludes rapid integration and it generates disincentives to experiment or take risks. Because of all these considerations, it is logically impossible to infer from this chapter something like an assertion that europhiles should support unchanged recourse to the rule of unanimity. What is suggested is the more modest proposition that they should keep the various effects of monotonicity in mind, including the one, fully positive from their perspective, that has played a role in reaching the present level of integration. Conversely, some europhobes might want to qualify their support to the rule of unanimity as a major safeguard against further integration. Inasmuch as they are above all annoyed by monotonicity, they should pay attention to the two sides of increasing recourse to majority-voting.

Notes

I am grateful for the comments made on earlier versions of this chapter by participants in the CESifo conference, especially by my discussant, Stefan Voigt, as well as for the very useful suggestions included in two referee reports.

1. Various sets of assumptions that may underlie the adoption of a gradualist approach to social transformations are analyzed theoretically by Roland (2000) and in the literature he cites. None of these sets fit well with the reasoning developed in this chapter. However, I do not no attempt here at a formal explication of that reasoning.

2. All constitutions, including those of unitary states, do evolve substantially in the course of time. See Voigt (1999) for an analysis stressing the distinction between explicit and implicit constitutional change.

3. See also Roland (2000, p. 37).

4. In the form of the side-payments and compensations that may prove necessary to reach the unanimity required for the adoption of new constitutional provisions.

5. The theory of fiscal federalism exerts a strong influence in this regard. Guido Tabellini (2002), however, follows it only in part; in particular, he insists that income distribution should not be transferred to the EU level. Some approaches to European integration are inspired by economic analyses of federalism completely different from the theory of fiscal federalism (see Breton 1996; Breton and Ursprung 2002; Salmon 2003b). They are also somewhat dissonant with interpretations of the European Union (such as the one I propose in this chapter) that stress its evolving characteristics.

6. Schneider (1996) and Berglöf (2003) are particularly interesting illustrations of this work by economists.

7. *The Economist* (2000) argues in a text entitled "Our Constitution for Europe,": "What needs to be fixed is ... its constitutional underpinnings. First and foremost this means renouncing the guiding concept of 'ever closer union,' an idea enshrined in the Union's pseudo-constitution. Ever closer union, taken seriously, is a commitment to permanent constitutional revision—and Europe's leaders do take it seriously. Earlier agreements oblige them to seek further integration, they often point out. End of discussion. It is too late now, they say, to start asking where or whether integration should stop. Actually, it is not too late—except in the sense that the answer is already long overdue. Europe's leaders are right about what the existing treaties say. Therefore, plainly, those agreements must be changed."

8. This interpretation is fully compatible with the assumption of aggregate uncertainty mentioned earlier. Even in world of high aggregate uncertainty, it is easy for anyone, and thus also for any politician, to predict that a bureau placed at the center of the system will try to expand its activities and influence. See note 15 below.

9. Some legal scholars claim that the *acquis communautaire* constitutes "an untouchable hard core, that is, an absolute substantial restriction implicitly imposed on any revision" (see Jørgensen 1999, p. 12). The argument I develop does not follow this, I think questionable, line.

10. On all these facts, and many more, see Jørgensen (1999).

11. The European Council meets regularly as a "summit" of heads of government and the president of the Commission. A very important role is played by the Commission,

and in particular its president, in decision-making by unanimity among the member states.

12. That is, a collective decision on an issue that satisfies each member on its own merits.

13. See Buchanan (1975, ch. 5).

14. As observed by several authors, periods of apparent nonactivity often conceal inconspicuous decisions that turn out later to have great importance.

15. This does not imply that Mitterrand and Thatcher were irrational. First, they did not have exactly the same priorities as those of their parties (this is particularly true of Mitterrand). Second, over time it is normal for some early objectives to prove incompatible, which explains why a number of objectives had to be abandoned. Third, more generally, unwanted and unforeseen consequences of rational decisions are the major implication of the aggregate uncertainty referred to earlier (e.g., see Roland 2000, p. xxvi, 2). See note 8 above.

16. An alternative hypothesis, and one that is more convenient in political terms, is that increased attachment to one collective leads to no decrease in the attachment to the other (e.g., see Wallace 2000). No transfer of attachments is then needed to generate ties. This alternative hypothesis forms the basis of much of my discussion in my 1995 paper though it is disregarded here.

17. In one of the models, the loyalty of citizens is viewed as a factor of production in the sense that it contributes positively to the efficiency of policies. When two levels of governments are considered, attachments are level-specific in the short run. At any point in time, there is thus a constraining distribution of attachments between the two levels. In the longer run, attachments can be transferred from one level to the other. The productive efficiencies of policies is at a maximum when the allocation of resources or powers between the two levels matches the distribution of attachments.

18. This interpretation reflects better the psychological state of the six original members than that of countries that later joined.

References

Ackerman, B. 1997. The rise of world constitutionalism. *Virginia Law Review* 83: 771–97.

Berglöf, E., et al. 2003. *Built to Last: A Political Architecture for Europe*. London: CEPR.

Breton, A. 1996. *Competitive Governments: An Economic Theory of Politics and Public Finance*. Cambridge: Cambridge University Press.

Breton, A., and H. W. Ursprung. 2002. Globalization, competitive governments, and constitutional choice in Europe. In H. Kierzkowski (ed.), *Europe and Globalization*. Houndmills, Basingstoke: Palgrave Macmillan, pp. 274–301.

Buchanan, J. M. 1975. *The Limits of Liberty: Between Anarchy and Leviathan*. Chicago: University of Chicago Press.

Cooter, R. 2000. *The Strategic Constitution*. Princeton: Princeton University Press.

Dewatripont, M., et al. 1995. *Flexible Integration: Towards a More Effective and Democratic Europe*. London: CEPR.

Jørgensen, K. E. 1999. The social construction of the acquis communautaire: A cornerstone of the European edifice. *European Integration online Papers (EioP)*, 3(5) (http://eiop.or.at/texte/1999-005a.htm).

Kirchgässner, G., and W. W. Pommerehne. 1996. Tax harmonization and tax competition in the European Union: Lessons from Switzerland. *Journal of Public Economics* 60(3): 351–71.

McKay, D. 2000. Policy legitimacy and institutional design: comparative lessons for the European Union. *Journal of Common Market Studies* 28(1): 25–54.

Persson, T., G. Roland, G. Tabellini. 1997. The theory of fiscal federalism: what does it mean for Europe? In H. Siebert (ed.), *Quo Vadis Europe?* Tübingen: Mohr, pp. 23–41.

Roland, G. 2000. *Transition and Economics: Politics, Markets, and Firms*. Cambridge: MIT Press.

Salmon, P. 1995. Nations conspiring against themselves: An interpretation of European integration. In A. Breton, G. Galeotti, P. Salmon, and R. Wintrobe (eds.): *Nationalism and Rationality*. Cambridge: Cambridge University Press, pp. 290–311.

Salmon, P. 2002. Decentralization and supranationality: the case of the European Union. In E. Ahmad and V. Tanzi (eds.): *Managing Fiscal Decentralization*. London: Routledge, pp. 99–121.

Salmon, P. 2003a. Accounting for centralization in the European Union: Niskanen, Monnet or Thatcher? In J.-M. Josselin and A. Marciano (eds.), *From Economic to Legal Competition: New Perspectives on Law and Institutions in Europe*. Cheltenham: Edward Elgar, pp. 165–91.

Salmon, P. 2003b. Assigning powers in the European Union in the light of yardstick competition among governments. In M. J. Holler, H. Kliemt, D. Schmidtchen, and M. E. Streit (eds.), *Jahrbuch für Neue Politishe Ökonomie*, vol. 22: *European Governance*. Tübingen: Mohr-Siebeck, pp. 197–216.

Schneider, F. 1996. The design of a minimal European Federal Union: some ideas using the public choice approach. In J. Casas Pardo and F. Schneider (eds.): *Current Issues in Public Choice*. Cheltenham: Edward Elgar, pp. 203–20.

Tabellini, G. 2002. Principles of policymaking in the European Union: An economic perspective. Paper prepared for the Munich Economic Summit, CESifo, Munich.

The Economist. 2000. Our constitution for Europe. October 26.

Vaubel, R. 1994. The political economy of centralization and the European Community. *Public Choice* 81 (1–2): 151–90.

Voigt, S. 1999. *Explaining Constitutional Change: A Positive Economic Approach*. Cheltenham: Edward Elgar.

Wallace, W. 2000. Collective governance: The EU political process. In H. Wallace and W. Wallace (eds.): *Policy-making in the European Union*, 4th ed. Oxford: Oxford University Press, ch. 19.

Winer, S. L. 2000. On the reassignment of fiscal powers in a federal state. In G. Galeotti, P. Salmon, and R. Wintrobe (eds.): *Competition and Structure: The Political Economy of Collective Decision-Making*. Cambridge: Cambridge University Press.

4 Rights and Citizenship in the European Union

Dennis C. Mueller

4.1 Introduction

Two of the fundamental elements of any constitution are the definition of citizenship for the polity, and the delineation of the set of rights that accompany citizenship. These are separate questions, although, as we will see, they raise similar issues and thus will be treated jointly in this chapter. The approach taken will be that of what has come to be called "constitutional political economy." Namely I will analyze the properties of rights and citizenship in the context of a society of rational, self-interested individuals who define a set of rights and criteria for citizenship as part of a constitution written to advance their collective interests. The society in question in this case is the European Union, and so the approach envisages an assembly of representatives of Europeans from the current EU countries meeting to write a new constitution to govern their collective lives.

The nature of the questions addressed is such that there is no "bottom line," in the sense of a list of specific rights and a definition of citizenship, that appears at the end of the chapter. The goal is rather to identify the salient properties of rights and citizenship to serve as a guide to a constitutional assembly, which would in fact have to make up such a list and define the criteria for citizenship. An important contribution of the chapter is to distinguish the relationship between the *structure* of the European Union, in particular, whether it is organized as a *federation* or a *confederation*, and the characteristics of the set of rights and definition of citizenship that should be chosen.

Sections 4.2 and 4.3 are concerned with the definition of citizenship. Here the focus is on the right or privilege of voting. What criteria should a constitution establish for allowing a person to vote? Section 4.2 takes up the question in the abstract; section 4.3 discusses the issue in the context of the European Union.

Sections 4.4 and 4.5 are concerned with rights. Once again, the first of these examines the general characteristics of rights, and the second applies the analysis to the European Union. In section 4.6 the concept of rights is used to discuss some of the issues raised by the Convention for the Protection of Human Rights and Fundamental Freedoms and the Charter of Fundamental Rights of the European Union. The final section draws some conclusions, and discusses the relevance of the discussion for the deliberations of the constitutional convention currently taking place, and for future constitution writing in the European Union.

4.2 Defining Citizenship[1]

To begin, let us imagine a group of people living on Utopia, an isolated island in the Blissful Ocean. They have decided to create a state. The potential set of citizens is thus easily identified as all individuals currently living on the island.

Optimal Citizenship with Homogeneous Preferences

Consider first the case where every individual on the island has the same preference function and income. The purpose in forming a state is to provide a single, lumpy public good, G. Since all potential citizens have the same preference functions, they realize that the optimal provision of the public good will involve equal tax shares. In the absence of crowding, each citizen's share of the public good's cost falls as the size of the polity increases, and its optimal size is infinity. Utopia is a small island, however, and therefore the possibility of crowding must be taken into account. Let each citizen's utility, U, be written as a function of her private good consumption, X, the public good, and the size of the polity, n.

$$U = U(X, G, n). \tag{4.1}$$

Since all individuals pay the same fraction of the public good's costs, we can define the prices of the public and private good to make $X = G/n$. Using this expression to replace X in (4.1) and maximizing with respect to n and G yields

$$\frac{G}{n}\frac{\partial U}{\partial G} = -\frac{\partial U}{\partial n}. \tag{4.2}$$

Utopians maximize their expected utilities by limiting the population's size so that the marginal gain from adding another person to the island in terms of a reduced share of the public good's cost just equals the marginal cost from increased crowding caused by this person.

If the n satisfying (4.2) is larger than the population of the island, then the task of individuals at the constitutional stage is simple. All current residents are made citizens. Moreover it will be in the interests of the current residents to allow immigration up until the optimal community size is reached. The situation is potentially more complicated when the optimal population size for Utopia is smaller than its current level.

One possibility here would be to make all current residents citizens, and allow free emigration. If other islands like Utopia exist where the population count is less than optimal, Utopians will have an incentive to migrate to them up until the point where the population of Utopia is optimal.

A second possibility is that no such attractive options for emigration exist. Utopians will then have no other recourse but to make everyone a citizen, prohibit immigration, and perhaps take steps to reduce the population of Utopia by discouraging births.

Optimal Citizenship with Heterogeneous Preferences

Consider now the consequences of citizens having different preferences. Let there be two groups, the Blues and the Greens. The sole public good to be provided is a highway across the island, whose cost will be shared equally by members of both groups. It is technologically infeasible once the highway is built to prevent members of either group from using it. Blues favor a high-quality, four-lane highway that will allow high driving speeds with minimal traffic snares. Greens favor a low-quality, two-lane highway where the low speed and heavy traffic create many delays. Looking forward to the postconstitutional stage, both groups can see that if everyone on the island is made a citizen, the outcome of the political process will be a compromise where some parts of the highway have four lanes, and other parts only two. Both groups can expect higher utilities if they are free to construct the highway as they prefer. It will not make sense for the Greens to construct a two-lane highway alongside of a four-lane one. Knowing this, the Blues have an incentive to form the state by themselves, that is to define citizenship for Blues only, and build a four-lane highway. This is obviously true if individuals at the constitutional stage know whether they will be Blues or Greens in the postconstitutional stage. But it is also possible that *all* Utopians unanimously agree to form a state in which only Blues have citizenship from behind the veil of ignorance. A sufficient condition for such a unanimous agreement would be, for example, that the Blues be in the majority and the utility gain for each Blue from choosing the type of highway equals the loss to each Green.[2]

If the Blues are in the majority, they could achieve the same outcome by granting Greens citizenship, and simultaneously selecting the simple majority rule as the voting rule to be used for making collective decisions in the postconstitutional stage. Here we have reached an important result. For the majority group the definition of citizenship and the choice of voting rule may be substitutes. A group with an absolute majority of the population can ensure that it dictates all outcomes in the postconstitutional stage *either* by excluding members of the other group(s) from citizenship *or* by choosing a voting rule requiring a majority below that which they have, say, a simple majority. Buchanan and Tullock (1962) introduced the concept of *external costs of collective decision-making* and used it to define the optimal voting rule from the point of view of citizens at the constitutional stage. In our example, inclusion of the Greens in the collective decision process creates a negative externality for the Blues, an externality that they can eliminate either by excluding the Greens from collective decision-making entirely or by effectively excluding them through the choice of a voting rule.

The same two options do not exist for a minority group. If the Greens constitute 35 percent of the population, they cannot dictate outcomes in the postconstitutional stage by choosing a one-third majority rule at the constitutional stage, for the Blues easily satisfy this requirement. The Greens can ensure that their most-preferred options win only by creating a state in which only they have the right to decide for the combined community.[3]

Although limiting citizenship to only certain groups is a *possible* outcome of the constitutional process, when individuals have heterogeneous preferences, it is of course not an inevitable one. The possibility exists that both groups obtain citizenship and compromises emerge out of postconstitutional politics when individuals define citizenship from behind the veil of ignorance. The likelihood of this happening increases if we expand the number of postconstitutional collective choices and allow for more groups, so that every group has a chance of being part of the majority on some future issues. Although such assumptions increase the likelihood of inclusive definitions of citizenship, they do not guarantee it when individuals choose definitions of citizenship that maximize their expected utility. With sufficient preference heterogeneity, the expected utility of an individual at the constitutional stage will be maximized—*even from behind the veil of ignorance*—by excluding some groups from affecting future collective choices. This can always be accomplished by excluding these groups from citizenship. When these groups constitute a minority of the population, they can be effectively excluded even when granted citizenship, by choosing the simple majority rule as the community's voting rule.

Optimal Citizenship with Heterogeneous Preferences and Separated Communities

Imagine now a second island, Polyana, not too far from Utopia. All Utopians have identical preferences for public and private goods as do all Polyanians, but the preferences of the two groups differ from one another. In addition to the public goods that each island can supply to itself, a set of public goods exists that could benefit both islands, if jointly supplied to them. The citizens of both islands contemplate forming a larger polity—the United Islands—to provide the public goods that would benefit both.

Obviously both Utopians and Polyanians will have to be citizens in this new polity if it forms. Neither group would agree to join a community in which they were obligated to pay taxes for a public good but were denied the opportunity to help determine its quantity and their tax shares. If the United Islands comes into existence, both groups will have to have citizenship and be represented in the assembly that makes decisions for the new polity.

Equally obviously, the voting rule used in this assembly *cannot* be the simple majority rule. If the assembly were formed by parties competing for votes across the two islands, and seats in the assembly were allocated according to the number of votes each party received, then two parties would take seats in the assembly—a Utopian Party and a Polyanian Party. If Utopia had the largest population, it would win a majority of seats in the assembly and could dictate the choice of public goods and tax shares under the simple majority rule. But citizens on Polyana would never agree to the use of the simple majority rule in the assembly, if they wished to maximize their expected gains from membership in the new state. If Utopia has α fraction of the population of the two islands, then any voting rule requiring more than α fraction of the votes in the assembly would require an agreement between both parties to reach a decision. De facto such a voting rule would be equivalent to the unanimity rule, and it would cost the two islands nothing as against requiring a majority greater than α if they wrote this voting rule into their constitution.

With all citizens of Utopia having identical preferences, they could be optimally represented by sending a *single person* to the representative assembly, as could all Polyanians under the assumption that they have homogeneous preferences. In this situation the new state could be optimally constituted as a *confederation* of the two island communities with the elected governments of each island sending delegations to an assembly that would make decisions for the greater polity under the unanimity rule.

As noted, the citizens of either island would only agree to join the larger polity if they were granted citizenship in it. What citizenship rights should exist in this new polity with respect to the two island polities? If a Polyanian migrates to Utopia, should she both retain her citizenship in the United Islands *and* be able to take up citizenship and vote in Utopia?

Under the assumptions that we have made about the preferences of the two groups, the answer to this question is not necessarily yes. If migrants from the other island are allowed to vote in local elections, *and their votes affect the collective decisions made*, costs will be imposed on the island receiving migrants. There may also be offsetting benefits, of course, if an island's population is smaller than the optimal size, for example. But, when a confederation is the optimal political structure for joining groups of geographically separated people with heterogeneous preferences, the presumption must be that migration will entail costs, and each lower level polity may find it optimal to minimize these costs by not granting migrants from other parts of the confederation voting rights in their polity.

Optimal Citizenship with Dispersed Populations and Heterogeneous Preferences

Imagine now that Polyana and Utopia both contain mixtures of Blues and Greens, with each group as before having identical preferences that differ from those of the other group. Now it would not be possible to select a single person from one island who could accurately represent all of its citizens, and a confederation of the two islands may also no longer be optimal. If the government of Utopia is controlled by the Blues, then they would presumably send a delegation to the United Islands' assembly that only represented Blues. The Greens on Utopia would be unrepresented in the larger polity. In this situation having parties compete for votes across the two islands should produce an assembly in which the Greens and Blues would be represented in proportion to their numbers on the two islands.

Assuming that there are some public goods that benefit only the residents on a single island, a *federalist* political structure is likely to be optimal in this situation. Each island's government makes collective decisions for the island's residents, and an assembly representing citizens across the two islands makes decisions for the larger polity. In such a federalist system the presumption would be in favor of allowing migrants to take up full citizenship on either island if they move, since Blues and Greens are found on both islands and each must have chosen political institutions to accommodate this heterogeneity.

4.3 Citizenship in the European Union

The Costs of Under- and Overcrowding

The costs of under- and overcrowding must be viewed in two contexts: as migration into and out of the European Union, and as migration within the European Union.

The prognosis for all EU countries is for steadily aging and declining populations. Immigration is one possible way to partly offset the negative effects of these demographic changes. Thinking only in terms of population size would suggest that the EU adopt a fairly liberal policy with respect to allowing immigration and granting citizenship.[4] Indeed, when one only contemplates the demographics, one might entertain the notion of introducing policies that discourage emigration, particularly by young people. Such policies do not directly raise issues of citizenship, however; they fall rather under the heading of rights.

A knottier question is raised by migration within the EU. A resident of community A who contemplates moving to community B considers only her expected future utility levels in the two communities. If she acts rationally and selfishly, she ignores any externalities caused by her migration. A consequence of this is that communities, which are particularly attractive places to live and work, are likely to attract more than the optimal number of migrants, unattractive communities are likely to suffer from excessive emigration. These problems raise questions both with respect to the rights of citizens to freely move about, and with respect to citizenship itself.

The nature of these questions can be seen by considering the following questions. Who owns the Riviera? All Europeans? The French and Italians? Only those holding property there?

One might argue that it belongs to everyone in Europe, on the ground that one's place of birth is determined by chance, and someone lucky enough to be born in southern France has no more right to the Riviera than someone born on a remote island off the coast of Scotland. To argue otherwise would be to say that the Scot is condemned by birth to a life of toil and hardship, while the Frenchman is entitled to a life of comparative bliss. Accepting the proposition that the Riviera belongs to all Europeans *would not imply*, however, that all Europeans can move to the Riviera. The costs of congestion remain, and an optimal set of policies is going to include measures that discourage people from migrating from Scotland to the Riviera. Claiming that the Riviera belongs to all Europeans will affect the nature of these policies, however. If every European has an equal claim to utility arising from one's place of residence, then the optimal policies to discourage excess migration to the Riviera will involve taxes on those living on the Riviera and perhaps subsidies to those living in places like northern Scotland.

If, on the other hand, the Riviera belongs to those who are now there, then the optimal set of policies to discourage immigration will involve taxes on the migrants. Current residents are then entitled to permanently higher welfare levels than people born into less attractive environments.[5]

Does a person born and raised in Venice think of herself first of all as a Venetian, as an Italian, or as a European? If one of the former, she is probably going to feel that she is entitled to introduce taxes and regulations that "keep Venice for the Venetians." More generally, the answers to these questions have implications for how readily people should be allowed to take up residence and citizenship within the European Union.

The Costs of Heterogeneity

The European Union has been created and evolved as a result of a series of agreements among representatives of the member countries. Its history has been one of a confederation therefore, and it operates today more as a confederation than as a federation. The major decisions regarding EU expansion, the Common Agricultural Policy (CAP), and so on, are made by representatives of the current governments of the EU members, as befits a confederation. If we are to assume that this political structure is the optimal one for the European Union, then it follows from the discussion of the previous section that the preferences of EU citizens must be homogeneous with respect to EU-wide policies within a given country and heterogeneous across them.[6] With such a distribution of preferences, there are likely to be substantial costs from the migration of individuals across countries, if migrants are allowed to take up citizenship fairly soon after arriving in a different country. By extension, serious costs would be imposed on citizens of the current member countries if the citizens of new entrants into the European Union were allowed to freely migrate into existing member countries and to take up citizenship there.

These considerations imply that the provisions regarding citizenship in the Draft of Article 7 of the Constitutional Treaty[7] could impose costs on member countries. The second entry of Article 7 reads

Citizens of the Union shall enjoy ... the right to move and reside freely within the territory of the Member States; [and] the right to vote and to stand as a candidate ... in municipal elections in their Member State of residence under the same conditions as nationals of that State.

If the Union's optimal structure is that of a confederation, then allowing immigrants from other EU countries to vote in municipal elections would increase the heterogeneity of the electorate in these elections, worsening the outcomes for local citizens. The force of this provision is, of course, reduced by limiting it to municipal elections, since in most member countries municipal elections are of little consequence, but one expects that the Article would eventually lead to voting rights at the national level in their country of residence for all EU citizens.

On the other hand, it might be the case that preferences are heterogeneous regarding EU-wide policies *within* each country. People opposed to the CAP exist in every country, as do its supporters. An advocate of a strong EU-foreign policy is as likely to be found in Denmark as in Portugal. If this assumption more accurately describes the distribution of preferences regarding EU-wide policies, then the free migration of individuals may actually *improve* political outcomes at the national and local levels of government by allowing individuals to resort themselves into communities of more homogeneous tastes.[8] A second implication of such a distribution of individual preferences is that the EU's decision-making structure is poorly designed. Decision-making power should reside with the European Parliament and not with the Council or Commission, and the Parliament's membership should be determined in elections across the entire European Union and not just within each member country.[9] Thus we can conclude that the assumptions one makes about the distribution of preferences across the European Union have important implications for both the definitions of citizenship within each country and whether the EU would be best structured as a federation or a confederation.

4.4 The Nature of Constitutional Rights

Among the many elements that must go into a constitution is a voting rule to be used for making future collective decisions. Although the unanimity rule would ensure that no future collective action would harm any citizen, the associated decision-making costs argue against it. Some qualified majority rule of less than unanimity is likely to be optimal for many decisions.

Now consider the decision calculus of an individual at the constitutional convention. She must look into the future and envisage all of the possible issues that might come up and then decide on the optimal voting rule for each. Given the uncertainties at the constitutional stage this is an impossible task. It is, however, reasonable to assume that an individual at the constitutional stage can envisage broad categories of issues and choose a voting rule for deciding these. On any particular issue, a citizen will be on either the winning or the losing side. Let s be her gain if she is on the winning side, and $u(s)$ her utility from this gain. Let t be her loss if she is on the losing side, and $v(t)$ her utility loss. The probability that she is on the winning side, $p(m)$, is an increasing function of the required majority to pass an issue, m, reaching a maximum of 1.0 under the unanimity rule.[10] An individual at the constitutional stage would then maximize her expected utility by balancing the gains from increasing the required majority and thus her chances of being on the winning side of an issue against the increased decision-making costs accompanying a rise in m. It is reasonable to assume that these decision-making costs, $d(m)$, not only increase with m, but increase at an increasing rate $(d'(m) > 0$, and $d''(m) > 0)$. An individual's expected gain from a future collective decision can then be written as

Rights and Citizenship in the European Union

$$G = p(m)u(s) - [1 - p(m)]v(t) - d(m) \qquad (4.3)$$

Maximizing (4.3) with respect to m yields

$$p'(m)[u(s) + v(t)] = d'(m) \qquad (4.4)$$

as a first-order condition. The left-hand side of (4.4) is the marginal gain from increasing the required majority and thereby reducing the chance of being on the losing side, the right-hand side is the marginal cost of increasing m and thereby increasing decision-making costs.

Different types of collective decisions will have different gain and loss functions. To get more of a handle on which voting rule is optimal for which types of decisions, we need to assume something about these gains and losses. A simple way to approach this issue is to assume that the loss to someone on the losing side of an issue is proportional to the gain to a winner, $t = bs$, $b \geq 0$. It is then easy to show that the majority satisfying (4.4), m^*, increases with b. Some possibilities are illustrated in figure 4.1. To the left of $m = 0.5$, the outcome under a qualified majority rule is undefined as mutually inconsistent proposals can win, and so the $d'(m)$ curve has only been drawn starting at $m = 0.5$. For many categories of decisions the marginal gains lines are likely to resemble g_1 and g_2, and the simple majority rule will be optimal. For a

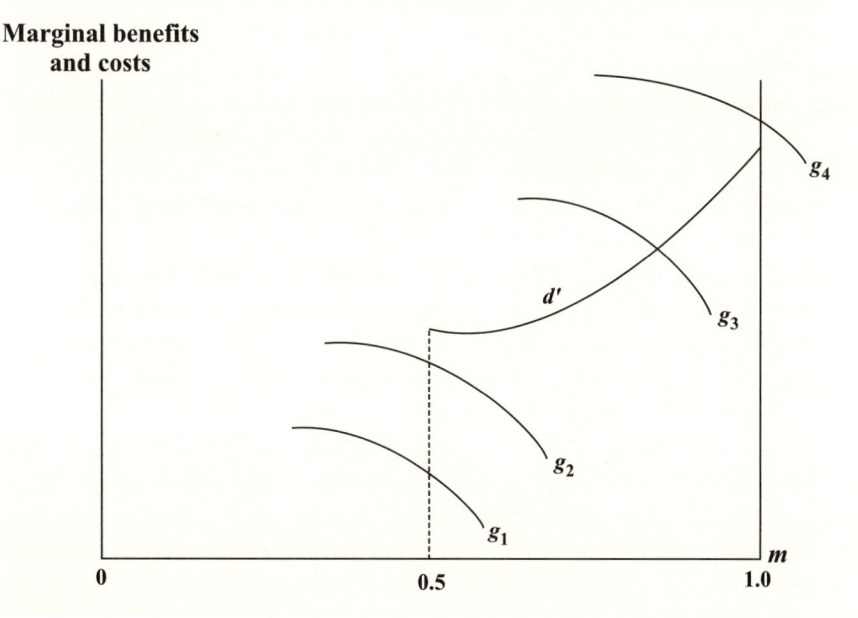

Figure 4.1
Possible optimal majorities

high value of b, however, the marginal gains curve will look like g_3, and some qualified majority greater than 0.5 will be optimal. When the expected loss to the loser under a collective decision becomes very large relative to the gain to a winner, the marginal gains curve looks like g_4, and the unanimity rule becomes optimal.[11]

Consider first the simple action of wiggling one's toes. This action carries with it a small gain for the actor, and does no harm to anyone else. If the community had to vote on whether a person wishing to undertake this action should be allowed to do so or not, the simple majority rule would certainly be the optimal rule, and one assumes any proposal to allow someone to wiggle their toes would achieve the required majority, as no one has an incentive to vote against such a proposal. There are an infinite number of such actions giving a small utility gain to the actor at no loss to the community (wiggling one's ears, scratching one's toe, etc.), and thus the transaction costs of voting on all of them would be immense. Citizens at the constitutional convention would minimize future decision-making costs by allowing individuals to undertake any action that is not specifically prohibited.

When an action creates a negative externality, like burning trash in an urban area, the community will want to be able to prohibit it, and thus the optimal constitution will allow future collective decisions to prohibit certain actions creating negative externalities. Trash burning might fall into the category of actions for which the simple majority rule is optimal.

Now consider the action of practicing one's religion. Religions often require their members to wear certain clothing, refrain from eating certain foods, or undertake other actions that, for whatever reasons, irritate some people in the community—that is, religious practices sometimes create negative externalities. As such one must anticipate that at some time a majority of the community might choose to prohibit a religious practice of a minority, if this were possible under the simple majority rule. Such a collective action might be expected to impose a large loss in welfare on members of the religious minority, however. If the externality caused by the religious practice were modest, the characteristics of this collective action would fit those for which the unanimity rule is optimal. If all citizens at the constitutional stage perceived the loss of being prevented from practicing one's religion as very large relative to any loss of those experiencing a negative externality from this practice, *and they were uncertain over whether they would be in the religious minority subject to a future prohibition*, all citizens might well vote to protect the freedom to practice one's religion by requiring that any prohibitions of religious practices obtain the unanimous support of the community.

If those experiencing a loss of utility from a minority's religious practices were a large enough and rich enough group, they might be able to offer members of the minority a sufficiently large bribe that they would willingly give up the practice in question and a ban would pass even under the unanimity rule. But if the constitution drafters were correct in choosing religious practices as a set of actions to be prohibited only by unanimous agreement (i.e., the loss to those prevented from acting is very large relative to the externality it causes), any bribes offered are unlikely to be large enough to produce unanimity. When placing bans on religious practices under the protection of the unanimity rule, the constitution framers must therefore anticipate that much time and energy will be wasted in idle debates and votes on proposals to ban certain religious practices that in the end fail to achieve unanimity. Realizing this, the constitution framers can economize on future decision-making costs by placing a *right* to practice a religion into the constitution, whereby a constitutional right is defined as a prohibition against any person or group of persons—including the entire community—interfering with an individual's freedom to undertake the protected action.

Three features of constitutional rights under this theory need to be noted. First, explicit rights will be defined only for actions capable of generating sufficiently strong negative externalities to elicit efforts by some members of the community to restrict them. Even if wiggling one's toes gives great enjoyment, no constitutional protection in the form of an explicit right to act will be afforded if it is unlikely that this action will ever generate a negative externality. Even actions that provide considerable benefits for the actor need not be protected, if they are not expected to be challenged.

Second, there is an inherent tension between constitutional rights and the normative principles justifying majoritarian democracy. When the institutions of explicitly defined rights and the simple majority rule are both found in a constitution to deal with situations where individual interests conflict, these situations should differ dramatically in the perceived losses imposed on the different sides from curtailing the action. The simple majority rule is optimal for resolving a negative externality, when an individual at the constitutional stage expects the utility gain from undertaking the action to equal the loss it causes.

Rights are defined precisely where the simple majority rule is not optimal, because the expected gains and losses from a ban are dramatically different, and the constitution framers wish to preclude its use. Because rights will be defined only when significant losses are expected for those prevented from acting relative to the losses imposed on others, disputes over rights are likely to be emotionally charged, as they pit a perhaps substantial majority that feels harmed by the action against an intense minority that benefits from it.[12]

Third, the kinds of constitutional rights defined by this theory are inherently *relative*, and thus they differ from many other definitions of rights, which see them as being *absolute* in some meaningful sense. In a community where everyone is a member of the same religion, it may not occur to anyone that someone would ever challenge practicing this religion, and the constitution may therefore not explicitly protect religious freedom. If a country has suffered greatly under the dictatorial rule of a political party, it may choose after the dictatorship falls to ban the party and any books that defend this party or promote its ideology. In another country that has never suffered under a dictatorship such bans might be precluded by a constitutional right to "free speech." The nature of the actions explicitly protected as constitutional rights should vary across communities depending on their particular histories, the preferences (values) of their citizens, and their expectations of the future benefits and costs of allowing the actions.

4.5 Defining Rights in the European Union

There are essentially three questions that must be addressed with respect to rights within the European Union. Should there be rights defined at the European Union level? If the answer to this question is yes, should they be the only rights in the EU or should member countries also be free to define their own sets of rights? If rights are defined at both levels, to what extent should it be possible for EU-level rights to "trump" member country rights?

Rights are of importance only in communities with heterogeneous interests. A right to free speech becomes important only when there is disagreement among members of a community over what books should be allowed to be printed. The answers to our three questions depend once again on the assumptions we make regarding the distribution of preferences across the European Union and the nature of these preferences.

Assume, to begin, that the distribution of individual preferences across the European Union is such as to justify a confederate structure—preferences are homogeneous within each country and differ across countries on at least some issues. It follows from the discussion above that individual member countries will wish to define *different* sets of rights. The answer to our second question is definitely yes, and the answer to the first is likely to be no. Consider, for example, rights involving *habeas corpus* protections. Such rights can be defended by the logic defined in the previous section, *if* at the time a constitution is written all citizens believe that a person held in jail without being charged and convicted of having committed a specific crime suffers a great loss relative to any possible negative externality that his release would impose on the rest of the community. The latter condition would require that the probability that this person would commit a crime if released would be relatively small, and the severity of any crime he committed would also be small. Now suppose that country X contains a small terrorist group, which has for many years kidnaped and killed innocent citizens. In this country the conditions needed to justify a right to be quickly charged and convicted of a crime to be held in prison may not be fulfilled. From behind a veil of ignorance *all citizens* may agree that the government should be allowed under certain circumstances, as say following several terrorist attacks, to arrest and detain suspected terrorists without charging them with particular crimes. Quite obviously in county Y, where no history of terrorism exists, citizens may feel quite differently and the constitution will contain a clause guaranteeing strong writ of *habeas corpus* protection. When preferences and circumstances differ across communities, no single set of rights is likely to be optimal for all.

It is, of course, possible with respect to a particular right that all citizens in all EU countries have the same preferences, even though they differ with respect to other rights issues. Even this situation does not require that the right in question be defined at the EU level rather than at the nation state level. Each member country can simply place the particular right in question into its own constitution, and all member country constitutions will be identical with respect to this right. This option is superior to defining a right at the EU level, given the assumption that preferences can differ across countries. Indeed, a time may come when the citizens of a country wish to redefine a particular right, and this would not be possible if it is defined at the EU level. Suppose, for example, that at one point in time citizens in each

EU country decide to protect a person's "right to life" by prohibiting capital punishment. Following a series of terrorist assassinations, the citizens of X reach the conclusion that their right to life would be better protected, if capital punishment were introduced for terrorist acts of murder. Even if one believes that the citizens of X are misguided in their judgments about the deterrence effects of capital punishment, it does not seem justifiable that citizens in Y and Z, where terrorism is not a problem, should be able to prevent citizens in X from changing their constitution in a way that *they* believe will be to their benefit.

Constitutional rights at the EU level can be defended using the theory of rights outlined above if we assume that individual preferences are distributed across Europe in such a way as to make a federalist structure optimal. Consider, for example, the right to practice a religion. Catholics are spread across Europe as are Protestants, Jews, and members of other religions. Every European is aware that religious minorities have been discriminated against in the past, and can contemplate such discrimination in the future. There are two sets of assumptions under which this knowledge might lead a European to want to see a religious freedom right defined, *and to prefer that it be defined at the EU level* rather than in the country of which she is a citizen.

Assumption number one is that our European is sufficiently mobile that she can well imagine living in almost any of the EU countries sometime in the future. Today she lives in Y where a majority of the citizens practice the same religion as she does, but tomorrow she may be living in Z where her religion is in the minority, and she does not want to run the danger of religious persecution. Thus EU-wide rights can be optimal when citizens with particular sets of preferences can be found across all of Europe, and Europeans are sufficiently mobile that they can imagine being in the minority at some future point in time.[13]

While the first rationalization of EU-wide rights rests on the assumption of real uncertainty about future positions, the second rests on the assumption of artificially imposed uncertainty. When contemplating what actions should receive rights protection, the European citizen steps behind a Rawlsian veil of ignorance and contemplates being a citizen of every other country. She does this not because she realistically expects to reside in another country, but as an ethical act. She contemplates being in the religious majority and being in a religious minority and wishes to protect people in the latter situation regardless of where they might live.

For this chain of reasoning to justify an EU-wide right, the European when she steps behind the veil of ignorance must contemplate being any other European and not just any other citizen of her nation state. Behind the veil of ignorance her answer to the question, "what are you?" must be "a European" and not "an Italian" or "a Venetian."[14] The ethical European identifies first of all not with people of her nationality but with all Europeans.

If either of these justifications for the existence of EU-level rights is accepted, so that the answer to the first question posed above becomes "yes," then the answer to the third question also is yes. The only justification for defining rights at the EU level is to be able to "trump" national and local majorities that may try to tyrannize over minorities in particular contexts.[15]

4.6 Citizen Rights within the European Union

Before closing this chapter, I will pause to examine the situation as it pertains to citizen rights within the European Union today, and as may be the case under a new European Union Constitution.

Today a European Union citizen has two sets of rights—one defined in the constitution of the nation state of which she is a citizen, a second defined in the Convention for the Protection of Human Rights and Fundamental Freedoms. Adoption of Article 5 of the proposed first 16 articles of the Constitutional Treaty would make the Charter of Fundamental Rights of the European Union part of the EU Constitution and give an EU citizen essentially three sets of constitutional rights. In this section I will discuss the status and content of a citizen's rights at the European level. To save space I will refer to the Convention for the Protection of Human Rights and Fundamental Freedoms as simply the *Convention*, and the Charter of Fundamental Rights of the European Union as the *Charter*.

Citizen Rights under the Convention

The Convention was first ratified by the members of the Council of Europe in 1950, and has been amended several times since. It contains 59 articles and is some 15 pages long, although only the first 18 articles (five plus pages) contain definitions of rights and freedoms, the remaining articles describe the European Court of Human Rights, which arbitrates the Convention, the procedures under which it operates, and so on.

The rights defined under the original Convention are in two senses subsidiary to those defined in the national constitutions. A citizen can seek satisfaction under the rights defined in the Convention only "after all domestic remedies have been exhausted" (Article 35). Thus a citizen's rights are in the first instance those as defined in the constitution of the nation state which has granted him citizenship.

The second sense in which the Convention's rights are subsidiary to those of the nation states is that many of the rights defined by the Convention are *conditional* on their not being in conflict with a national law. For example, Article 2 states that, "No one shall be deprived of his life intentionally *save in the execution of a sentence of a court following his conviction of a crime for which this penalty is provided by law*" (emphasis added). Article 4 prohibiting slavery and forced labor explicitly exempts involuntary military service. Article 10 protects freedom of expression "subject to such formalities, conditions, restrictions or penalties as are prescribed by law and are necessary in a democratic society," and so on. Several of the articles of the Convention explicitly state that the protected freedom is conditional on it not having been curtailed by legislation at the national level, and thus these rights are relative in that sense.

When no such conditions are present in the defined right or they are not fulfilled, the rights defined at the national level are subsidiary to those defined in the Convention. Its final judgments are binding on the countries that have accepted the convention. All current EU members have accepted the Convention.

Citizen Rights under the Charter

The Charter contains 54 articles devoted to defining rights and freedoms and runs to some 15 pages. An additional 83 pages of "notes" serves to explicate the meaning of the broad language contained in the Charter. Like many modern constitutions it is overly long and contains many articles in which the nature of the protection offered is ambiguous. Article 35, for example, ensures "a high level of human health protection," while Articles 37 and 38 ensure high levels of environmental and consumer protection. Article 33 offers the family "social protection."

Some of the articles are redundant or contradictory. Article 21, for example, states that, "Any discrimination based on any ground such as sex ... 16 additional criteria ... shall be prohibited." The first sentence of Article 23 goes on to ensure "equality between men and women." Such equality would, one would think, already have been ensured by the prohibition against discrimination on the grounds of sex contained in Article 21. Remarkably and contradictorily, the second sentence in Article 23 explicitly *allows* for discrimination on the grounds of sex, *when it leads to "specific advantages in favour of the under-represented sex."*

Some articles merely offer commentary or advice. The second provision under Article 12, for example, informs us that "Political parties at Union level contribute to expressing the political will of the citizens of the Union." A profound observation without doubt, but in what sense does it define a "fundamental right"?

Enough has been said to suggest to the reader that many of the articles of the Charter would not find support among large numbers of European citizens as currently drafted. Should the Charter's definitions of rights become binding on all citizens and countries, conflicts with local preferences and laws would seem inevitable. Unlike in the original Convention many articles in the Charter do not explicitly defer to national laws and policies. Article 2 explicitly forbids capital punishment and thus would, presumably, preclude any country's introducing capital punishment for any type of crime, however serious. Article 5 prohibits slavery and forced labor and would, under a liberal interpretation, make conscription for military and civil service unconstitutional. Articles 11 and 12 ensuring freedoms of expression and association would, under a liberal interpretation, make Germany's and Austria's laws regarding the Nazi party unconstitutional. It is difficult to see how the long and broad set of rights defined in the Charter would not result in numerous conflicts with member countries over existing and future laws.

Relationship between the Convention and the Charter

The Charter was drafted by a special committee set up by the European Union and was signed by representatives on the European Parliament, the Council and the Commission in December of 2000. Article

2 of the draft of a new European Constitution, which appeared in the fall of 2002, leaves open the question of whether the Charter would merely be mentioned in the Constitution or would be included in full as a "bill of rights." Nevertheless, Article 2 proclaims "respect" for human rights as defined in both the Convention and the Charter. As we have seen, however, the nature of the rights defined in the two documents is often quite different. While the Convention would allow a country to introduce capital punishment, the Charter would forbid it. Which interpretation should be binding? The sweeping and often ambiguous language of the Charter would open the door for considerable constitutional disagreement over the status of both existing and future national laws. The adoption of the Charter as a binding part of a European Union Constitution would lay open the danger of continual legal strife between member countries and the Union, and of the eventual dismemberment of the Union.

4.7 Conclusions

The optimal criteria for defining citizenship and delineating citizens' rights in the European Union rest crucially on the distribution of preferences. If the distribution of preferences justifies a confederate structure of the European Union, as exists now, then rights should be delineated in the constitutions of the member countries, and no EU-level rights should exist. Member countries should be free to impose strict conditions for obtaining citizenship even on citizens from other European countries. Citizen rights defined at the EU level, on the other hand, can be defended, if one assumes (1) that individual preferences are dispersed across the Union, and thus every country contains people with similar preferences to the other countries, (2) that individuals within the Union are highly mobile, or (3) that they tend to identify first of all with other Europeans rather than people from their own countries, when making ethical choices.

Up to the present, mobility across borders within the European Union has been surprisingly low, and few people seem to think of themselves as Europeans first and Swedes or Greeks second. These facts would seem to favor leaving definitions of citizenship and rights to the individual countries. As we have seen, the Charter defines numerous broad rights which, if they were liberally interpreted, would run afoul of current or potentially future actions by national parliaments. The continual assassinations by terrorists in Spain have led some people in that country to propose introducing the death penalty for terrorist murders. If Spain were to do so, and the Charter were part of a European constitution, Spain would be in violation of the constitution. Would the other EU countries expel Spain from the European Union for such a violation? Would the EU be improved by such an expulsion?

The preamble to the Charter begins with the words "The peoples of Europe...." In its second sentence, however, it goes on to proclaim the existence of *universal* values, which it intends to define in the Charter. The use of the word *peoples* suggests that Europe is made up of a heterogeneous mixture of different groups of people. Thus the first two sentences of the Charter illustrate the tension between the heterogeneous nature of Europe, and the desire to impose homogeneous definitions of rights and citizenship.

The US Constitution begins with the words "We the people of the United States...." Although it would have been common at the time of the Philadelphia Convention for people to think of themselves first of all as Virginians or Pennsylvanians and second of all as Americans, the drafters of the US Constitution recognized a degree of homogeneity among the colonists—forged by their common effort against England in the Revolutionary War—that made it possible for them to think they were drafting a constitution for *a people* rather than for a set of peoples. That the drafters of the Charter apparently perceived that they were drafting a document for a diverse collection of *peoples* should be cause for concern about the nature of the document.

A noticeable difference between the United States and Europe is that American politicians think of themselves as, and act to a greater degree as, servants of the citizens. If the citizens are concerned about crime, then the politicians pass tougher laws, and build more jails and gas chambers, regardless of "expert opinion" questioning the efficacy of such actions. In Europe, however, political leaders seem more often to believe that citizens *ought* to think and behave as the experts and politicians think that they should.

Recent election results in the Netherlands, France, and other EU countries have revealed that the leaders of the major parties are greatly out of touch with the thinking of many voters regarding issues like immigration and crime. Large numbers of voters in these countries seem to have opinions on issues such as these that run against what has been defined by the elites of Europe as "politically correct." A similar danger looms with respect to a new constitution for the European Union.

The occasion of writing a new constitution might have seemed like the perfect opportunity to involve the citizens of Europe in "the European Union project"—an opportunity to correct "the democratic deficit" in the Union. The obvious way to accomplish this would have been to involve citizens in the process of convening the convention by, say, having them elect delegates to the convention. Instead, the delegation to the convention is a mixture of members of the political elite which already governs the European Union (e.g., members of the Commission and the EU Parliament), and delegates chosen from the parliaments and governments of the member countries, delegates chosen in the same way that the members of the assembly that drafted the Charter were chosen—by the political elites of each country. Consequently there was no direct participation by European citizens in the selection of the delegates, and most EU citizens undoubtedly have no knowledge of the identity of *their* representatives.

This method of selecting delegations is not unlike that used to select delegations from the colonies to the constitutional convention in Philadelphia in 1787. Perhaps the final document produced by the European Convention will be just as good or even better than the US Constitution. The task of the delegates in Philadelphia was made considerably easier by the absence of antifederalists at the convention (Riker 1987). Those who did attend were thus left free to replace a loose confederation of colonies with what would eventually become a tight federation of states. A disproportionately large fraction of the delegates at the convention in Belgium appear to be favorably disposed to a more centralized and federalist Union, and the first draft of the European constitution would move Europe a major step in this direction.

The adoption of the US Constitution led to a rapid "meltdown" of state sovereignty, as is illustrated by the following statement by a member of the First Congress: "Among the first sentiments expressed in the first Congress was that Virginia is no more. That Massachusetts is no [more], that Pennsylvania is no more, etc. We are now a nation of brethren" (quoted by Berns 1988, p. 140). Enthusiasts for European integration also perhaps envisage a meltdown of state sovereignties should a constitution be adopted that creates a strong federalist structure. Even if such a constitution were adopted, however, it would be difficult to imagine the representatives at the first parliamentary session under the new constitution proclaiming, "Italy is no more; France is no more." The cultural differences across Europe today seem far greater than one imagines them having been in the American colonies at the end of the eighteenth century. To neglect these differences when writing a new constitution for Europe is to court considerable conflict and an eventual unraveling of the whole enterprise.

Notes

1. The discussion in this section draws on Mueller (2002a).

2. Let U_B and U_G be the utilities that a Blue and Green experience if their preferred form of public good is provided, and V_B and V_G be the utilities that each experiences if the other group's preferred form is provided. Then sole citizenship for Blues is optimal from behind the veil of ignorance if

$$pU_B + (1-p)U_G > pV_B + (1-p)V_G,$$

where p is the probability of being a Blue. If $p > 1 - p$, then this condition is satisfied when

$$U_B - V_B = V_G - U_G.$$

3. Thus the only way whites could dictate outcomes in South Africa was by denying blacks voting rights. Blacks, on the other hand, can dictate outcomes even when whites are allowed to vote under the simple majority rule.

4. Of course, one can have a liberal policy toward immigration and a stringent policy with respect to granting citizenship, as several EU countries have had, but I assume here that immigration will be greater, the more attractive it is, and granting citizenship under reasonable conditions is one way to increase the attractiveness of coming into the European Union.

5. For further discussion of the costs and issues arising from citizen mobility, see Mueller (2003, ch. 9).

6. It could be, of course, that individual preferences were homogeneous both within and across the member countries. No disagreements on EU policies would then arise, and all decisions could be made using the unanimity rule. There is considerable evidence against this being the case.

7. Draft of Articles 1 to 16 of the Constitutional Treaty, Brussels, February 6, 2003.

8. The classic reference here is, of course, Tiebout (1956). See also, Inman and Rubinfeld (1997) and Mueller (2003, ch. 9).

9. For further discussion, see Mueller (1997, 2002b).

10. Specifically, I assume $p'(m) > 0$, $p''(m) < 0$, and $(m = 1) : (p(m) = 1)$.

11. The discussion to this point reproduces in a slightly different way the classic treatment of the choice of a voting rule by Buchanan and Tullock (1962, pp. 63–91). See also Mueller (2001).

12. For further discussion of these issues, see either Mueller (1991) or Mueller (1996, ch. 14).

13. Note that having given sets of preferences dispersed across Europe does not suffice to justify EU-wide rights. A person with a particular set of preferences in a community

in which he is in the majority has no reason to wish to define a right with respect to this set of preferences. Such a right becomes in his self-interest only if he might leave the community.

14. The issue of how wide an individual's frame of reference will be is discussed in Mueller (1974).

15. For a discussion of the constitutional trumps issue in the context of US federalism, see Gillette (1997).

References

Berns, W. 1988. The writing of the Constitution of the United States. In R. A. Goldwin and A. Kaufman (eds.): *Constitution Makers and Constitution Making*. Washington, DC: American Enterprise Institute, pp. 119–53.

Buchanan, J. M., and G. Tullock. 1962. *The Calculus of Consent*. Ann Arbor: University of Michigan Press.

Gillette, C. P. 1997. The exercise of trumps by decentralized governments. *Virginia Law Review* 83: 1347–1417.

Inman, R. P., and D. L. Rubinfeld. 1997. The political economy of federalism. In D. C. Mueller (ed.): *Perspectives on Public Choice*. Cambridge: Cambridge University Press, pp. 73–105.

Mueller, D. C. 1974. Achieving the just polity. *American Economic Review* 64: 147–52.

Mueller, D. C. 1991. Constitutional rights. *Journal of Law, Economics, and Organization* 7: 313–33.

Mueller, D. C. 1996. *Constitutional Democracy*. Oxford: Oxford University Press.

Mueller, D. C. 1997. Federalism and the European Union: A constitutional perspective. *Public Choice* 90: 255–80.

Mueller, D. C. 2000. Capitalism, democracy and rational individual behavior. *Journal of Evolutionary Economics* 10: 67–82.

Mueller, D. C. 2001. The importance of uncertainty in a two-stage theory of constitutions. *Public Choice* 108: 223–58.

Mueller, D. C. 2002a. Defining citizenship. *Theoretical Inquiries in Law* 3: 151–66.

Mueller, D. C. 2002b. Constitutional issues regarding European Union expansion. In B. Steunenberg (ed.): *Widening the European Union*. London: Routledge, pp. 41–57.

Mueller, D. C. 2003. *Public Choice III*. Cambridge: Cambridge University Press.

Riker, W. H. 1987. The lessons of 1787. *Public Choice* 55: 5–34.

Tiebout, C. M. 1956. A pure theory of local expenditures. *Journal of Political Economy* 64: 416–24.

5   Enlargements and the Principles of Designing EU Decision-Making Procedures

Mika Widgrén

5.1 Introduction

Experiences on earlier enlargements and especially the Nice reforms demonstrate that the design of decision-making procedures and voting rules in EU institutions belong to the most cumbersome parts of membership negotiations. Since the institutional arrangements and decision-making in the EU are not based on clear constitutional rules this creates unnecessary additional costs for enlargements and potential secession. The lack of underlying principles in the design of decision-making rules also unnecessarily increases pressures and demands to re-negotiate the rules.

The Nice Summit in December 2000 confirms the difficulties that may arise when enlargements and institutional reforms are tied together.[1] The main argument behind the need of the reform was the fact that large member states have weaker representation and less power in the Council than their share of EU population would suggest while for the smallest countries the reverse holds. Since the current candidate countries are mainly small nations the problem was seen more urgent in the eyes of EU leaders than before. This started the reform process soon after the 1995 enlargement.[2] In the Council of Ministers, the Treaty of Nice introduced the first re-weighting of member states' voting rights since the establishment of the European Community in 1957.[3]

The determination of voting rights in the Council looks automatic but, in practice, it is far from that. With this respect there are three striking features. First, new entrants' voting rights have always been negotiated as a part of their accession treaties and, second, as the system—both before and after Nice—puts member states into categories all countries within one category having the same number of votes, the assignment of groups to the new entrants have always been a tough question in membership negotiations.[4] A third striking aspect is the fact that the current system, still in power till the enlargement, has not been updated to reflect changes in member states relative sizes.[5] In sum, it seems that eastern enlargement was used to reform (and update) the system without regarding the two first shortcomings of the system.

As the entry of new member states requires incumbent countries' unanimous agreement, threats of vetoing a candidate country's entry can be used to gain in negotiations on required reforms in institutional rules or in general in EU decision-making. To avoid the bias to decision-making institutions caused by the seek of short-run gains, the task of the constitution is to design the institutional structure and the decision-making rules using acceptable transparent principles that are neutral to changes in membership and that can be automatically revised if the basis of these principles change.

The objective of this chapter is to assess EU decision-making procedures and, related to them, two well-known principles of designing legitimate institutions in terms of their neutrality to membership. We argue that in normative sense the constitutional rules should obey the following two principles

1. The EU as a union of states and a union of citizens (USC)
2. One-person–one-vote principle (OPOV).

In a federation, the former gives equal weights to the union of states legitimacy and the union of citizens legitimacy. In a confederation the latter gets a lower weight and in purely intergovernmental approach it diminishes to zero.

Figure 5.1 gives the structure of our analysis. We assume that the constitution gives general desirable goals for the institutional structure in the European Union and the consequent decision-making rules (i.e., procedures, voting rights and majority rules) are defined to achieve the goals. Examples of the former could be like "all EU citizens should be equally represented" or "the European Parliament and the Council should be equal decision-makers." The equilibrium analysis is then carried out to determine the policy implications of the legislative procedures, and ex ante assessment of the equilibrium analysis reveals what kind of principles the legislative procedures are built upon and how stable or neutral to membership these principles are.

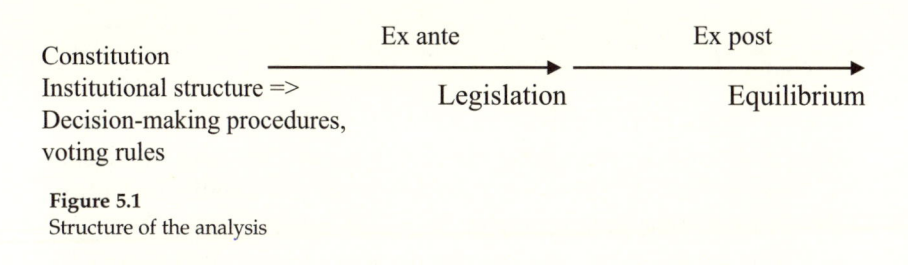

```
                        Ex ante              Ex post
Constitution         ─────────────►    ─────────────►
Institutional structure =>    Legislation       Equilibrium
Decision-making procedures,
voting rules
```

Figure 5.1
Structure of the analysis

5.2 The Tools

Influence is a crucial element in any decision-making institution. The role of the decision-making rules or, more generally, institutional design is to affect power relations.

Theoretically the quantitative analysis of decision-making rules can be divided into two distinct methods based on cooperative and noncooperative games. Scholars of cooperative game theory apply different power indexes, mainly for assessing the implications of different decision-making rules on agents who are assumed to have no particular preferences. The agents form winning coalitions, which then implement, in the analysis, unspecified policies. Individual chances of being part of and influencing a winning coalition are then measured by a power index.[6] By disregarding individual preferences, we can observe this approach to fit well in the evaluation of constitutional rules.

The noncooperative approach, on the other hand, evaluates explicit decision procedures over a well-defined policy space.[7] In this approach the conclusions are based on equilibrium analysis, which requires detailed information regarding the agents' preferences. As such, the noncooperative approach does not fit the analysis of constitutional rules, but if one considers the several realizations of agent preference constellations, similar conclusions can be drawn on performance of the constitutional rules. This adaptation can also be seen as a bridge between the two game-theoretic approaches.[8]

The cooperative approach fits the institution design when the rules are understood simply as voting weights and a vote threshold that is required for the passage of a proposal. It is the method that fits, for example, the assessment of power distribution in a single decision-making body like the Council. Among the cooperative one useful tool in the analysis of constitutional rules is the Penrose-Banzhaf measure (PBM),[9] which can be written as

$$\beta_i = \frac{s_i}{\sum_{i=1}^{n} s},$$

where s_i refers to the number of winning coalitions in which i has a swing position (i.e., can swing the coalition from winning into losing by changing his vote). Power is thus defined as one's ability to contribute to the existing state of affairs. To assess relative power, the PBM is often normalized by dividing the number of individual swings by the total number of swings; this is then referred to as the (normalized) Banzhaf index (NBI).

Interinstitutional aspects play a significant role in the design of decision-making rules and procedures. For instance, the EU Treaties define explicitly the actors that are involved in decision-making, the procedures used, and the way the decisions are made, namely the sequence of moves. This cannot be evaluated appropriately by the cooperative approach, since it cannot take strategic interinstitutional or procedural aspects of EU decision-making into account.

Consider a simple agenda-setting game where an institution makes a legislative proposal to a decision-making body that either accepts or rejects the proposal. By the simultaneous coalition-based approach, all winning coalitions must contain the acceptance of the agenda-setting institution plus a required majority in decision-making institution. This approach completely disregards the fact that the agenda setter moves first—decision-making is procedural not simultaneous. Suppose, for simplicity, that the agenda setter is a single player and the passage of a proposal requires unanimous acceptance in the decision-making body. Then the power index approach suggests that each player in the latter is as powerful as the former, but this is not trivially true since the agenda setter moves first.

The criticism toward classical power indexes does not, however, mean that the core of power index approach, namely the definition of power as a player's marginal contribution, is useless. In a strategic procedural environment, this application leads us quite naturally to define power as a player's expected marginal contribution to the equilibrium outcome (see Napel and Widgrén 2004 for a detailed discussion). This strategic power index can be written as

$$\xi_i = \int_A \frac{\partial \chi(\lambda_i, \lambda_{-i})}{\partial \lambda_i} dP,$$

where χ is the equilibrium outcome of a (spatial) voting procedure as a

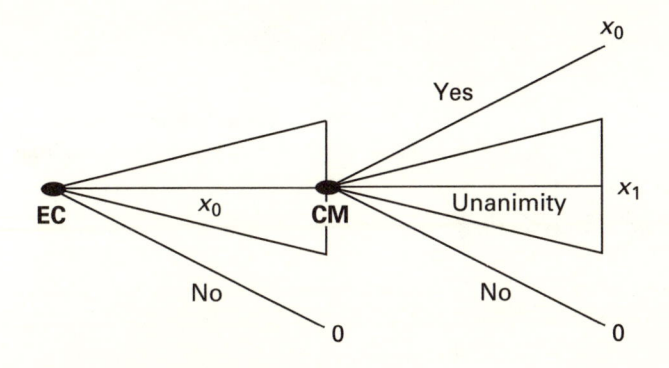

Enlargements and Principles of Designing EU Decision-Making

[Figure 5.2: diagram showing EC proposing X_0 to CM, with branches Yes leading to X_0, Unanimity leading to X_1, and No branches leading to 0]

EC: European Commission
CM: Council of Ministers

Figure 5.2
Consultation procedure

function of player i's (spatial) preferences λ_i and other players' (spatial) preferences λ_{-i}, A denotes the policy space of the game, and P gives the a priori probability distribution of players' ideal policy positions, meaning their spatial preferences in the policy space A. In the following we assume that $A = [0, 1]$, the unit interval where the current state of legislation is normalized to zero and that actors' ideal policy positions are uniformly distributed on $[0, 1]$.

5.3 Investigating the EU Institutional Structure

The European Union has three main decision-making bodies: the Commission, the Council, and the European Parliament (EP). Its two main decision-making procedures are consultation and co-decision (see figures 5.2 and 5.3 for the sequence of moves in co-decision procedure). The most fundamental difference between the two procedures is that the former relates to intergovernmental cooperation whereas the latter is more supranational and federalist oriented. In consultation procedure (see figure 5.2), say the Commission proposes X_0 and the Council decides. The proposal X_0 passes if it gets the qualified majority support in the Council. A unanimous Council decision can be used to amend the Commission's proposal, and then X_1 is the outcome. The Commission can also decide to not to propose, and then the legislative status quo prevails. The same procedure can lead the Council to reject the

EC: European Commission
CM: Council of Ministers
EP: European Parliament
CC: Conciliation Committee

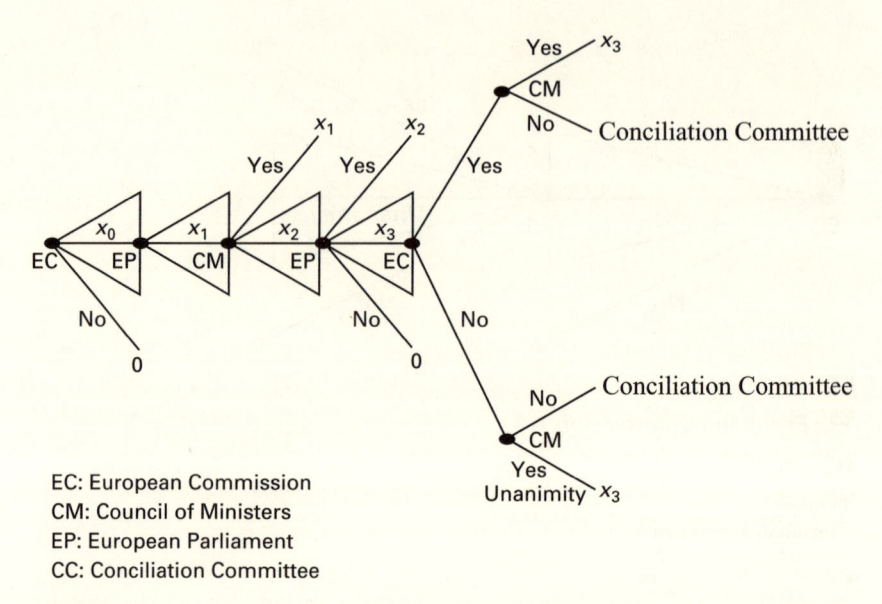

Figure 5.3
Co-decision procedure

proposal. The Commission thus exerts agenda-setting power and gatekeeping power and the Council decision-making power. In the consultation procedure, the EP can only express its opinion on a proposal but this does not bind either the Council or the Commission.

In our one-dimensional policy space, the equilibrium outcome of consultation procedure can be described as follows: The Commission picks the majority coalition where the swing-player's ideal point is very close to the Commission's ideal point. If it is closer to the Commission's ideal point than to the legislative status quo, then the Commission's ideal policy passes. If it is not, then the Commission makes the closest swing-player only a weakly better off with the proposal than with the status quo. In our strategic power measure above, this means that, in the former case, the Commission and, in the latter case, the swing-player can exert a small change in the outcome. Over several preference configurations swing-players and their positions will vary. The strategic power index computes the players' average impact in a uniformly distributed ideal policy position space.[10]

The co-decision procedure is more complicated. The main difference from the consultation procedure is that co-decision empowers the EP. Figure 5.3 gives a detailed description of the co-decision procedure.

First, the Commission submits a draft proposal to the EP, which can accept a proposal as it is or propose amendments. Whether original or amended, the proposal is submitted to the Council, which can accept it or propose further amendments. Council acceptance leads to the outcome X_1 in figure 5.3. If the Council proposes amendments, the procedure continues with a proposal X_2, which can be then accepted, amended, or rejected by the EP. This stage of the procedure gives the EP some agenda-setting powers if the EP decides to propose amendments to the proposal X_2.

The EP proposal X_3 is then studied by the Commission, which can reject or accept it. Note, however, that the Commission's view does not bind the Council, which is the next mover. This is because by overruling the Commission's view, the Council can start conciliation with the EP. In practice, this means that the EP and the Council can together amend the Commission's proposals, and as this does not require unanimous acceptance in either of these bodies, co-decision can in fact restrict the Commission powers significantly.

The Conciliation Committee controls the core phase of the procedure. It is co-chaired by the president of the European Parliament and the member state that is holding presidency in the Council. Before the Committee meets, the member state that holds presidency has a leading role as the agenda-setter and the gate-keeper. To put this into a more general perspective, another way to model the decision-making in the Conciliation Committee is by a simple agenda-setting model, whereby the executive takes the initiative. The executive can be the member state that is holding presidency in the Council or an elected president. Where the former scenario emphasizes intergovernmental approach as it gives agenda-setting power to each government on rotating basis, the latter scenario gives the agenda-setting power to a separate supranational institution. Let us refer to these models more generally as the executive model.[11] This way we can observe better the role of the Commission. If we assume that the president has two hats, then we have the Commission's president acting as president of the Council as well.

The logic behind the equilibrium outcome is similar to that of the conciliation procedure described above. The agenda-setter, seen now as president, needs a majority support in the Council and an absolute majority in the EP. In each preference configuration the president exerts power if both the EP and the Council swing-players have their ideal policy positions closer to the president than to the legislative

Table 5.1
Impact of Nice reforms on main EU institutions' consultation procedures

	CM	EC	CM(E)	EC(E)	Differences (CM)	Differences (EC)
Q = 71%	0.813	0.531	0.744	0.592	−0.069	0.061
Q = 74%	0.922	0.477	0.831	0.549	−0.092	0.072
Difference	0.109	−0.054	0.086	−0.043	0.017	0.018

Table 5.2
Impact of Nice reforms on main EU institutions' co-decision procedures

	CM	EP	CM(E)	EP(E)	Differences (CM)	Differences (EP)
Q = 71%	0.658	0.178	0.668	0.173	0.010	−0.005
Q = 74%	0.731	0.162	0.727	0.162	−0.004	0.000
Difference	0.073	−0.016	0.059	−0.011	0.069	−0.016

status quo. If this is not the case, either the EP or the Council swing-player can exert power, depending on which one is closer to the legislative reference point (i.e., is more reluctant to shift the current state of affairs).

The consultation procedure is purely a matter of intergovernmental negotiation. For this reason it can be best applied in policy domains that depend on cooperation. The extent of supranationalism involved can be measured by the Commission's power relative to the Council. Within the Council, the OPOV principle generally holds (see section 5.5).

The co-decision procedure can be seen as federalist. It is here that both OPOV and USC principles hold. Union of states and citizen rule guarantee equal weights to the EP and the Council. As more weight is given to the Council's constitution, this shifts co-decision toward intergovernmental cooperation.

Table 5.1 shows the effects of Nice reforms on majority threshold before and after the enlargement and the effects of enlargement with under pre-Nice and post-Nice quota. Table 5.2 gives the corresponding effects in co-decision procedure.[12] The total effect can be computed either by taking the effect of enlargement under the old threshold and then the threshold effect or by taking the effect of the change in thresh-

Enlargements and Principles of Designing EU Decision-Making   93

old and then the effect of the enlargement under the new threshold. The total effects are shown on the two rightmost columns of the third row. As before EP refers to the European Parliament, CM to the Council, and EC to the Commission. In both tables columns 2 and 3 give the pre-enlargement figures, columns 4 and 5 post-enlargement figures, and columns 6 and 7 the differences.

Table 5.1 shows that both the Council and the Commission gained somewhat in consultation procedure as a result of Nice reforms. More generally, this procedure is close to an intergovernmental take-it-or-leave-it agenda-setting game. With the exception of the very high quotas, the membership size seems to benefit the agenda-setter, who presides in the Commission, whereas the legislature, meaning the Council, seems to diminish in power. The balance is restored between the two enlargements, as member states receive incentives to increase the vote threshold as decided in Nice. It is worth noting, though, that each member state lost power after each enlargement because the number of member states in the Council increased.

In consultation area, the threshold in the Council is reached when the power balance between the Commission and the Council is 67 percent in the EU15 and remains the same in the EU27. Figure 5.4 demonstrates this more generally. It shows the effects of enlargement on strategic power measures of the Council and the Commission. The former is increasing with the Council quota and the latter is decreasing. The figure shows that the effect of the enlargement is almost monotonic with the quota. Even at high quotas the Council loses power, and the Commission gains. However, at unanimity rule, the Council gains, and there are no significant effects for the Commission. From the viewpoint of interinstitutional power this makes unanimity rule stable, as there are no strong incentives to deviate from it when the membership expands. Figure 5.4 suggests that a two-thirds majority also imparts stability.

In the European Union, the consultation procedure was the only legislative procedure until 1986 and unanimity rule was the only voting rule until 1966. The 1966 Luxembourg compromise made it possible to adopt unanimity rule to serve national interests even where majority decision was possible. A qualified majority vote was mainly plugged into a new procedure introduced to serve the Single Market Program. Today unanimity is still more often applied in consultation than in co-decision procedures.

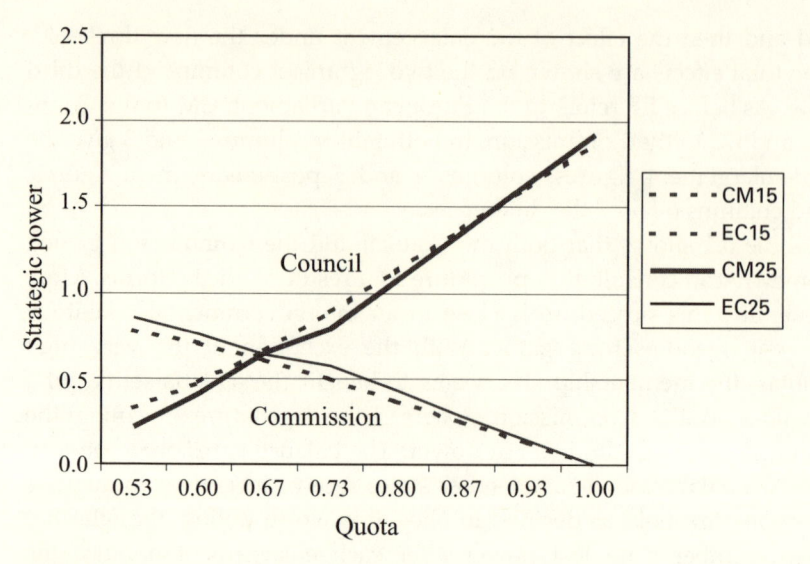

Figure 5.4
Strategic power in consultation procedure

If unanimity rule is desirable for an interinstitutional balance of power, what might explain the deviation from it in the European Union since the late-1980s. One explanation may be that in enabling interinstitutional balance of power, it effects an intra-institutional distribution of power. In relative terms, the big countries lose more than the small countries as the membership expands and unanimity rule is applied. This issue is explored more in detail in section 5.5.

In co-decision procedure the impact of the enlargement is practically zero (see table 5.2). The main difference between the procedures is that the magnitude of effects is smaller in the consultation procedure. In consultation procedure, the equilibrium outcome is determined by the policy positions of the median voter in the Commission and the pivotal player in the Council (the legislative initiator). In the co-decision procedure, the policy positions of the pivotal player in the Council and the median voter in the EP are both that of decision-maker in the Conciliation Committee. In both cases the source of Council gains is the fact that it uses qualified majority threshold whereas the Commission and the EP use absolute majority. The increase of the quota from 71 to 74 percent benefited the Council as can be seen in table 5.2.

Figures 5.5 and 5.6 show the impact of the enlargement on the interinstitutional balance of power in co-decision procedure for EU-27. The

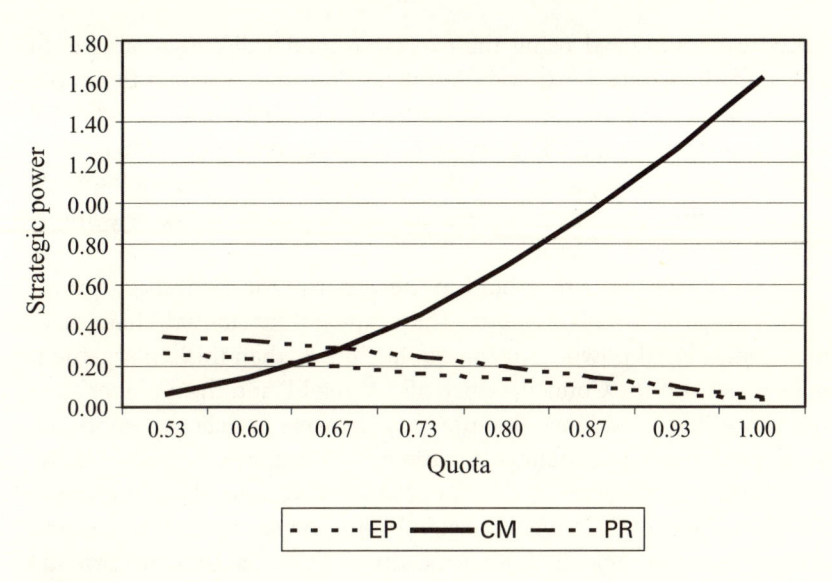

Figure 5.5
Strategic power in co-decision procedure

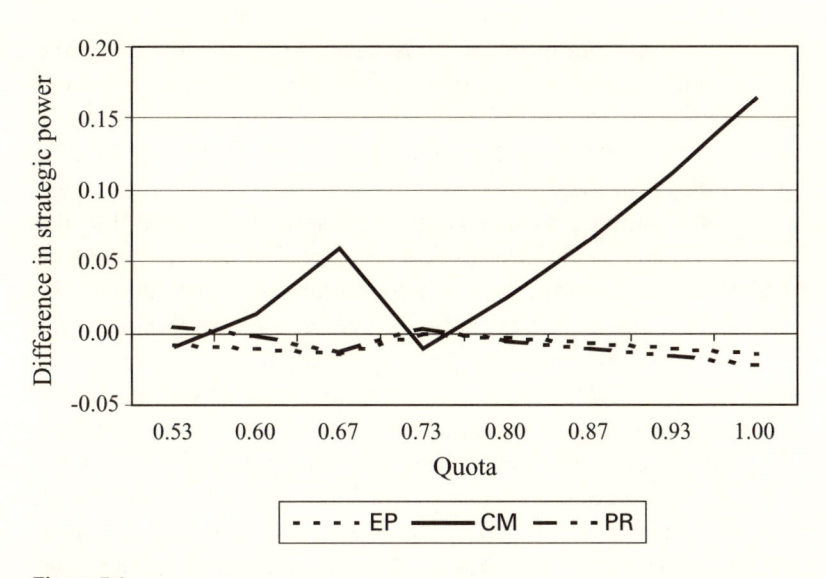

Figure 5.6
Impact of expanding membership on strategic power in co-decision procedure

procedure is modeled using the executive model discussed above. In figure 5.5 the Council exerts more power than the EP when the quota exceeds 62 percent, though the executive is more powerful than the EP regardless of the quota. The division of power between the executive and the Council is equal at two-thirds majority rule. This corresponds to consultation procedure where the Commission is the executive, which is intuitively plausible.

For the current vote threshold in the Council, the co-decision procedure is neutral to enlargement. There are no substantial changes in inter-institutional power. For the quotas higher than this, enlargement gains power for the Council, which affects the EP and the member state that is holding presidency. In sum, any increase in majority quota decided in Nice can be explained by attempts to balance the power in the consultation procedure. In the co-decision procedure, the old and the new threshold coincide with nonsignificant power changes. It is worth noting, however, that in both procedures the enlargements provide incentives for member states to increase the Council quota.

The executive model of the co-decision procedure can be divided into two "subgames." Where the executive has agenda-setting power in the Conciliation Committee, the relationship between the executive and the Council is close to that of the consultation procedure. Where this is not the case, the conciliation committee can be modeled as an alternating offers bargaining between the median voter in the EP and the pivotal player in the Council.

In a weak executive scenario, which corresponds rather well to the current co-decision procedure, there is a clear first-mover advantage in the Conciliation Committee. In relative terms, the advantage works in favor of the Council. If it is the first mover in the Conciliation Committee, it is more powerful than the EP regardless of the quota. If the EP offers first, the Council is more powerful provided that the quota exceeds two-thirds, as in consultation procedure between the Commission and the Council. The main reason for this asymmetry is that the ideal policy position of the pivotal player in the Council is likely to be more biased toward the legislative status quo than toward position of the median voter in the EP. This works like patience in normal bargaining setup.[13]

In the powerful executive scenario of figure 5.5, the distribution of power between the Council and the EP is neutral to the enlargement. If the executive is the rotating Council presidency, the Council is more powerful than the EP. This roughly corresponds with the case where the Council is the first mover in alternating the bargaining offers. The full influence of the Council is the vertical sum of the CM and PR curves in figure 5.5.

If the executive is a separate institution, there are two possible schemes. First, there is the double-hat scheme whereby the elected Commission president acts as the president of the Council as well, and second, there is the scheme where that presidents of the Commission and the Council are treated as two different institutions, whereby the latter might be elected by a qualified majority of the Council. Figure 5.4 includes the impact of these schemes in the co-decision. If the Commission president becomes the head of the Council, the PR-curve reflects the increased power of the Commission. However, although some power is shifted to the Commission, the Council still maintains its powerful hold based on the current quota. If a separate president is chosen, the PR-curve transfers the power to this person, and the Commission is pushed out to a gate-keeping role. The important, and potentially far-reaching implication, is that co-decision becomes inefficient in the case of a rotating presidency.

5.4 Inefficiency of Co-decision

An institution's capability to act or make decisions is often used to assess decision-making efficiency.[14] The main drawback of such an efficacy measure is its lack of strategic aspects. An abstract measure of an institution's capability to act can be simply obtained by computing its share of the majority of all coalitions. Such a picture of strategic aspects can give a different and a more procedure related picture on the sources of inefficiency.

As the status quo is normalized to zero in the analysis, all stakeholders are on the same side of the status quo and there are always gains from trade. That is to say, there always exists a proposal that makes all players at least weakly better-off than the existing state of affairs.

A common feature in both the consultation and co-decision procedures is that any Commission proposal can be amended and the amended proposal can then be accepted without the Commission's consent. In the consultation procedure, a unanimous Council vote will suffice and, in the co-decision procedure, the Conciliation Committee becomes involved. This weakens the Commission as an executive power and also makes both procedures inefficient. Since the

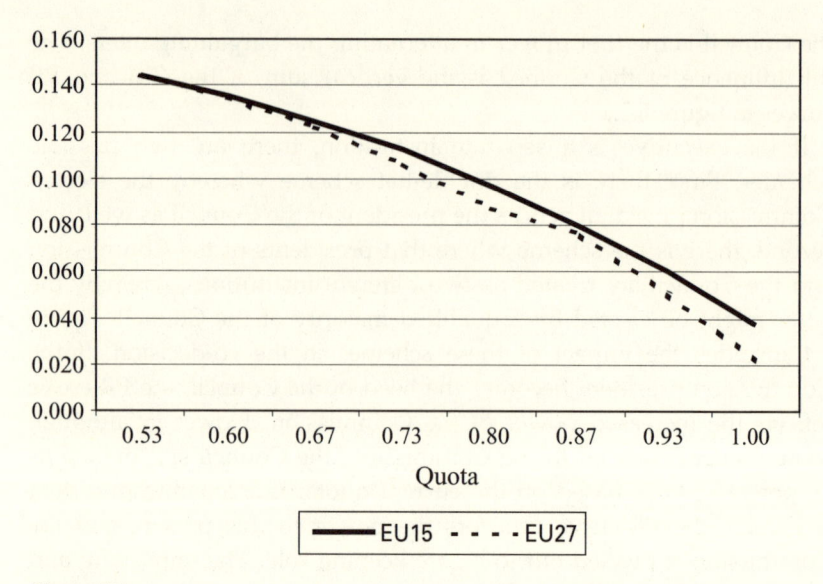

Figure 5.7
Probability gatekeeping bias in co-decision procedure

Commission exerts gate-keeping power, it may decide to not to make a proposal if it foresees an outcome that will be worse than the legislative reference point, the status quo. This way a status quo bias is created and hence inefficiency results because not all gains from trade can materialize. Note that some gains can still be obtained from trade in the sense that all actors prefer less integration or more decentralization. This way the status quo bias can become a centralization bias.

Figure 5.7 demonstrates this. It shows the probabilities of a status quo bias, that is, the percentage of issues where the Commission has incentives to use its gate-keeping power in legislative equilibrium. The figure gives the probabilities before and after enlargement as the quota in the Council is allowed to vary.

The conclusions that can be drawn from figure 5.7 are quite opposite to those based on passage probabilities. First, increasing the quota in the Council decreases inefficiency, and second, enlargement has practically no effect. The first phenomenon can be explained by the fact that a higher threshold decreases efficacy in the Conciliation Committee. That makes it less likely that the Commission will use its gate-keeping power. The outcome in the Conciliation Committee is then biased toward the status quo because of the quota used in the Council. The price of improving efficiency is deteriorating efficacy, which might limit the scope of EU decision-making superfluously. Using the current threshold gives the probability of status quo bias of more than one-tenth, which is substantial. Theoretically this means that every tenth decision that could have benefited all is not taken.[15]

One important difference between the co-decision and consultation procedures is that in the former the Council and the EP use the same quota in the Conciliation Committee as when they decide on Commission proposals. In the consultation procedure, amendments require a higher quota for their passage than do Commission proposals. In the co-decision procedure, a similar differentiation with the vote thresholds in the Conciliation Committee and on Commission proposals will lower the status quo bias toward gate-keeping without necessarily deteriorating efficacy in their passage. It is worth noting, however, that this solution only reduces inefficiency; it is not able to eliminate it completely.[16] That would give more powers to the Commission in the procedure. Another even more straightforward solution would be to make the Commission politically accountable, but that would not eliminate the inefficiency either from the procedure per se. A third alternative would be to take the Commission's role as an initiator and share it with another supranational institution, namely the EP.

5.5 Equal Representation of EU Citizens

In the 2000 intergovernmental conference, the Commission proposed a simple dual (SD) majority voting rule to the Council. The SD rule reflects the union of nations and union of citizens principle. The way it is applied is to subject all legislative proposals to acceptance by a majority of member states and a majority of EU citizens. It is worth noting that the SD rule is not weighted voting. The governments of member states do not have voting weights; rather, whether a proposal passes depends on the combination of the two majorities, which then determines the distribution of power among the member states.[17]

The Commission's proposal to the Council reflects more generally a voting rule typical of federal states. For instance, in the United States the majority vote of the states is relegated to the Senate and the majority vote of citizens to the House of Representatives. As both chambers become equal in power, as in the United States, the proposal treats only the national distribution of power and gives the same conclusion in one- and two-chamber decision-making. In the EU co-decision between the Council and the Parliament there are similarities to the federal system but the Council and the Parliament use different quotas.

One-person–one-vote (OPOV) principle is a cornerstone in the design of democratic institutions interested in the fair allocation of power in a federation or in two-tier decision-making.[18] Citizens in large states have less power in choosing their national government than citizens in small states. As a result large states compensate in their Councils by using voting weights. The right compensation that ensures the OPOV principle is known as the square-root rule, due to Penrose (1946). Applied to the EU Council, a fair power distribution among countries is determined by each country's square-root share of the EU population. Hence the fair power of country i is written

$$\beta_i^* = \frac{\sqrt{p_i}}{\sum_{j=1}^{n} \sqrt{p_j}},$$

Where p_i denotes the population of country i and β^* the fair (Banzhaf) index of power.

Table 5.3 gives the summary of differences between normalized Banzhaf indexes when two alternative dual majorities are used in the Council of the EU15 and EU27. The difference that we use is the sum of squares of the differences between the actual Banzhaf indexes and the fair ones. In the table, D50 refers to simple dual majority, which is the absolute majority of states and citizens, D62 refers to absolute majority of states and 62 percent majority of citizens,[19] and D74 to absolute majority of states and 74 percent majority of citizens. The alternatives SD50, SD62, and SD74 refer to similar dual majorities where, for the absolute majority of member states, 50 percent, 62 percent, and 74 percent majority of member states' square-rooted population is needed

Table 5.3
Sum of squares of differences between the NBI and the square-root rule ($\times 10^{-3}$)

Rule	EU15	EU27
D50	2.166	2.037
D62	3.588	2.690
D74	5.805	6.234
SD50	6.100	4.668
SD62	0.100	0.057
SD74	0.252	0.051
Nice weights	0.749	5.494

respectively to pass legislation. (We will refer to these rules as square-root dual majorities.) The last rows of each table give the results in terms of the Nice reform.

The results of the three categories suggest, not surprisingly, that square-root weights give a power distribution that is very close to the square-root rule. This is a common feature of classical power indexes. When the number of players increases, the power measures converge to voting weights if the variance of weights is relatively small. In the category of square-root dual majorities the performance is almost as good, but excluding the case where an absolute majority of square-rooted population is needed (SD50); here in terms of equal representation of EU citizens, it turns out to be the worst voting rule. In the category of dual majorities, simple dual majority performs the best.

Figure 5.8 confirms and generalizes the results in table 5.3. The figure shows the sums of squares of the differences between the fair power indexes based on the OPOV principle and the actual vote indexes where the Nice weights and square-root dual majorities are used. Common to both models is a wide range of equally good majority rules. For the Nice weights there are practically no differences in the range of thresholds between 55 and 80 percent. The performance of the square-root dual majorities is quite stable between 55 and 70 percent. Note, however, that the square-root dual majorities perform better than the Nice weights can do at their best between the 50 and 90 percent quotas. The most important conclusion that can be drawn from table 5.3 and figure 5.8 is that the square-root dual majorities seem to fit best the OPOV principle in the Council. Moreover the rule is as transparent as the simple dual majority rule proposed by the Commission, which would serve as the second-best solution here.

Figure 5.8 also explains why unanimity rule is not stable in the Council, although both procedures indicate a tendency toward it. The difference between OPOV principle and actual voting power increases rapidly as the quota gets higher. This is unfavorable to large countries where the deviation occurs. Interestingly, both procedures show more stable results of majority rule than the unanimity rule, and this is where the difference toward the OPOV principle is minimized.

5.6 Conclusions

In this chapter, I considered the EU decision-making procedures and voting rules. My particular focus was on their neutrality to the

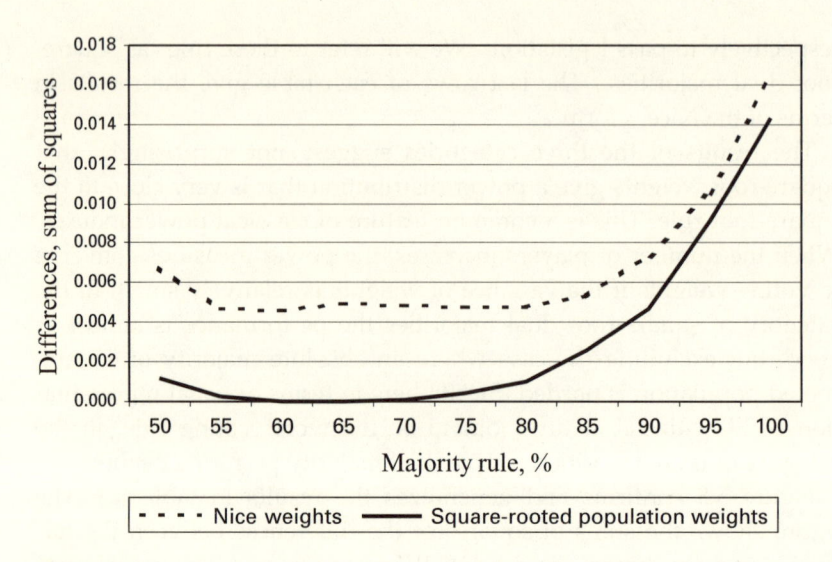

Figure 5.8
Difference between the OPOV principle and actual power scores in two weighting schemes

membership. I assessed the interinstitutional power of the two main EU decision-making procedures, their efficacy and efficiency in decision-making, and the impact of expanding membership on national distribution of power in both procedures. My objective was to study how some general constitutional principles can contribute to the design of EU decision-making and how neutral decision-making rules can be derived from such principles.

As the chapter demonstrates, the interinstitutional power in EU procedures is relatively neutral to expanding (or decreasing) the membership. This especially holds for the co-decision procedure. Both procedures provide incentives toward unanimity rule if the quota is decided by member states' governments, but both procedures observe majority rule.

At the two extremes are alternatives to the OPOV design of the European Union: the purely intergovernmental union and the USC principle. The former design suggests strengthening the Council and weakening or removing the roles of the Commission and the EP. In the latter case there would be a co-decision relationship between the EP and the Council with a relatively strong, but accountable, Commission. By the current rules used in the consultation procedure, the Council would be the more powerful actor. Despite its role as the initiator, the Commission will exert less power. The difference is not very big though. The consultation procedure is not therefore purely intergovernmental. As it fails to meet the USC principle, it does not belong to the policy domains that pertain to Union competence but rather to the policy domains that are organized under enhanced cooperation. The results suggest that a two-thirds majority vote would balance the power between the Commission and the Council.

The co-decision procedure fits better to the USC principle. As the chapter shows, exercising the strong official executive role can be a member state holding the presidency or an elected president. If this person is also the president of the Commission, then the power of president brings the power of the Commission to the procedure. The former model makes the Council the most powerful actor and makes it impossible to obey the USC principle. The role of the EP is weaker, and there exist no Council quotas that make the EP an equal partner to the Council.

Another feature of the procedure is the Commission's role. The Commission's gate-keeping is diminished as the Council and the EP use the same threshold in the Conciliation Committee and when they decide on Commission proposals. That makes the procedure inefficient. The likelihood of inefficiency is neutral to membership, however.

A possible way to deal with this inefficiency problem is to apply higher thresholds in the Conciliation Committee on deciding the Commission proposals. Another may be to make the Commission politically accountable to the EP and the Council, and thus diminish harmful effect of its gate-keeping. Neither solution removes the problem completely, however.

Yet a different approach may be to divide the power to initiate between the Commission and the EP. As the EP sits on the Conciliation Committee, this would make the procedure efficient. It could raise the competition for proposals, which could then be eased by introducing a powerful executive position. A double-hat presidency might work, where the president of the Commission is also the president of the Council. The problem with this solution is the potential centralization bias it would facilitate, and this could be avoided by introducing a situation whereby the EP can work as a co-initiator with the Commission.

The distribution of national power is another important aspect of EU institutions. The intra-institutional distribution of power currently does not have much effect on the interinstitutional distribution of power, but EU enlargements will affect intra-institutional power and the performance of the USC and OPOV principles. This is why this question is analyzed separately. The results suggest a trade-off between OPOV and USC principles in arriving at a constitutional base for decision-making rules in the European Union. It turns out that a simple dual majority rule that takes the USC rule literally does not work very well in representing citizens but it appears to be an improvement over the current weighting approach. The so-called square-root dual majorities are as transparent as (simple) dual majorities and carry out a power distribution that is practically identical with that of the fair distribution.

Notes

The author is grateful for Gerrit Köster, the conference participants, and two anonymous referees for beneficial comments.

1. In the case of eastern enlargement the Treaty of Nice defines candidate countries' voting rights in the Council and numbers of seats in the European Parliament and consequent vote threshold in the Council. Strictly speaking, the latter is, however, defined for EU27 and this must still be negotiated since only 10 new countries will join in the first phase in May 2004. Possible rejection of the Accession Treaty in any candidate country would require still another negotiation round.

2. Note that there was a debate on votes in the Council before Austria's, Finland's and Sweden's entry as well. That finally led to so-called Ionnina compromise whereby 23 votes minority of the total 87 votes in the Council can postpone the acceptance of a proposal by three months and put in under reconsideration. Qualified majority that is needed for passage of a proposal is 62 votes, i.e. 71 percent. The compromise was a result of some member states' claims for increasing the quota to 65 out of 87 votes, which is nearly 75 percent.

3. In 1973 the original numbers of votes were multiplied by 2.5 and Luxembourg's votes only by 2. This, of course had a small re-weighting effect as well. Since 1973 the incumbent countries' numbers of votes have remained the same.

4. In terms of their populations, Sweden and Austria are rather close to middle-sized countries having five votes each. They also had this as their goal in membership negotiations. A new category of four votes was, however, established (see Hamilton 1991 or Widgrén 1994 for a more detailed discussion).

5. The best example is the Netherlands where the size of the population has increased by 60 percent since the time of the Treaty of Rome. See also Laruelle and Widgrén (1998).

6. See, for example, Laruelle and Widgrén (1998), Baldwin et al. (2000, 2001), Felsenthal and Machover (2001), and Leech (2002) for recent applications of traditional power indexes. Felsenthal and Machover (1998) and Nurmi (1998) include a more general discussion of index-based power analysis.

7. See, for example, Steunenberg (1994), Tsebelis (1994, 1996), Crombez (1996, 1997), and Moser (1996, 1997).

8. See Steunenberg et al. (1999) and Napel and Widgrén (2003, 2004).

9. It is often referred simply to as the Banzhaf index or measure; see, however, Felsenthal and Machover (1998).

10. For a more formal treatment, see, for example, Steunenberg (1994) and Napel and Widgrén (2004).

11. The third alternative is to interpret the procedure as (alternating offers) bargaining game between the EP and the Council (for details, see Napel and Widgrén 2003).

12. Here we disregard the effects of the changes in inter-Council distribution of power. According to the earlier results the power distribution within the Council does not have a significant effect on interinstitutional distribution of power at the aggregate level.

13. See Napel and Widgrén (2003) for details.

14. For applications on the eastern enlargement, see, for example, Baldwin et al. (2000, 2001), and on the 1995 enlargement, Widgrén (1993, 1995).

15. In the consultation procedure, a status quo bias does not exist in the above-mentioned sense. A unanimous Council vote can amend the Commission's proposals, but the likelihood of amending them in a way that leads the Commission to use its gate-keeping power is very small. In the EU15 the probability of status quo bias in consultation procedure is $1.9 \cdot 10^{-6}$ and in the EU27 even smaller.

16. A solution that requires the unanimous consent of both the EP and the Council would not in practice remove it but would decrease efficacy dramatically.

17. A simple dual majority can be interpreted as a weighted vote with an additional safety-net that guarantees support from the absolute majority of the member states.

18. For earlier analysis on the EU, see Laruelle and Widgrén (1998).

19. The choice of 62 percent is due to the Nice reform, which defines the voting rule in the Council as a mix of voting weights and the D62 rule.

References

Baldwin, R., E. Berglöf, F. Giavazzi, and M. Widgrén. 2000. The EU Reforms for Tomorrow's Europe. CEPR Discussion paper 2623.

Baldwin, R., E. Berglöf, F. Giavazzi, and M. Widgrén. 2001. *Nice Try: Should the Treaty of Nice Be Ratified? Monitoring European Integration 11*. London: Centre for Economic Policy Research.

Crombez, C. 1996. Legislative procedures in the European Community. *British Journal of Political Science* 26: 199–228.

Crombez, C. 1997. The co-decision procedure in the European Union. *Legislative Studies Quarterly* 22: 97–119.

Felsenthal, D., and M. Machover. 1998. *The Measurement of Voting Power: Theory and Practice, Problems and Paradoxes*. Cheltenham: Edward Elgar.

Felsenthal, D., and M. Machover. 2001a. Myths and Meanings of Voting Power. *Journal of Theoretical Politics* 13: 81–7.

Felsenthal, D., and M. Machover. 2001b. The Treaty of Nice and qualified majority voting. *Social Choice and Welfare* 18: 431–64.

Garrett, G., and G. Tsebelis. 1999a. Why resist the temptation to apply power indices to the EU. *Journal of Theoretical Politics* 11: 291–308.

Garrett, G., and G. Tsebelis. 1999b. More reasons to resist the temptation to apply power indices to the EU. *Journal of Theoretical Politics* 11: 331–38.

Garrett, G., and G. Tsebelis. 2001. Even More Reasons to Resist the Temptation to Apply Power Indices to the EU. *Journal of Theoretical Politics* 13: 99–105.

Holler, M., and M. Widgrén. 1999. Why power indices for assessing EU decision-making? *Journal of Theoretical Politics* 11: 321–30.

Kirman, A., and M. Widgrén. 1995. European economic decision-making policy: Progress or paralysis? *Economic Policy* 21: 421–60.

Laruelle, A., and M. Widgrén. 1998. Is the allocation of power among EU states fair? *Public Choice* 94: 317–39.

Laruelle, A., and F. Valenciano. 2002. Assessment of voting situations: The probabilistic foundations. Discussion paper 26/2002. Departamento de Economia Aplicada IV. Basque Country University, Bilbao.

Leech, D. 2002. Designing the voting system for the Council of Ministers of the European Union. *Public Choice*, forthcoming.

Moser, P. 1996. The European Parliament as a conditional agenda setter: What are the conditions? A critique of Garrett and Tsebelis. *American Political Science Review* 90: 834–38.

Moser, P. 1997. A theory of the conditional influence of the European Parliament in the cooperation procedure. *Public Choice* 91: 333–50.

Napel, S., and M. Widgrén. 2001. Inferior players in simple games. *International Journal of Game Theory* 30: 209–20.

Napel, S., and M. Widgrén. 2004. Power measurement as sensitivity analysis: A unified approach. *Journal of Theoretical Politics*, forthcoming.

Napel, S., and M. Widgrén. 2003. Modelling codecision bargaining. Mimeo.

Nurmi, H. 1998. *Rational Behavior and the Design of Institutions*. Cheltenham: Edward Elgar.

Penrose, L. 1946. The elementary statistics of majority voting. *Journal of the Royal Statistical Society* 109: 53–57.

Steunenberg, B. 1994. Decision-making under different institutional arrangements: Legislation by the European Community. *Journal of Theoretical and Institutional Economics* 150: 642–69.

Steunenberg, B., D. Schmidtchen, and C. Koboldt. 1999. Strategic power in the European Union: Evaluating the distribution of power in policy games. *Journal of Theoretical Politics* 11: 339–66.

Tsebelis, G. 1994. The European Parliament as a conditional agenda setter. *American Political Science Review* 88: 128–42.

Tsebelis, G. 1996. More on the European Parliament as a conditional agenda setter: Response to Moser. *American Political Science Review* 90: 839–44.

Tsebelis, G., and G. Garrett. 1997. Why power indices cannot explain decision-making in the European Union. In D. Schmidtchen and R. Cooter (eds.): *Constitutional Law and Economics of the European Union*. Cheltenham: Edward Elgar.

Widgrén, M. 1994. Voting power in the EU and the consequences of two different enlargements. *European Economic Review* 38: 1153–70.

Widgrén, M., and S. Napel. 2002. The power of a spatially inferior player. *Homo Oeconomicus* 19: 327–43.

6

The Deadlock of the EU Budget: An Economic Analysis of Ways In and Ways Out

Charles B. Blankart and
Christian Kirchner

6.1 The Normative View of the EU Budget and Its Positive Alternative

EU spending is largely a matter of redistribution. Huge sums of money are transferred from the member states to Brussels and back to the member states. Only about 15 percent of the budget is spent for Union-wide public goods.[1] There is a widespread view that EU spending is inefficient. Redistribution is said to be excessive, while the provision of Union-wide public goods is held to be too small comparatively. Many economists believe that a reallocation of the budget will generate welfare gains. Guido Tabellini illustrates the common belief:

> From the perspective of cost and benefit analysis, it seems obvious that there would be large payoffs to more central provision of public goods in the areas of defence foreign policy, and of aspects of internal security, border patrols, immigration policy. The abolition of borders between EU countries carries with it the need to centralise aspects of law enforcement against organised crime. Moreover the recent terrorist attacks have made it absolutely clear that the challenges in these areas are global and require a co-ordinated European response. The positive spill-over effects and the economies of scale for foreign and defence policy, international security, border patrols and immigration policy are very large.... Currently the EU budget is mainly devoted to finance the re-distributive programs of the EU.... Now the whole discussion on the EU budget only concerns who gains and who loses, and in particular which countries are net beneficiaries or net payers, and by how much. No attention is paid as to whether the money is well spent for the average European tax payer, or whether reallocations across alternative programs are desirable. Enlargements, with the large disparities between rich and poor countries, will make the political debate on the EU budget a nightmare. (Tabellini 2002, pp. 17–19)

Although good arguments can be made in support of Tabellini's view, some questions remain: Why is there so much redistribution?

Why does the European Union as an institution that has been founded for promoting free exchange in a common market spend most of its budget on redistribution? And why is redistribution so persistent? Why are some member states consistent net payers and others consistent net receivers? All these questions cannot be answered by a cost-benefit analysis of the traditional public finance type. It requires a rigorously positive analysis of the incentives, costs, and constraints of political decision-making.

Our analysis starts from the *theory of incomplete contracts* as developed for constitutions by Buchanan (1975), Brennan and Buchanan (1985), and others. Its purpose is the design of rules at the contractual level which will be executed later at on the postcontractual level. While decisions at the contractual level may be unanimous, their later execution may cause problems. We will distinguish two alternatives:

1. Some decisions made at the *contractual level* do not require further decision at the postcontractual level if the rights and duties of the parties have been reasonably well specified. The contract should simply be executed. Possible misinterpretations of the terms of contract that may emerge in time are not to be reconsidered in the political process but by courts. This holds, in particular, for contractual redistribution, whereby redistribution is predesigned in the contract and can take place according to the agreed-upon rules.

2. It has to be anticipated at the contractual level, however, that some contractual provisions are incomplete and that new issues will emerge at the *postcontractual stage*. Therefore it has to be agreed at the contractual level how to decide such issues as they come up. The subsequent enforcement of these decision rules is often not called into question. It is simply assumed that the decisions according to these rules will be binding because the rules themselves had been agreed-upon unanimously.

The second assumption will be relaxed here. Rules to settle postcontractual issues do not, in general, generate unanimously accepted outcomes. There will be winners and losers. The latter may reject the outcomes if they have the power to threaten to terminate the contract. But their threat has to be credible. In this chapter, we make the simple assumption that a threat is only credible for the larger partners or for a coalition of partners without whom the contract cannot be maintained and that the credibility of threat is strong in the early stages of a con-

Deadlock of the EU Budget 111

tractual arrangement, as long as the ties of cooperation that evolve under the contract are still loose. Therefore there is not much to lose by terminating memberhip. In time, however, these ties become more intense, the costs of exit rise, which makes the threat of exit less credible, and the postcontractual decisions following from the application of the constitutional rules become binding.

This basic reasoning will now be applied on the budget of the European Union. In the Treaty of Rome of 1957 we can find contractual rules of redistribution of type 1, which are applied without further decisions at the postcontractual level, and rules of type 2, which require redistributive decisions at the postcontractual level. Had the Treaty been designed as a fully complete contract, postcontractual redistribution would not be an issue. But the Treaty of Rome was typically an incomplete contract (see upper part of figure 6.1). Therefore postcontractual decisions on redistribution had to be expected. Redistribution did, however, not only take place according to these agreed-upon rules but also through threat.

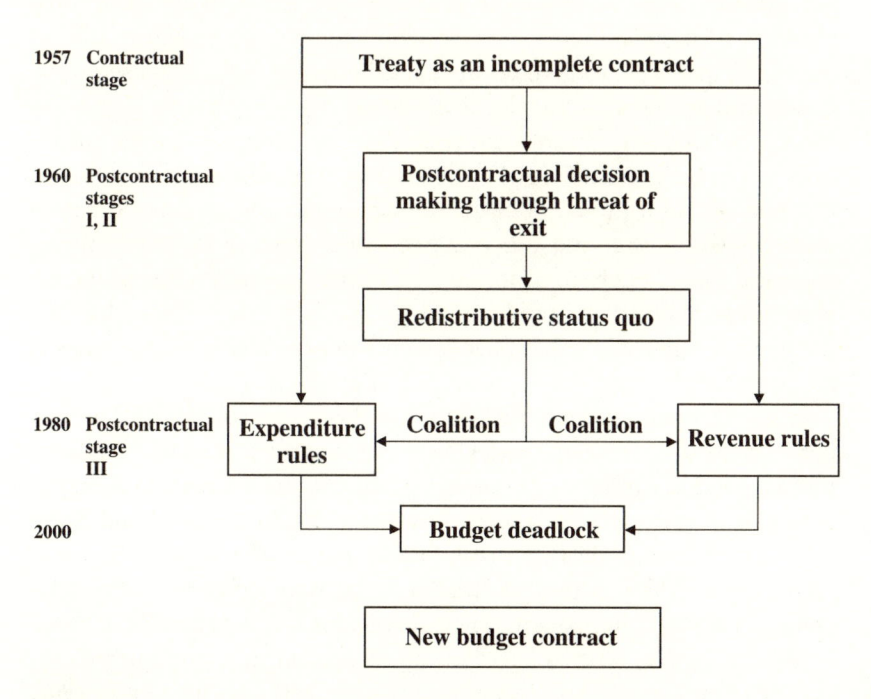

Figure 6.1
Budgetary rules and budgetary outcomes, 1957–2000

Rules were dominated by threat, in particular, in the early decades of the existence of the Community (see middle range of figure 6.1). Member state governments that had alternative policy options and were able to harm the other member states with terminating their membership could thereby enforce their distributive goals in the budget. As cooperation in the Common Market grew, however, the threats became increasingly less credible. It became obvious that the loss from terminating membership would be too large. Therefore threat as an instrument of influence in apportioning the budget was gradually displaced by the rules as they are written in the Treaty (see lower range of figure 6.1).

These rules, however, are far from perfect. They separate the expenditure side of the budget from the revenue side and therefore generate opposing coalitions on either side of the budget. The expenditure side is dominated by net receivers, the revenue side by net payers, and both groups exert veto power. The result is that of a budget deadlock dominated by redistribution with fixed allocation of benefits and burdens per member state. Union-wide public goods are unlikely to be provided in a larger amount, as those who benefit from redistribution in the status quo have to give up their priviledges to finance these public goods and those who pay for the budget are reluctant to pay more money because they cannot earmark their contibutions for the provision of public goods. To put it differently: The allocation of burdens and benefits, as it came out of the threatening period, generated a new redistributive status quo that has been preserved or locked in thereafter and that is likely to continue after eastern accession. A change toward more Union-wide public goods is unlikely to be achieved under the present rules. We rather believe that a new additional set of rules is required for allowing decisions on public goods.

In the *literature* one can find roughly three approaches to the budgetary process in the European Union. A first group of authors concentrates on a description of the design of the budgetary rules and on the decisions that have been taken: Messal (1989, 1991), Messal and Klein (1993), Peffekoven (1994), Strasser (1991), EU Commission (1995), and Lienemeyer (2002). Although this literature only describes what happened, not why it happened, it is valuable, for it serves as a "database" on which our hypotheses can be built. A second group of authors argue that "power politics dictate the EU's budget" (Baldwin et al. 1997, p. 157). We have benefited a lot from their work whose view we share. But we should be able to predict more precisely when and what power counts. A third group of authors such as Widgrén (1994), Hosli (1996), Peters (1996), and Raunio and Wiberg (1998) tries to assess mainly voting power in the Council and to predict the changes of power when the Union is enlarged toward Eastern Europe. But they do not confront their predictions with the decisions taken on budget allocations. There is still a gap, as far as we know, between budget decision-making rules and budgetary outcomes. Vaubel (2001, p. 36) has mentioned recently the problem of the different types of rules and coalitions, one on the expenditure and one on the revenue side, but without deepening his observation. In this chapter we contribute some of our insights to understanding this problem.

Before going into the analysis of the distributional consequences of these rules and the emergence of the budgetary deadlock in section 6.3, we give a breakdown of the actual budget incidence in section 6.2. In section 6.4 we widen the scene and discuss new budgetary procedures to overcome the deadlock. Our conclusions follow in section 6.5.

6.2 The Budget Incidence Today

The compilation of data on the incidence of the EU budget is not simply a statistical problem. These data represent a political issue that alone could be a subject of a public choice analysis. Politicians, in general, tend to avoid talking about money. They prefer to give great speeches on the future of the European Union and its achievements rather than to talk about the financing involved. The budget implying the question of who has to pay how much and for whom is postponed as long as possible in the political process in order to maintain the impression of harmony among the political fellows. In the rhetoric it is said that the budget is too small to be of major relevance. It is true that in the early years of the European Economic Community the budget was only about 80 million euro. But it has risen by about factor of a 1,000 to nearly 90 billion euro in 2001. Even today the budget costs are only about 1.13 percent of EU GNP in 2000 (see figure 6.2). But 1.13 percent is still a remarkable sum of money when compared to the resources of a smaller member state, such as Denmark, whose total government sector including social security is about the same absolute size. Despite these facts the problem of redistribution is often set aside.

The general distaste of talking about redistribution and who pays is also reflected in the Commission's policy of not publishimg data on the net incidence of the EU budget. They argue that statistical numbers

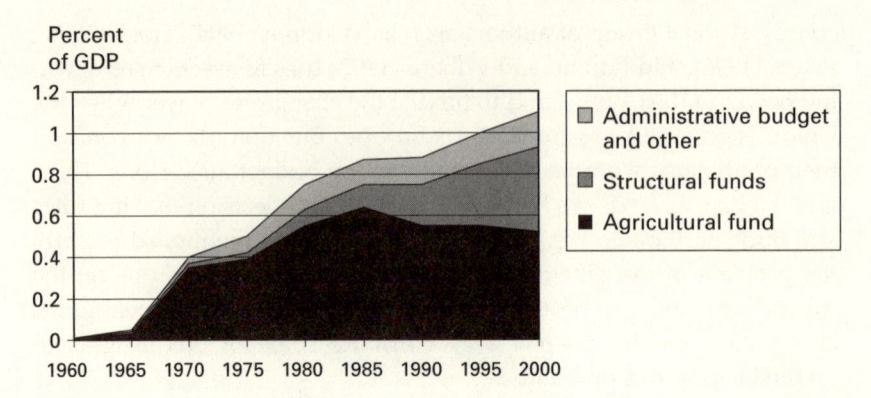

Figure 6.2
The budget of the European Union in percent of GDP, 1960–2000

cannot be allocated to individual member states and that they did not reflect the true benefits derived from EU membership (EU Commission 2001). Only after the insistence of the German government, the Commission gave in and has started to publish data since 1994 (Stegarescu 1999).

In its statistical breakdown the Commission publishes only so-called operative expenditures—about 90 to 95 percent of the budget. It is said that only those expenditures have a redistributive effect that can be allocated to member states (EU Commission 2001). Operative expenditures encompass mainly expenditures for the Common Agricultural Policy (CAP) and for the structural policy. The assumption presumably is that these budget allocations can be valued one-on-one among member states. The willingness to pay 1 euro is for the contributing member state the same as the willingness to accept 1 euro for the receiving member state regardless of rent-seeking costs and the welfare costs of raising funds. Even if we accept this assumption, the calculations remain distorted when the Commission confronts these expenditures with each member state's total contributions to the Union. Since contributions are larger than operative expenditures, too many member states end up as apparent net contributors.

To put it differently, if we add the money equivalent of what the Commission calls "the advantages accruing to the member states from the Union" (EU Commission 2001, p. 6) to each member state's receipts, each of them might turn out to be a net receiver. But what are these public good values shared by all members; in particular, what is the value of the Common Market protected by the Council, the Commission and the European Court of Justice? We assume that the total willingness to pay for the maintenance of the Common Market and for the other public goods by the European citizens represented by their national governments is at least as large as their costs as reflected in the administrative budget and that each government's willingness to pay can be approximated by the member state's share of intra-Community trade. The intuitive reason is as follows: large member states benefit from the Common Market because of their large volume of intra-Community trade and small member states benefit because they may have above average intra-Community export quotas relative to their GNP in order to benefit from the division of labor in the larger market. In table 6.1 we have added the administrative expenditures allocated on each member state according to this rule to the operative expenditures as calculated by the European Commission. These were then subtracted from each member state's contributions to the common budget yielding the total net payer/net receiver position of each member state. A minus mark means that the member state is a net payer.

It turns out that Germany, the Netherlands, Austria, Sweden, and the United Kingdom were net payers while the remaining ten member states were net receivers in the year 2000. Germany was by far the largest net contributor not only in the 1990s as documented in the table but, as sparse available data seem to indicate, also back to the late 1960s (e.g., see later tables 6.3 and 6.4).

There are a number of statistical problems behind these data that we will not discuss here. But it is astonishing to see that no less than six institutions calculate and publish data on member states' net contributor/receiver positions and that all of them come to similar results though their methodologies and reasonings may be different.[2]

Germany's persistent net payer position has led to substantial irritation in the political discussion. Normative and positive arguments are intertwined, which does not help to clarify the issue. Some say that Germany for its mere size and income level, in being the largest country and among the richest member states (number 3 in per capita income), should be a net contributor. But when we take France and the Benelux states together, they aggregate to similar size and income levels, and their aggregated net contribution is nearly zero. Taking, alternatively, the United Kingdom and the Benelux states together, we come to an aggregated net payer position, but it is not even half the size of

Table 6.1
Net receipts from the EU budget, 1994–2000 (in € mil)

	1994	1995	1996	1997	1998	1999	2000	Total net payments, 1994–2000	Population in median year 1997 (in 000s)	Total per capita payments, 1994–2000
Germany	−9,631	−10,389	−9,643	−9,794	−7,173	−7,578	−7,230	−61,437,3	82,052	−748,76
Austria	0	−539,4	−28,6	−551,4	−391,6	−355	−170,4	−2,375,9	8,072	−294,33
Belgium & Luxembourg	597,5	1,081,2	646,8	232,3	188,7	359,6	558,4	3,664,5	10,602	345,64
Denmark	554,2	644,9	415,6	280,4	154,3	279,4	402	2,730,9	5,284	516,83
Finland	0	14,5	157,5	128,6	−10,6	−102	376,6	658,7	5,140	128,16
France	−441,4	−210,9	−182	−645,3	−108,6	859,5	200,5	−528,1	58,609	−9,01
Greece	4,062,3	3,654,4	4,091,7	4,416,1	4,798,6	3,888,8	4,496,7	29,408,5	10,499	2,801,07
Ireland	2,086,2	2,201,5	2,543	2,955,3	2,513	2,137,7	1,910,3	16,347	3,661	4,465,17
Italy	−1,011	461	−1,352	219,7	−1,007	−312,1	1,710,7	−1,291	57,512	−22,45
Netherlands	244,2	−48,6	−701,7	−490,4	−964,8	−1,198	−901,6	−4,060,7	15,611	−260,12
Portugal	2,112,2	2,696,8	2,971,5	2,849,8	3,160,1	3,026,3	2336,8	19,153,5	9,946	1,925,75
Spain	3,876,7	8,005,6	6,311,2	6,041,2	7,449,2	7,758,3	5832,9	45,274,9	39,323	1,151,36
Sweden	0	−447,4	−384,2	−902,4	−570,9	−671,4	−827	−4,437	8,846	−501,58
United Kingdom & Northern Ireland	2,157,4	−2,080,6	178,2	403,2	−3,062	−2,265	−2,505	−7,173,9	58,009	−123,67

Source: Own calculations based on data of the European Commission and of the *Statistical Yearbook of The Federal Republic of Germany*.
Notes: Trade figures of Belgium and Luxemburg are not available separately. Total net contributions of Finland, Austria, and Sweden are from 1995 to 2000. They have been inflated by 7/6 to make them comparable with those of the other member states.

Germany's net contribution in 2000. Others argue that one should not look at the relatively small net payments but rather at the gross payments of the whole budget because only the latter reflect the whole benefit of the EU agricultural and structural policies. Yet the question remains why redistribution should require large gross payments first, before net payments come out. Finally it is said that longer time spans have to be considered and that figures have to be calculated per capita. But the result does not change. Germany remains the largest net payer with 750 euro per capita from 1994/95 up to 2000 followed by Sweden with 502 euro per capita. Further net payers are Austria, the Netherlands, and the United Kingdom while Italy and France manage to just break even.

Although Germany's large net payments may anger the German taxpayer, they are of little analytical interest. What matters from a public choice point of view is rather the causes creating permanent net payer positions, on the one hand, and net receiver positions, on the other. Why are some member states destined to become net payers while others have the privilege to remain net receivers?

6.3 Explaining Redistribution through the Budget

In this section we return to the budgetary process mentioned in our introductory remarks in section 6.1. Following figure 6.1 we will distinguish among four stages of budgetary decision-making: a contractual stage and three postcontractual stages I, II, and III when the distributive struggles occur. We predict that the (re)distributive outcome will be defined in the postconstitutional stages I and II according to the relative exit and nonentry opportunities of the member states and according to their size. Large member states with considerable options outside the Community are in a stronger position to attract budgetary resources than large member states with few outside alternatives and small member states that are not so relevant for the survival of the Community. The importance of these threats will level off in stage III. This is because as interfirm ties become closer and firms grow together, the costs of exit rise and governments can make fewer credible threats that to leave the Community if their budgetary demands are not fulfilled. We predict roughly that among the EU15, France, the United Kingdom, and Spain with its southern allies will be in the group of winners, while Germany and some smaller member states will be in the losers' group.

The Contractual Stage: The Treaty of Rome 1957

The original purpose of the Union, as laid down in the Treaty of 1957, was to establish a Common Market and not a system of redistribution among member states. In Article 2 of the Treaty, redistribution is not even mentioned:

The Community shall have its task by establishing a common market and by progressive approximation of economic policies, to promote throughout the Community a harmonious development of economic activities, a continuous and balanced expansion, a growing stability, the raising of the standard of living and closer relations among Member States. (Article 2, 1957)[3]

Redistributive needs show up only in later articles. Article 40 of the Treaty of 1957[4] mentions the establishment of agricultural guidance and guarantee funds, and Article 123 the establishment of a European Social Fund.[5] By these two funds there was to be achieved a fair distribution of the benefits through the Common Market. It appeared then to the fathers of the European Economic Community that industrialized and export-oriented member states such as Germany would gain from free trade in the Common Market, but that such gains were much less certain for the more domestically oriented economies such as Italy and France. Their governments' fear was that the rents of integration would be shifted out of their countries. Therefore both Italy and France aimed at institutionalized claims on the rents to be guaranteed through the Community budget. The Italians wanted their workers to be helped by the Social Fund so that they could overcome their structural problems and transform their economy from an agrarian to an industrialized one, and the French wanted their farmers to be subsidized through the agricultural guidance and guarantee funds. Market intervention through funds appeared to be a rational way for the Italian and French governments to preserve a claim on the rents of integration. Only through these funds could they be sure of obtaining their desired share of the Common Market. The wisdom then was that with the higher growth of intracommunity trade in manufactured goods, the structural divergence would become larger in the less adaptable markets such as labor and agriculture and as would the budgetary transfers required to compensate the losers. Lump sum payments, in contrast, would have required renegotiations every year and were therefore regarded as not as reliable as funds.[6]

As funds were part of the Treaty, they were not unilaterally terminable and could only be removed by an unanimous decision. They became part of the *acquis communautaire*. Given that there is always at least one loser when a fund is abolished, it is difficult to see how unanimity could be achieved. Therefore a persistent element of redistribution was built in the European Economic Community from the very beginning.

Criticisms of the funds' efficiencies and calls for their abolishment are therefore ill founded. There were no alternative arrangements at the disposal of the French and Italian governments in 1957 that could secure permanently the rents of the Common Market. It soon became clear that only the arrangements framed in the constitutional Treaty were secure. Any inefficiencies and deadweight losses they generated should not come up as a surprise to the economist.

The founding fathers of the European Union were not unaware of the expansionary potential built in these funds. They took the precautionary (neither necessary nor sufficient) measure to split the budget into three parts: an administrative budget (covering the administrative expenditures of the Commission, the Council, and the Court of Justice), an agricultural budget (representing the subsidies to farmers through the guiding and guarantee funds), and a social budget (for training and reintegrating workers affected by the structural change). This way the members of the Council could continually control spending. It turned out, however, that the control was insufficient as the decided-upon procedures were weak.

Postcontractual Stage I: France and the Financing of CAP, 1958–1970

In the early years of the Community, from 1958 to 1970, spending was distributed quite differently among the three budgets. The administrative and the social budgets grew moderately, while the agricultural budget exploded (see figure 6.2). The explanation can be found in the different contractual rules applicable to these funds.

The administrative budget and the social budget were financed by fixed share contributions, as laid down in Article 200 of the Treaty (see table 6.2). To the administrative budget, the three large countries, Germany, France, and Italy, each had to contribute 28 percent. To the social budget, France and Germany each contributed 32 percent while Italy contributed 20 percent. Changes were subject to unanimity.

Table 6.2
Percentage share of administrative expenditures and the Social Fund, 1957–1970

Member state	Administrative expenditures	Social fund
Belgium	7.9	8.8
Germany	28.0	32.0
France	28.0	32.0
Italy	28.0	20.0
Luxembourg	0.2	0.2
Netherlands	7.9	7.0

Source: Treaty of Rome, 1957, Article 200; see Peffekoven (1994, p. 44).

Expenditures of the social budget were also regulated with subsidies granted on a matching basis of 50 percent. So there were no "free goods" from the fund for the member state governments. Governments of the larger member states had to calculate the incremental cost of each additional program. The smaller member state governments could not freely expand their programs because they needed the contributions and the consent of the larger member states. Under these constraints the size of the Social Fund remained small in this early period. It developed as planned by the Treaty and required little postcontractual decision-making. Hence the result confirms our hypothesis made in section 6.1 on contractual redistribution.

The Agricultural Fund was designed quite differently. First, the extent of the agricultural market was defined openly in Article 38 (par. 3) of the Treaty of 1957.[7] It was not exactly defined how many or which products had to be subsumed in the agricultural fund. Second, neither the system of price guarantees nor that of structural aid to farmers provided for national co-financing. Third, the contribution shares that each member state had to pay to the Agricultural Fund were not fixed in the Treaty. They were negotiated periodically in the Council.

The results confirm again our hypothesis of section 6.1: when contractual rules are incomplete, collective decisions must be made at the postcontractual stage amid the politics in progress where the outcome depends on decision rules applied. Responsibility for the budget rested mainly with the Council, which had to apply a qualified majority rule according to Article 148 (par. 2) of the Treaty of 1957.[8] But it has to be considered that qualified majority rule (as any non-unanimity rule) only works if the outvoted minority concedes because the stakes in the Community are so high that it would lose more in leaving the

Table 6.3
Percentage share to Agricultural Fund, 1962–1970

Member state	7/1962–6/1965[a]	1965/66	1966/67	7/1967–12/1969[b]	1970
Belgium	7.90	7.95	7.95	8.10	8.25
Germany	28.0	31.67	30.83	31.20	31.70
France	28.0	32.58	29.26	32.00	28.00
Italy	28.0	18.00	22.00	20.30	21.50
Luxembourg	0.20	0.22	0.22	0.20	0.20
Netherlands	7.90	9.58	9.74	10.35	10.35

a. Fixed shares only. Variable supplementary shares (according to a member state's net imports of particular farm products) are not included.
b. Only for guiding expenditures and for guaranty contributions not covered by customs revenues (90 percent of which was transferred to the Community).

Community than in accepting an objectionable decision. In these early years, however, the stakes the member states had in the Community were still small. Private business ties were not well developed. Therefore an exit threat was credible and potentially harmful when made by a larger member state (see section 6.1).

Taken together, these theoretical elements of contractual and post-contractual decision-making explain why the agricultural budget developed so differently from the social budget and why its rules were capable of bringing the Community to its first deep crisis. The vagueness of the contractual rules tempted the French government to extend the agricultural fund in a way that was disapproved by the other member states. The French claims were outvoted by the Council in fall 1965. But, because the Community was very young and the stakes were still small, the French government, under President Charles de Gaulle, chose to exit and jeopardize the Community's future. In fall 1965 the French government decided to boycott all future meetings of the Council until the unanimity rule was formally resumed; this came with the so-called Luxembourg compromise of January 29, 1966. What we can learn is that the unanimity rule crowds out qualified majority rule where a credible exit threat exists.

Table 6.3 shows how extensive the bargaining must have been in the agricultural budget proceedings of the early 1960s. Five different distributions of country contribution shares were made since the common agricultural fund was introduced in 1962. These shares formed the basic units on which further increments or decrements were negotiated from year to year. The outcome was fundamentally different from the policy in the Social Fund whose volume remained negligible throughout this early period.

To summarize: The Social and the Agricultural funds show the relevance of strict versus weak contractual budget rules. In the case of the Social Fund, postcontractual collective decision-making was avoided because its size was already delineated in the Treaty. In the case of the agricultural fund, however, collective decision-making was shifted from the contractual to the postcontractual stage, where collective decisions were taken under the French government's threat to leave and jeopardize the integrity of the Community. The budgetary consequences can be seen in the steep increase of agricultural spending in figure 6.2 after 1965. Indeed, the Luxembourg compromise prevailed in the Council for the next twenty years.

Postcontractual Stage II: Britain and Spain/Portugal/Greece, 1971–1986

Threats to exit the Community led to budget decisions also in the following period of its history, 1971 to 1986. The big issue was the UK rebate on contributions to the budget. The origin of this dispute was a decision on what constituted the *"Community's own resources"* in 1970.[9] Then the tripartite budget with earmarked contributions was relinquished in favor of a unitary budget financed initially by two sources of revenues: revenues of customs and other levies and contributions by member states based on their respective standardized VAT bases. Later these two resources became known as "traditional own resources" and "VAT own resources." Formally a decision on Community's own resources had the character of a change in the Treaty, and it remained valid until a new decision on the Community's own resources replaced it. Thus the status quo could only be changed by unanimity (Lienemeyer 2002, pp. 205–14). We will return to the consequences of this rule in the next subsection.

The expected political advantage of the unitary budget was that the revenue side would be separated from the expenditure side of the budget, and so any open discussion could be eliminated on the distribution of the burden of the Common Agricultural Policy (CAP). Moreover it allowed the development of the new system of structural funds out of the existing Social Fund and the Guidance Department of the agricultural fund without the need to respect the former percentage contributions (see table 6.2).

Table 6.4
Net receipts from EU budget, 1981–1984 (in € mil)

Member state	1981	1982	1983	1984	∑ 1981–84
Belgium	320	310	210	330	1,170
Denmark	280	280	330	500	1,390
Germany	−1,770	−2,320	−2,300	−2,950	−9,340
Greece	160	690	940	990	2,780
France	540	0	10	330	220
Ireland	590	740	770	920	3,020
Italy	780	1,520	1,320	1,710	5,330
Luxembourg	270	250	270	280	1,070
Netherlands	220	350	370	510	1,450
United Kingdom	−1,380	−1,820	−1,910	−1,950	−7,060

Source: Messal (1991, p. 113) and own calculations.
Note: Calculations exclude benefits from public goods.

The expectation that looser rules on the expenditure side and rate base payments on the revenue side facilitated the discussion on the distribution of the financial burden was, however, not fulfilled. When the United Kingdom joined the Union in 1973, it was supposed to accept the system of Community's own resources of 1970 as an *acquis communautaire*. It had not only to waive all its customs revenues to the Community but also to contribute to the VAT own resources. Given that British agricultural imports were large and own (subsidized) agricultural production relatively small, compared to those of other member states, the overall balance resulted in a large net transfer in favor of the Community, which was unacceptable to the British taxpayers (see table 6.4). While this problem could have been negotiated relatively easily under the previous system of earmarked budgets with country-specific contribution shares, it became a question of allocating benefits and costs of a common pool under a unitary budget in which quid pro quo was eliminated. Under the threat that the British citizens would vote against EC membership and the United Kingdom would leave the Community, the Council granted several yearly rebates and repayments up to 1984 when a permanent rebate was conceded in the own resources decision of the Council and the member states.[10]

Threat rather than formal decision-making rules also determined the concessions made to the coalition of the Spanish, Portuguese, and Greek governments at the time of their accessions in 1984 and 1985 and later when the single market was at stake in 1986. In the early 1980s it was not improbable to think that these nations might fall to populist socialism or communism. Hence their outside alternatives had to be considered as tempting compared to membership in the Community. As the EC member states would have felt uneasy with communist neighbors in the east as well as in the south, they were quite willing to pay the price to bring and keep these countries in their fold.[11] As a result real spending on structural funds doubled in the 1980s (see figure 6.2).

To summarize: The concessions made to France and to Spain and its allies on the expenditure side and to the United Kingdom on the revenue side emphasize the relevance of member states' capacity to make threats relative to formal decision rules in early stages of Union development. Not all member states, however, were equally able to make credible threats to terminate membership. Germany, for example, had no credible alternative to its membership in the Community. Although its net payments were at least as large as those that the United Kingdom was expected to make, it was unable to exert threat. No one seriously could think that Germany was in a position to leave the Community. Geographically sandwiched between France and the Comecon, it had nowhere to reach but to fill the gap left by the British rebate, and this further increased its net payer position. Similarly, while some smaller member states such as the Benelux, Austria, and Sweden could threaten to stay outside, they were too small for their withdrawal to endanger the survival of the Community, so they lacked this bargaining tool for attracting budgetary resources. In the next decade all but Belgium remained net payers. Altogether the net receiver or net payer positions of France, Spain and its allies, the United Kingdom, and Germany depended not only on the common rules laid down in their own resources decisions but to a large extent also on their relative exit options.

Postcontractual Stage III: The Budget under Qualified Majority/ Unanimity Rule, 1987–2003

Over the following years the power of governments to force budget decisions by threat of exit[12] kept on abating. Member states grew closer, and firms made cross-border investments. The network of ties that emerged made the notion of exit increasingly less practicable.[13]

As it became evident that member states had entrenched themselves firmly in the Community, it was possible to depart from the Luxembourg Compromise of 1966 and return gradually to the collective decision rules of Article 148 in the Treaty of Rome.[14] A first step was the Single European Act of 1987 where qualified majority rule was extended to the issues of the single market. A second step was the compromise of Ioannina of 1994 where a qualified majority was maintained (even with Austria, Finland, and Sweden as new members) but the minority required for blocking an issue (temporarily) was set at 23 votes (26 percent) instead of 25 votes (29 percent) out of 87 votes. The actual end point of this development was the Treaty of Amsterdam by which qualified majorities were accepted for Council decisions in more fields than ever before.

On the expenditure side of the budget, the return to qualified majority rule after Amsterdam had only minor effects (see table 6.5). Net receivers obtained a comfortable blocking minority of 32 votes in the Council, strong enough to maintain the status quo of the allocation of Union's budgetary resources on agriculture and structural funds. The net payers took on a minority position as well. They have only 35 votes. Two member states, France and Italy, break even with 10 votes each.[15] Even a proposal to reallocate some of the redistributive funds to provide public goods is not likely to be accepted by the blocking minority of actual net receivers. This is because the costs of reduced transfers are likely to be borne by them while the benefits accrue typically to all member states.

On the revenue side, the principle of a status quo oriented unanimity has been maintained since the first decision on own resources of 1970.[16] Hence an existing decision can be replaced only by a new unanimous decision (Article 269 of the Treaty). This principle has important consequences for the net budget incidence. When the incidence of expenditures drifts away from the incidence of revenues (for the reasons given above) and net payers positions are built up, then there is no way for the net payers to rid themselves of their burden. They are not able to reduce the general contribution rates nor to shift their own burden onto the shoulders of the net receivers. Both attempts will fail to be accepted by the latter. There is only one way for the net payers to protect their interests: to veto proposals coming from the net receivers and further increase their contributions to the Union's own resources. Thus veto is the only way for net payers to protect themselves against the growing demands of net receivers. Any promises to net payers that higher contributions will be used for Union-wide public goods cannot be taken seriously. Under general fund financing it is up to net receivers to channel these funds to themselves.

Table 6.5
Net receipts per capita, 1994–2000, and distribution of votes, 1995

	Net receipts (€)	Votes in Council (abs)	Shapely weight (%)	Population share (%)
Austria	−294	4	4.5	2.2
Belgium	346[a]	5	5.5	2.7
Denmark	517	3	3.5	1.4
Finland	128	3	3.5	1.4
France	−9	10	11.7	15.7
Germany	−744	10	11.7	22.0
Greece	2,801	5	5.5	2.8
Ireland	4,465	3	3.5	1.0
Italy	−22	10	11.7	15.4
Luxembourg	346[b]	2	2.1	0.2
Netherlands	−260	5	5.5	4.2
Portugal	1,926	5	5.5	2.6
Spain	1,151	8	9.6	10.5
Sweden	−501	4	4.5	2.4
United Kingdom	−124	10	11.7	15.8
Qualified majority		62		
Blocking minority		25		
Total	..	87	100.0	100.0

Source: For calculations, see table 6.1 and *Wissenschaftlicher Beirat beim Bundesministerium für Wirtschaft und Technologie* (1999).
Note: The data of Austria, Finland, and Sweden were adjusted for seven years of membership.
a. Includes Luxembourg.
b. Includes Belgium.

To summarize: Decision-making on the EU budget has resulted in a redistributive deadlock. Net receivers can use their blocking power to object to any reallocation of resources away from their narrow own interests, and net payers, anticipating net receivers' power to attract the additional resources, will veto any increase in their burden. However, net payers cannot enforce a decrease of their burden, for net receivers will not permit this under unanimity rule. Therefore the status quo is a stable equilibrium. Preserving the status quo means that the net budget incidence from the power play in the postcontractual stages I and II will be preserved. Tabellini's call for more public goods to be provided will remain politically unnoticed.

It is important so see the effect of the status quo related unanimity rule for decisions on Union's own resources. Had the net payers the possibility to unilaterally terminate an existing own resources decision, all member states would be under pressure to discuss budget revenues and expenditures de novo. The separation of revenues from expenditures would be abolished, and substantial reforms might become possible. Though such a change is desirable, it is irrelevant to our discussion, as no unanimity can be found to support it. Therefore it is unlikely that the EU budget process can be reformed by its own rules.

An example may illustrate how sensitive governments are to proposals on redistributing the burden. When, in anticipation of the Berlin summit of 1999, the German government made some tentative computations on the possibility of obtaining an UK type of rebate on its contributions, the Spanish government promptly responded by submitting a counterproposal suggesting that member states' contribution rates be raised progressively with GNP, the obvious effect being that the German government would pay more instead of less to Union's own resources.[17] The Spanish proposal was not mentioned at the summit, but it had the effect of taking the German proposal off the agenda, and the status quo was maintained.

If these deliberations are correct, the likely result is effectively one of no decision-making. The budget is likely to grow in line with the built-in rules. These rules are mainly defined by the ceiling of 1.27 percent of Union's GDP as assessed in the own resources decision of 1992. The ceiling was renewed in 1995 and in 1999, and it will remain at this level until 2006 when it may be prolonged again. Some readers may not be too unhappy with the deadlock because it guarantees a sort of "second best": as long as it is apparently not feasible to provide (more) Union-wide public goods, they may say, it is fortunate that the budget has a built-in stabilizer holding further growth down at the rate of growth of the Union GNP.

Anyone taking a critical view could object, first of all, that it is simplistic to focus only on the Council as a decision maker. There are other players such as the Commission that make mid-term projections and prepare the yearly budget. Moreover, although negotiations take place between the Commission and the Council, within the Council, ministers fight fiercely for their national interests as contributors and receivers of funds. The better they fight, the larger is the support they will receive from their voters at home where they have to survive in national elections. It may be criticized further that the European Parliament has not been taken explicitly into account. We justify the omission with the fact that the European Parliament has no right of initiative. It has only the right to decline or to change a budget proposal made by the Council in the field of nonobligatory expenditures or to reject the budget as a whole. But very much dissent between the Council and the Parliament cannot be expected. The national representatives have an incentive to fight primarily for their own national interests, meaning the interests of their voters at home.

Decision-Making Projections

What outcomes of the budgetary process can we expect in the future? To take the long-term view, we can consider two factors that will have a big impact on the budgetary process: (1) enlargement of the European Union to some 25 to 27 member states and (2) constitutional changes proposed by the Convention and adopted by member states in a new European Constitution.

Enlargement of the European Union
The impact of enlargement of the European Union is difficult to foresee. We must therefore rely on strong trends. The exit threats of the postconstitutional stages I and II will likely not reappear. The Union has become large enough to bear the exit of some of the new accession states. Therefore there is no threat of secession potentially comparable to that of France in the 1960s or the United Kingdom and Spain in the 1970s and 1980s. A healthy development is that a right of exit will liberally be granted by the proposal of a new European Constitution.[18] Therefore it can be expected that collective decisions will be made according to the rules written in the Constitution. Table 6.6 shows the voting power of the traditional net receivers, the traditional breakeven countries, and the traditional net payers along with the voting power of the accession countries, all weighted with the distribution of votes as decided at the summit of Nizza in 2000. Accession states have been taken together because roughly all of them are likely to become net receivers.[19] Along with the traditional net receivers, they can form a blocking minority routing to themselves the revenues of the agricultural and structural funds as in the past. Even if some of the earlier net receivers become net payers, net payers' total voting power will not rise enough to achieve a qualified majority. Adding net payers' votes

Deadlock of the EU Budget

Table 6.6
Status of voting power in the Council after eastern accession

Groups of member states	Number of votes	Percentage of votes
Net receiver states, 2003	95	29.6
Accession states, 2004	84	26.2
Breakeven states, 2003 (F&I)	58	18.1
Net payer states, 2003	95	29.6
Blocking minority	90	27.7
Qualified majority	232	72.3
Total	321	100.0

Source: See table 6.5.

to those of the budgetary breakeven countries will increase total votes of (net) payers from 95 to 153, which is still far away from the required qualified majority of 232 votes. Even if some more member states become net payers and join this coalition, the relative voting power will not change radically. So the net receivers should be able to maintain the sizes of the agricultural and structural funds and suppress public good programs. On the other hand, net payers could use their voting power to block any expansion of the budget. All in all, little change is expected, although the strain on the resources of the budget will clearly increase.

Impact of Constitutional Changes

A change of the budget policy could arise if the budget-balancing constraint is dropped (Article 269 of the Treaty of Amsterdam). An indication of this occurring comes from the European Investment Bank (Article 267 of the Treaty of Amsterdam), which is charged with the task of providing loans and securities to governments and firms in structurally backward regions and industries. Politicians may be tempted to soften the budget constraint through this backdoor, especially under the fiscal strain that is expected with the eastern accession (Blankart 1996).

A more dramatic change could have come from discussion in the Convention. The plan was to divide the European constitution in two parts: a constitutional part where changes are subject to unanimity and a policy part where decisions can be made by qualified majority rule. It has not been clear for a long time whether the revenue side is to remain in the constitutional part, however. There was strong pressure to put it into the policy part and to subject it to a qualified majority. Had this occurred or will occur in the future, a qualified majority of net receivers and break-even countries could dictate larger contributions and increases in the volume of the budget. But it is not likely that the larger budget will increase spending for public goods relative to redistribution given the large number of net receivers.

6.4 A Way out of Deadlock

In this section we consider circumstances where the unanimity rule on the revenue side and the qualified majority rule on the expenditure side are maintained. Hence we have both the deadlock and budget ceilings prolonged, as there is neither a substanial provision of public goods nor a budget explosion. We want to discuss for this case the solution of a separate supplementary budget. Such a budget could be used to break the deadlock and to provide for any needed Union-wide public goods.[20]

To set our various proposals within a realistic framework, we first present three conditions that appear to us to be the necessary prerequisites for any consensual agreement of member states on the budgetary issue:

1. *Separation.* Collective decision-making on public goods cannot take place within the existing budgetary rules. Net receivers can channel the means into redistribution, and in anticipation of net receivers' behavior, net payers can refuse to contribute. Therefore a separate budget, a public good budget, must be added to the "general budget" in order to prevent losers.[21]

2. *Veto.* The new budget procedure must be designed in a way that no party risks ending up in net payer position nor aggravating its existing net payer position. Thus some veto power must be part of the new solution.

3. *Contributions.* Since willingness to pay for public goods depends on a number of factors, such as the characteristics of the good, individual preferences, income, and price, the rules of financing must be flexible. They should take the form of contributions rather than rate base payments.

All in all, we are searching for a Pareto-superior procedure. Leaving inefficiencies of the existing system aside, we want to find a procedure that opens opportunities for public goods to be made available in the

Union on a consensual basis. This part of our proposal is purely positive. It can be taken up by any party that wants to gain votes. It differs from normative proposals targeted to a change of the existing rules implying winners and losers and hence opposition.

Wicksellian Unanimity

The strongest form of veto is use of the Wicksellian unanimity rule. All voters have a veto right, so no participant will end up being exploited. Also no vote weighting is necessary as under qualified majority rule. A major disadvantage is, however, that vetoes are costless to the voters. They can just say no and expect that someone else will take up the load of creating a new proposal. Therefore Wicksellian unanimity is a burdensome process not suitable for the European Parliament. Even in the Council, unanimity is practicable only for a few restricted decisions.

A way to make the unanimity rule more flexible is to allow unilateral termination of the existing arrangement after a certain period, say five years, by one or more parties. If no termination is requested, the arrangement is prolonged for another five years, and so on. Unilateral termination after the agreed-upon period puts the other members under pressure to find a new arrangement, to test whether the whole enterprise is still worth its cost, and to ensure that no member will be exploited in the long run. A member state may become net payer for some years but not for an indefinite period of time. A disadvantage is, however, that a new arrangement, though basically beneficial, may not be found because of excessive negotiation costs. Then the community of states might fall back into a precontractual stage. Such a disadvantage can be avoided by voting by veto.

Voting by Veto

Under voting by veto, as developed by Dennis Mueller (Mueller 1989), each of N participants submits a proposal on the size and the cost sharing of a public good to be provided. The status quo is added as a further proposal. Each participant has the right to eliminate—to veto—one proposal. Therefore she has an opportunity to compare and to evaluate the relative advantages of different proposals, one of which she can veto. A veto has a cost. For only those who make a proposal have the right to veto. Who may choose first, second, and so on, is determined by lottery. Eventually one proposal remains as the proposal that has not been vetoed and is therefore acceptable to all participants.

Each person has an incentive to take account of other participants' preferences when making a proposal in order to avoid its elimination. Since many alternatives are proposed and subject to a veto, there is more search and better solutions will come about. Every participant can protect herself from being exploited by vetoing the least desired proposal. So do all other persons, and the resulting proposal will be fair and efficient.[22]

A further advantage of voting by veto is that it produces no cycling because the procedure has a finite number of steps. For a given set of rankings and sequence of veto-voting, it produces a unique outcome (Mueller 1984). It is true that it may yield a different winner for the same set of rankings under a different order of veto-voting. But it has to be considered that the procedure produces incentives to select proposals that benefit all voters.

Among the possible disadvantages there are three main concerns. First, the procedure is often said to be unfair because it does not differentiate between large and small member states. All have the same voting power. Such an argument is actually misleading. The same would hold under unanimity rule. Even with the qualified majority rule, a group of small member states hold veto power. The advantage of the voting by veto concept is its inherent reciprocity. Any small member state is well advised to submit proposals that include the interests of large member states; otherwise, such proposals will be automatically vetoed by one of the large member states. The voting by veto concept thus does not provide undue influence of small member states but rather mitigates the power of large and small member states reciprocally.

Second, voting by veto is said to be complicated. This is actually not the case. The only additional work that is required compared to the usual voting is that each voter must establish a ranking of suggested alternatives. The elimination procedure is by computer, which can deliver the result within minutes.

Third, the number of participants may be relevant for the outcome. In a small group, participants may behave strategically, but in a large number, they may lack of the incentive to become actively involved in the voting process. These are two well-known characteristics of voting mechanisms. In so far voting by veto is not different it could be considered for the specific institution of the Council, which is neither very small nor very large. The Council will have 25 to 27 members after full accession, and 28 after Turkey joins. In competition policy a market with that many suppliers is regarded as fairly competitive.

What has been said for strategic behavior and active participation in voting also holds to some extent for collusion. With as much as 25 to 28 participants it is not easy to maintain voting discipline among colluders. Nevertheless, one could argue that collusion in politics is not prohibited by law.

We have in mind a kind of collusion in which all of the net receivers of the general budget (see condition 1 at the start of this section) submit identical proposals for the public good budget that exploit net payers, and the number of vetoes by the latter is not large enough to cancel out the number of net receivers' proposals. The procedure of voting by veto boils down to simple majority vote where the number of votes count. Such an outcome can, however, be avoided by secret voting.

Implementation of Voting by Veto in the Treaty

In Article 269 EC on financial provisions a third paragraph should be added; it should read as follows:

Additional to the general budget under the provisions of the preceding paragraphs of this article, there will be a second budget on expenditures for public goods to be provided by the European Union. For this budget the following procedural rules are binding: Each year every Member State has to submit to the Council a draft law for a regulation on the raising of revenues and for a regulation of expenditures from the Union's public goods budget according to the regulations issued by the Commission.[23] One draft law is last year's public goods budget. Member States have to exercise sequentially their right to eliminate one draft law each. Which Member State votes first, second, and so on, is determined by lot. The process stops when there is only one draft law left. This draft law, which is not vetoed, shall be adopted and put into effect by the Council.

6.5 Conclusions

Politicians pursue policies with regard to the EU budget that promote their re-election at home. On the expenditure side of the budget, they try to maximize the flow of resources toward their electorate, and on the revenue side they want to minimize their contributions to the budget. Both goals can be pursued simultaneously because the two sides of the budget are institutionally separated. A combined evaluation of costs and benefits does not take place. Any attempt of net payers and net receivers to connect, at least, partially, revenues to expenditures will be ineffectual. As under the principle of general fund financing no earmarking is enforceable, the budget will end in deadlock.

Some authors advocate connecting the two sides of the budget by giving the European Union the power to tax, thus making the European Parliament responsible for levying the taxes. President Romano Prodi has supported reforms in such directions at the opening session of the European Convention (Prodi 2002). In the Commission it is expected that such a system would strengthen representatives' responsibility before voters and simultaneously end the dismal discussion on which member state is net payer and which is net receiver (Goulard and Nava of the European Commission in a personal statement, 2002).[24]

There is, however, no indication that members of the European Parliament will act less egoistically in *spending* than ministers in the Council. This is because members of the European Parliament depend on the voting base of their home country. The more money they bring home, the more votes they will receive, and hence there is little hope of reaching a unanimous decision to abolish the common EU policies on which this spending takes place. EU policies are part of the Treaty and can only be replaced by a unanimity vote of the member states.[25]

A difference has, however, to be expected on the revenue side. If the European Parliament is given the power to tax, it will be able to increase taxes by less than unanimity. Under such a parliamentary regime tax increases will be much easier to enforce than under the present system of own resources, which requires unanimity of the member states for increasing contributions and hence taxes. Moreover it has to be expected that with a second and—with Turkey—a third round of accession, the income distribution in the Union will become increasingly skewed to the left, making redistribution increasingly attractive for a majority of voters and their representatives in the European Parliament.

In sum, in giving the responsibility for taxing and spending to a majoritarian European Parliament, we are likely to have a higher budget for redistribution. The provision of Union-wide public goods nevertheless will not be promoted by such a change. For that goal not majority vote but cooperation is required. Cooperation requires trust, which can only be achieved by a procedure where partners do not finding themselves in a position of being exploited. Our proposal for promoting both trust and cooperation is to allow voting by veto in the Treaty.

Notes

The authors are indebted to Pio Baake, Dennis Mueller, Ludger Schuknecht, and two anonymous referees for helpful comments.

1. European Commission, Haushaltsvademekum, 2000, p. 31. Expenditures for research, external activities, and administration (in relation to total expenditures, 2001) are regarded as contributions to unionwide public goods while member state specific expenditures have been defined as redistributive.

2. These are EUROSTAT, the European Court of Auditors, the EU Commission, the Federal Ministry of Finance of Germany, the Ministry of Finance of the Netherlands, and the Deutsche Bundesbank (Stegarescu 2001). For a critical review of the concept of net payer position, see Milbrandt (2000, pp. 42–46).

3. The original text of the Treaty of Rome is in German, French, Italian, and Dutch. Translation by the authors.

4. The new version of Article 40 can be found in Article 34 of the Treaty of Amsterdam.

5. The new version of Article 123 can be found in Article 146 of the Treaty of Amsterdam.

6. Early consideration of the compensation function of the EU budget is given by Folkers (1995).

7. The new version of Article 38 can be found in Article 32 of the Treaty of Amsterdam.

8. The new version of Article 148 can be found in Article 205 of the Treaty of Amsterdam.

9. Beschluss 70/243 des Rates vom 21 April 1970 über die Ersetzung der Finanzbeiträge der Mitgliedstaaten durch eigene Mittel der Gemeinschaft.

10. It has to be added that the establishment of the structural funds had also the specific purpose to increase British receipts in order to reduce the British net payer position.

11. For Greece, it was the problem of adherence as it entered already in 1981.

12. Or threat of nonentry in the case of Spain.

13. Vaubel (2001, pp. 108–15) argues that EU politicians and public officials often form circles of friendship, cultivate reciprocity, and logroll at costs to the public at large. Therefore inner ties can be presumed to promote coherence too.

14. A new version of Article 148 can be found in Article 205 of the Treaty of Amsterdam.

15. Strictly speaking, their net contributions totaled 9 and 22 euros respectively per capita over seven years total, amounting to 1 to 3 euros per capita each year, which is nearly no net contribution (see table 6.1).

16. 70/243/EGKS, EWG, Euratom, Abl., Nr. L 94 (1970), p. 19.

17. See H. Bünder, Die mühsame Suche nach dem richtigen Reformmodell, *Franfurter Allgemeine Zeitung* 193 (August 21, 1998), p. 12.

18. Article 46 of the Preliminary Draft of October 28, 2002.

19. Malta, Slovenia, Czech Republic, and Cyprus will receive an extra payment to keep them from being pushed into a net payer position.

20. Buchanan and Lee (1994) suggest that contributions to the EU budget be tied to member states' public expenditures. While this idea is attractive from an efficiency point of view, it is unlikely to be acceptable unanimously, for it creates winners and losers. The European Constitutional group (1993) wants to avoid this problem by granting a veto right to net payers.

21. Some may object that the principle of the unity of the budget is violated. But it has to be remembered that the Union never had a fully integrated budget. The budget of the European Community of Coal and Steel (during its existence) as well as the budget on loans and credits has always been separated from the general budget (see Strasser 1991, pp. 46–49).

22. See Mueller (1989, pp. 139–45) as well as Mueller (1984).

23. The Commission could establish a public goods budget for each major public good.

24. Other reform proposals that have been made in recent years cannot be summarized here; see Heinemann (1998).

25. One way to lower incentives for representatives to maximize transfers to their home constituencies and instead to pursue more Union-wide goals is to merge all of Europe into one electoral district. The pros and cons are discussed in Blankart and Mueller (2004).

References

Baldwin R. E., J. F. François, and R. Portes. 1997. The costs and benefits of eastern enlargement: The impact on EU and central Europe. *Economic Policy* 24: 127–76.

Blankart. Ch. B. 1996. The European Union's debt question: A conceptional viewpoint. *Constitutional Political Economy* 7: 257–65.

Blankart, C. B., and D. C. Mueller. 2004. The advantages of pure forms of parliamentary democracy over mixed forms, Public Choice, forthcoming.

Brennan, G., and J. M. Buchanan. 1985. *The Reason of Rules: Constitutional Political Economy*. Cambridge: Cambridge University Press.

Buchanan, J. M. 1975. *The Limits of Liberty: Between Anarchy and Leviathan*. Chicago: University of Chicago Press.

Buchanan, J. M., and D. R. Lee. 1994. On a Fiscal Constitution for the European Union. *Journal des économistes et des études humaines* 5: 219–32.

EU Commission. 2001. *Aufteilung der operativen EU-Ausgaben 2000 nach Mitgliedstaaten.* Brussels.

EU Commission. 1995. *Die Finanzverfassung der Europäischen Union*. Luxembourg.

European Constitutional Group. 1993. *A Proposal for a European Constitution.* London: www.European-Constitutional-Group.org.

Folkers, C. 1995. Welches Finanzausgleichssystem braucht Europa? In H. Karl (ed.): *Regionalentwicklung im Prozess der Europäischen Integration.* Bonn: Europa-Union-Verlag, pp. 87–108.

Goulard, S., and M. Nava. 2002. A more democratic system for financing the EU budget: A challenge for the European Convention. Manuscript. European Commission, Brussels.

Heinemann, F. 1998. *EU Finanzreform 1999. Eine Synopse der politischen und wissenschaftlichen Diskussion und eine neue Reformkonzeption.* Gütersloh: Verlag Bertelsmann Stiftung.

Hosli, M. O. 1996. Coalitions and Power: Effects of Qualified Majority Voting in the Council of the European Union. *Journal of Common Market Studies* 34: 255–73.

Lienemeyer, M. 2002. *Die Finanzverfassung der Europäischen Union.* Baden-Baden: Nomos.

Messal, R. 1989. *EG-Finanzierung und Lastenverteilung—Die Reform des EG-Finanzierungssystems 1988.* Bonn: Stollfuss Verlag.

Messal, R. 1991. *Das Eigenmittelsystem der Europäischen Gemeinschaft.* Baden-Baden: Nomos.

Messal R., and A. Klein. 1993. Finanzlasten und Eigenmittelstruktur der europäischen Gemeinschaft. *Wirtschaftsdienst* 73: 375–83.

Milbrandt, B. 2001. *Die Finanzierung der Europäischen Union. Perspektiven für eine Osterweiterung.* Baden-Baden: Nomos.

Mueller, D. C. 1984. Voting by veto and majority rule. In H. Hanusch (ed.): *Public Finance and the Quest for Efficiency.* Detroit: Wayne State University Press, pp. 69–86.

Mueller, D. C. 1989. *Public Choice II.* Cambridge: Cambridge University Press.

Peters, T. 1996. Reform der EU-Abstimmungsverfahren. In M. E. Streit and S. Voigt (eds.): *Europa reformieren: Ökonomen und Juristen zur zukünftigen Verfasstheit Europas.* Baden-Baden: Nomos, pp. 85–97.

Peffekoven, R. 1994. *Die Finanzen der Europäischen Union.* Mannheim: Bibliographisches Insitut und Brockhaus AG.

Prodi, R. 2002. Speech at the opening session of the Convention for the future of Europe. Brussels. February 28.

Raunio, T., and M. Wiberg. 1998. Winners and Losers in the Council: Voting Power Consequences of EU Enlargements. *Journal of Common Market Studies* 36: 549–62.

Stegarescu, D. 2001. Zahlmeister und Nutzniesser der EU—Die Nettozahlungsposition als Vergleichsmasstab. Manuscript. Zentrum für Europäische Wirtschaftsforschung, Mannheim.

Strasser, D. 1991. *Die Finanzen Europas,* 7th ed. Luxembourg: Amt für amtliche Veröffentlichungen der EG.

Tabellini, G. 2002. Principles of policy making in the European Union: An economic perspective. *CESifo Forum* 3: 16–22.

Vaubel, R. 2001. *Europa-Chauvinismus. Der Hochmut der Institutionen.* München: Universitas.

Widgrén, M. 1994. Voting power in the EC decision making and consequences of two different enlargements. *European Economic Review* 38: 1153–70.

Wissenschaflicher Beirat beim Bundesministerium für Wirtschaft und Technologie. 1999. *Neuordnung des Finanzierungssystems der Europäischen Gemeinschaft.* BMWi-Dokumentation 455. Berlin.

7

Coordinating Sectoral Policy-Making: Searching for Countervailing Mechanisms in the EU Legislative Process

Bernard Steunenberg

7.1 Introduction

The Council of the European Union—or the Council of Ministers as it was initially called—has developed into a large number of different Council formations. When the European Community was established, the Foreign Affairs ministers represented the member states in the Council meetings. But soon these ministers started to invite one or more of their colleagues to assist or replace them (Westlake 1999, p. 59). The Transport Council and the Agriculture Council were among the first Council formations created in this way, followed by the Social Affairs Council. The number of different Council formations increased in the 1970s and 1980s. The heads of state and government first discussed this development in the Helsinki European Council (1999) and decided to limit the number of possible formations.[1] The amended rules of procedure for the Council adopted on June 5, 2000, limited the number of different Councils.[2] Besides the General Affairs Council in which the Foreign Affairs ministers of the member states meet, 15 other Councils were identified for specific policy sectors. The Seville European Council (2002) decided to lower the number further by merging the existing 16 formations into 9 new ones (European Council 2002, p. 23).[3]

Unlike national legislatures in which the parliament adopts new laws, the European Union (EU) allows sectoral Council formations to set its policies. Depending on the EU legislative procedure, sectoral ministers take final decisions on legislative proposals (consultation procedure) or adopt proposals in agreement with the European Parliament (codecision procedure). This decision-making structure of the Council has been challenged in the current discussions on institutional reform. In the White Paper on European governance, the European

Commission (2001, p. 29) noted that "[t]he Council of Ministers, in particular the General Affairs Council composed of Ministers for Foreign Affairs, has lost its capacity to give political guidance and arbitrate between sectoral interests," and concluded that there is a need to improve policy coordination. The member states as well as Union's High Representative for the Common Foreign and Security Policy (Solana 2002) have expressed similar concerns.

In this chapter, I address these legislative concerns and analyze the sectoral structure of the Union's decision-making process. In particular, I consider the ways in which different policies in the EU are currently coordinated and how changes in the Union's legislative process could strengthen policy coordination.[4] The sectoral structure of the Union's decision-making process has been overlooked in most analytical models of EU decision-making.[5] These models focus on the interactions between the Commission, Parliament, and a single Council in which the member states are represented, and regard shifts in power among these actors in the decision-making process. In effect they show that the Union is more like a parliamentary system, where the power of Parliament has increased under the codecision procedure.[6] However, this conclusion is questionable and may be partly the result of the limited focus of this established approach. Other models suggest a different view of the Union's decision-making. They take into account of the links between the national administrations and the policy-making process in Brussels. They argue that the Council structure has created a mode of interest representation that "cuts across the member states" and in which the sectoral ministers and other officials from various member states play an important role in the making of common policy (e.g., see Christiansen 2001, p. 152). In this view, sectoral policy-making contributes importantly to the Union's decision-making process, which may even outstrip the traditional national divide between member states. In this chapter I follow this perspective and focus on the countervailing mechanisms that are part of the Union's legislative process and that may improve policy coordination within the European Union.[7]

I base my analysis on game-theoretical modeling of the interactions between different Council formations and other EU actors. This way I am able to show that the General Affairs Council as well as the European Parliament have limited coordinating powers. Their powers can be labeled ex post coordination because they permit adaptations and changes after a proposal is drafted. The main problem with the General Affairs Council and Parliament is that its members cannot include in a proposal all the policy dimensions that are relevant to a policy problem. Coreper plays a more effective role because this committee participates in the preparation of the various initiatives. In addition it is a single committee that is not sectorally divided. Finally I show that the European Council, which is higher in the Union's hierarchy than the Council formations, could effectively coordinate different policies by preparing decisions that span various policy dimensions. Such an arrangement with an overarching European Council would fit a Union that is a confederation of states and not a federal or parliamentary model of Europe in which the European Parliament plays a central role in the legislative process.

The chapter is structured as follows: After discussing the extent to which sectoral policy-making has developed in the European Union, I show why sectoral policy-making is beneficial to certain political actors. However, when political actors have a general interest in EU policy and are also concerned by the policies set by other Council formation, sectoral policy-making has its drawbacks. I analyze several possible ways to counteract the consequences of sectoral decision-making, including coordination by the General Affairs Council, joint policy-making with the European Parliament, policy preparation by Coreper, and involvement of the European Council. I conclude the chapter with a discussion of the implications of my analysis for the reforms currently discussed in the European Union.

7.2 The Rise of Sectoral Policy-making in the European Union

The number of sectoral Council formations has grown over the years. Figure 7.1 presents the development of different Council formations in the period 1958 to 2002 based on various issues of the Official Bulletin of the European Union. Note that in the 1970s there were the largest number of formations. Whereas 8 different Councils met in the period 1967 to 1971 (the dotted lines in the figure indicate if a Council formation did not meet for some time), 20 formations were active around 1988, and this number was increased to 22 formations in 1996. This development is often related to the rising volume of the Union's legislative agenda. In their monograph on the Council of Ministers, Fiona Hayes-Renschaw and Helen Wallace indicated that "[i]n practice different specialised formations of the Council have emerged in response to the rhythm and volume of business in different policy

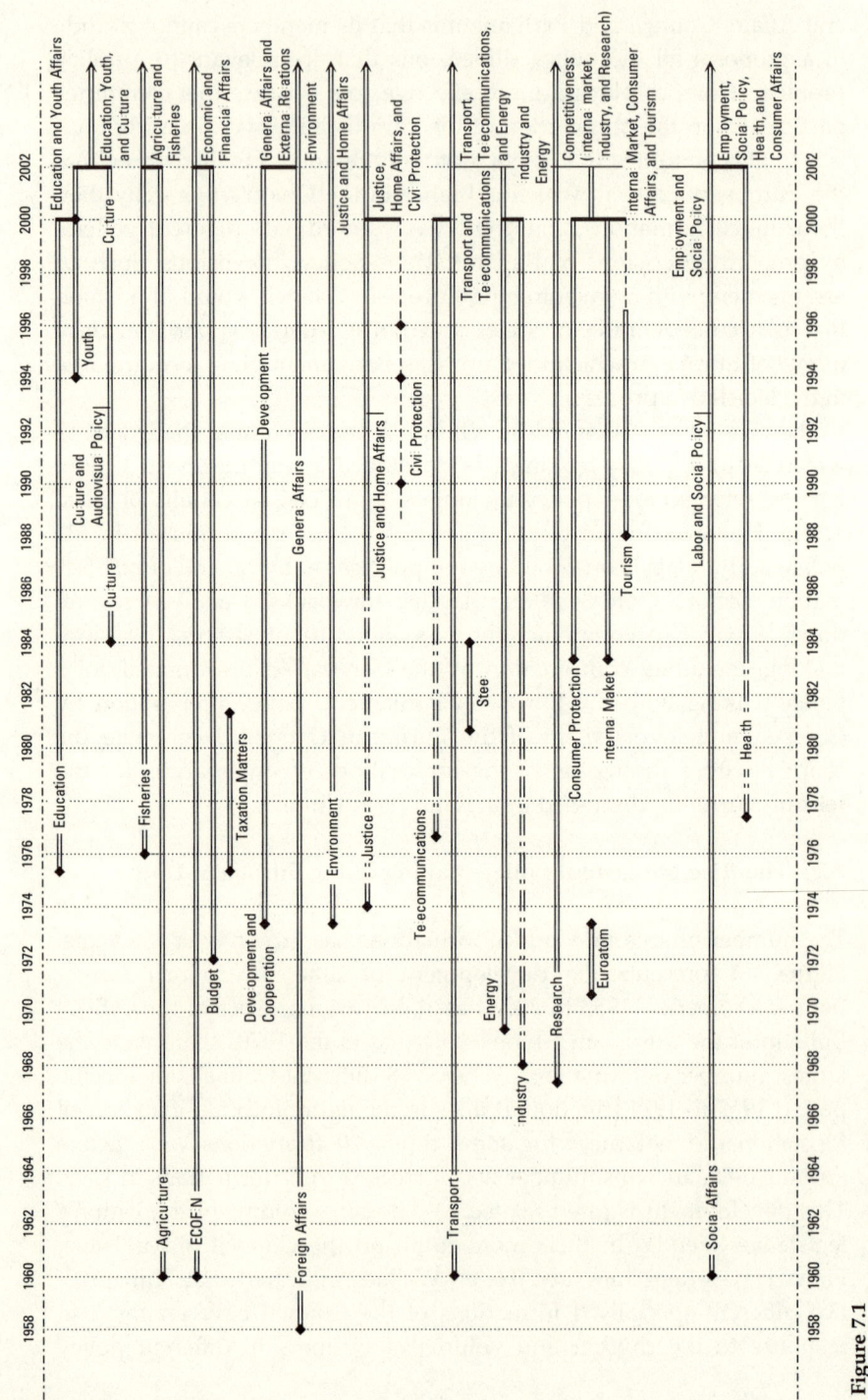

Figure 7.1
Different Council formations in the period, 1958–2002

areas" (1997, p. 29), which in their view is partly the result of "... changing fashions in public policy and shifting EU priorities" (1997, p. 33).[8] The meetings of the Internal Market Council, which began in 1983, and the large number of meetings of the Justice and Home Affairs Council from 1992 on illustrate the relationship with political priorities.

The increase in the number of sectoral Councils has not always been steady. Some Council formations were maintained for a number of years and then disappeared or were merged with others. The Civil Protection Council, for instance, only met five times in the period 1987 to 1996 and then became a separate Council formation. The Iron and Steel Council only met in the period 1981 to 1984. The Taxation Matters Council was active in the period 1975 to 1981. Still the total number of formations grew, and at the beginning of 2000, 20 different Council formations were active in the European Union. However, with the introduction of new Council's rules of procedure in June 2000, the member states officially recognized only 16 different Council formations. This was the first reduction of the number of different formations. The decision of the Seville European Council in 2002 brought this number down to only 9 formations.

The gradual specialization of Council formations may have reinforced the idea that sectoral ministers need to discuss their dossiers at the EU level. In discussing the rise of different Councils, Jan Werts indicates that it "... reflects a tendency by the specialized Ministers to manage by themselves European policy related to their portfolio" (Werts 1992, p. 163). This development of specialization in the Union's decision-making process has led to a further fragmentation of EU policy-making. As Hayes-Renschaw and Wallace have noted, cross-Council coordination is "very hit-and-miss," while the "... pronounced segmentation of work between policy areas and between Councils impedes coherent decision making and consistent treatment of subjects" (1997, p. 286). EU policy-making has become very sector oriented, while the link between these sectors and the subsequent policies has not received much attention.

Interestingly, the sectoral division in the organization of the Council is reflected in the structure of the European Commission as well as the European Parliament.[9] The different portfolios of Commissioners as well as the standing committees of Parliament, which discuss policy initiatives proposed in the Union, follow a similar sectoral divide and thus re-enforce the fragmentation of decisions made in the nine different Councils.

7.3 What Is the Attraction?

The first step in the analysis is to focus on the possible consequences of sectoral policy-making, where the decisions are made by ministers with similar portfolios and as members of the same Council formation. These ministers, like any other players, are assumed to have simple Euclidean and separable preferences over the policy dimensions that are involved. These preferences are single peaked so that each player has a preferred position, which is called the player's ideal point. The alternatives in this space are valued based on their distance; that is, the farther away an alternative is from the player's ideal point, the less it is preferred.

The ministers in the same Council formation share responsibility for a policy area, as is reflected in their portfolios. This is represented by a single dimension. In addition, and to simplify the analysis, I assume that these ministers, for example, in the Industry and Energy Council, have the same preferences.[10] The reasoning is that ministers with similar portfolios in the national political arena are faced with similar mechanisms that shape their preferences. These mechanisms can be either "capture" by special interest groups or "deliver" on policy promises to this sector as is necessary for political survival. The ideal point of this group of ministers, B, is denoted b. Similarly the ministers in a second Council formation, for example, the Environment Council, are responsible for a different policy dimension. The ideal point of this group of ministers, A, is denoted a. Finally the current state of affairs or *status quo*—the policy or situation without a common policy at the beginning of the policy-making process—is denoted q.

Each Council formation has unique (or monopoly) jurisdiction over the making of common policy in some area. When the Commission proposes a new policy in the area of energy, the policy is submitted to the Industry and Energy Council for approval. Based on the preferences presented in figure 7.2a, the Energy Council will agree on a new policy b. Similarly the Environment Council, which decides on any initiative in the area of environmental policy, will set a policy a (see figure 7.2b). The unintended consequence of these separate decision-making processes is that the resulting EU policy is simply the sum of decisions

a. Policy dimension concerning energy

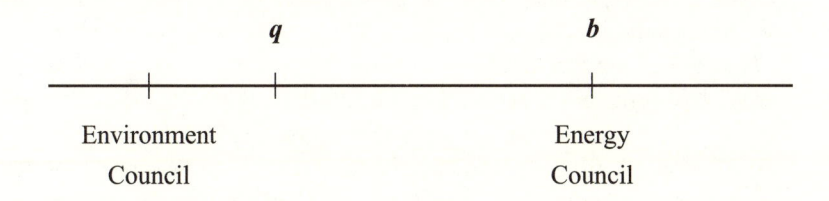

```
                    q                          b
────────┼───────────┼──────────────────────────┼────────
     Environment                            Energy
      Council                               Council
```

b. Policy dimension concerning the environment

```
                              a     q
────────┼─────────────────────┼─────┼─────────────────
      Energy                Environment
      Council                 Council
```

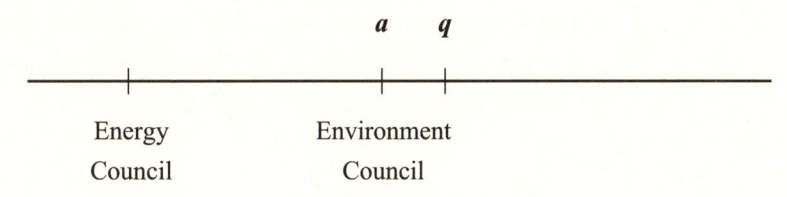

Figure 7.2
Decision-making by two sectoral Council formations

made by the sectoral Councils. Without any further coordination, the ministers in each Council formation, whether it be Industry and Energy or the Environment, are able to reach their preferred policy along the dimension for which "their" Council has jurisdiction.

This outcome differs from that of decision-making in national cabinets. In cabinet governments, policies are the result of agreement among ministers responsible for *different* policy sectors together with a "coordinating" prime minister. The national ministers with different portfolios have to negotiate a result that is acceptable to all of them, including the prime minister. As a consequence the resulting policy is based on the balancing of different sectoral interests and not only the interest of a specific sector. In the national context, a sectoral minister is mostly not able to get his or her most preferred policy, since this policy will not be feasible. However, the sectoral structure at the EU level offers different opportunities, since it leaves EU policy decisions in the hands of national ministers with *similar* portfolios. These ministers are now able to obtain a more preferred result, as they share interests. This advantage may explain the popularity of the "road to Brussels" and the expansion of policy-making at the European level (see Steunenberg 2003, pp. 9–12).

However, sectoral decision-making, as described, may not be preferred by ministers who have an interest in the policies represented by the "other" dimension of the policy space. As in the example of figure 7.2, energy ministers may be concerned with environmental policy, since high environmental standards may affect costs to energy producers. At the same time, ministers responsible for the environment may have an interest in energy policy, since some production methods may have a negative impact on the environment. This situation can be illustrated by placing the two policy dimensions—energy and environment—in a two-dimensional space for which each group of ministers, A and B, has two-dimensional preferences. In figure 7.3 the issues related to energy are reflected by the horizontal x-axis and to

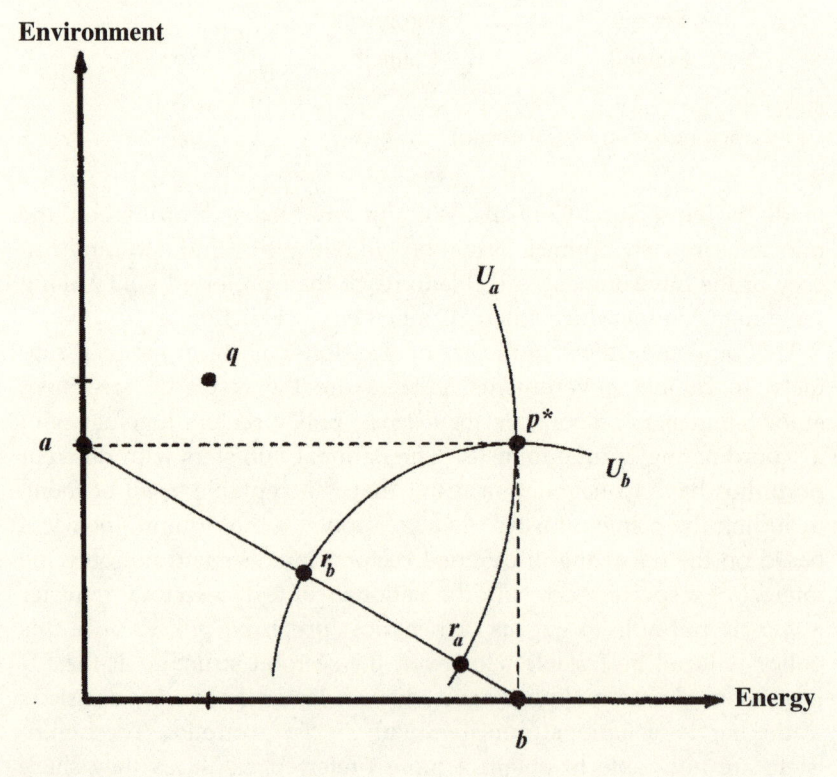

Figure 7.3
Two sectoral Council formations in a two-dimensional policy space

the environment by the vertical y-axis. The dimensional preference orderings for both sectoral Councils are kept the same as in figures 7.2a and b.

The outcome of uncoordinated sectoral policy-making, which occurs when the two groups of ministers have no say over each other's policy dimension, is presented as p^* in figure 7.3. This solution is not preferred by either of the two groups. Taking simple Euclidean preferences for this space, both groups of ministers prefer the range of policies found in the area below p^*, where their indifference contours U_a and U_b overlap. When these two Council formations engage in a bargaining process over a new policy, the resulting outcome will be found on the section of the contract curve (i.e., the line between the ideal positions a and b) between the points r_b and r_a. Because such a policy yields a higher utility level to both Council formations, it is Pareto preferred to the sectoral solution p^*.

The disadvantage of sectoral policy-making is that the other Council formations, which are not involved in the decision-making process, are faced with less beneficial outcomes. Since this problem can be mutual, several Council formations will benefit from a change of the current system. The decisions made by the Helsinki European Council (1999) and, more recently, the Seville European Council (2002) indicate that the member states are well aware of the problems related to insufficient coordination among different Council formations. While the Helsinki European Council limited the number of Council formations to 16, the Seville European Council merged them further to 9 formations. The ministers who were members of the merged formations participate as full members of the new formations. This structure has improved the coordination of policies *within* the merged Councils (see Steunenberg 2003, pp. 12–15), but it has not resolved the inadequate coordination *among* the remaining Council formations. How can the policy coordination between these Councils be improved?

7.4 Sectoral Policy-making versus Coordination: Countervailing Mechanisms

While several actors in the Union's legislative process could improve intersectoral policy coordination, I will look at four such actors, the General Affairs Council, the European Parliament, Coreper, and the European Council, as they can countervail the sectorally biased decisions of individual Councils formations.

The General Affairs Council[11]

The main idea behind the formation of Councils was that the General Affairs Council would coordinate the policy-making of the different sectoral Councils. However, based on past performance, most observers are rather skeptical about the coordinating abilities of the General Affairs Council. As early as 1979 an assessment by a committee of "three wise men" found that "the General Affairs Council has ceased to be general, either in the sense of directing the work of the separate Councils, or in the sense of providing a forum for the discussion of all new major issues" (Werts 1992, p. 162).[12] More recently, Geoffrey Edwards has noted that "[t]he initial idea was that Foreign Ministers in the General Affairs Council would exercise an overall 'control.' It soon proved not to be feasible" (Edwards 1996, p. 134).[13]

In assessing the coordinating abilities of the General Affairs Council, I propose to use a simple game-theoretical model in which the different players are allowed to make a choice at different stages of the game. The two sectoral Councils that are involved are the Environment Council and the recently formed Transport, Telecommunications, and Energy Council—or Energy Council for short. The ministers in these Councils have spatial (two-dimensional) preferences. However, they can only decide on a (one-dimensional) policy for which this Council has jurisdiction. These different policy areas are indicated by the horizontal and the vertical axes in figure 7.4.

The structure of the game is as follows: the Environment Council, which consists of ministers with ideal points at a, may decide to initiate a legislative process with a proposal. The General Affairs Council, whose foreign ministers have ideal points at GA, decides whether or not to intervene. If it does, the proposal is sent for review by the Energy Council, which consists of ministers with ideal points at b. The Energy Council may advise the General Affairs Council to accept or oppose the proposal. In the case of opposition, the proposal is referred back to the Environment Council for further discussion, which implies that it cannot be adopted in its present form. In this way the Energy Council can be modeled as a veto player who is able to oppose policy initiatives of the Environment Council. Of course, this is the way proposals made by the Energy Council are also subjected to veto by the Environment Council.[14]

Environment

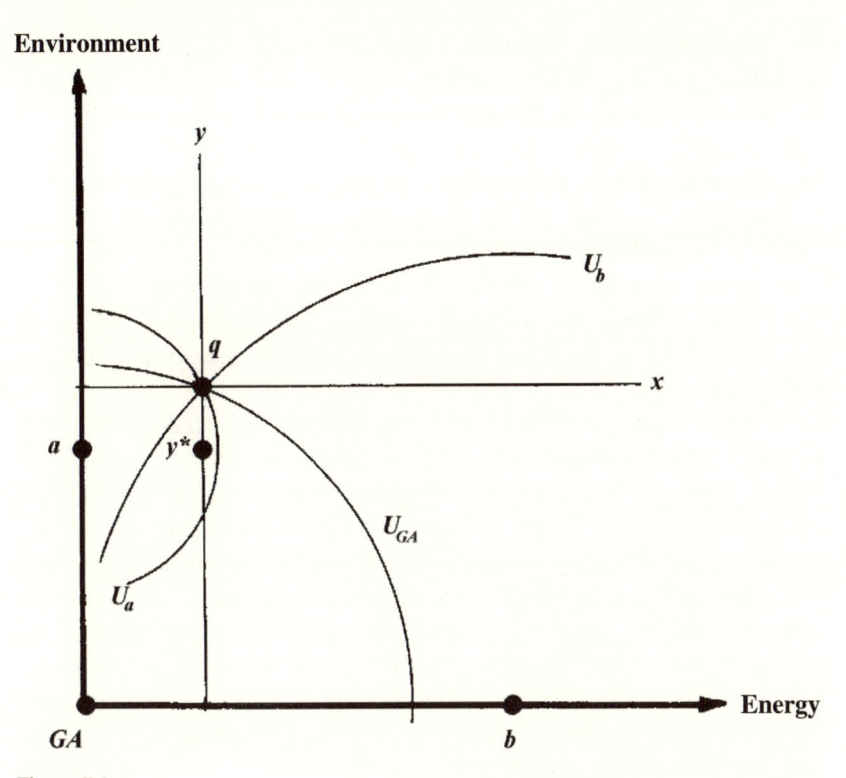

Figure 7.4
Decision-making by sectoral Council formations coordinated by the General Affairs Council

The outcome of this process is the new environmental policy y^* as presented in figure 7.4.[15] To the Environment Council this policy is the best possible outcome given the fact that this Council only has jurisdiction over the vertical policy dimension y. The General Affairs Council supports the new policy, since it prefers this policy to the status quo (its indifference contour with regard to q is U_{GA}). The Council does not want to reverse the proposal of the Environment Council. As the gatekeeper it will not open its gates and thus will not involve the Energy Council.

A policy-making process by the Energy Council can be approached in a similar way. Using the preference configuration as in figure 7.4, the Energy Council, which decides in the horizontal x-dimension, may propose a policy that can change the current state of affairs expressed by q. However, any proposal to the right of the status quo and along the horizontal policy dimension x that moves the energy policy closer to the ideal points of the Energy ministers will not be accepted by the General Affairs and the Environment Councils. Whenever the Energy Council releases a proposal, the General Affairs Council opens its gate and submits the proposal to the Environment Council. The Environment Council, which only accepts new policies within its indifference contour U_a, opposes the new measure. In opposing the change, the measure is referred back to the Energy Council. So, as there is no support for a change from the Environment Council or the General Affairs Council, the energy policy essentially remains the status quo.

The analysis suggests that the General Affairs Council could function as gatekeeper for different Council formations. From the moment one of the sectoral Councils makes a proposal, the General Affairs Council can involve another Council to join its opposition to the new policy. However, as is clear in the analysis, the General Affairs Council only intervenes when involvement affects its outcome. In all other circumstances, including cases where the General Affairs Council prefers the new policy to a current one despite the anticipated opposition, it keeps its gate closed and does not intervene. In other words, the General Affairs Council's coordinating role is weak, as is reflected in the literature on the European Union.

Another limitation to the influence of the General Affairs Council is that it can, at most, only "block" an initiative. It is rather powerless when many alternatives exist that are slightly more preferred than the status quo but are quite far away from the Council's most favored policy. As long as one sectoral Council has the authority to decide an issue, the other formations have limited means to challenge the decision. They cannot amend any policy proposal nor start a bargaining process with either Council formation over the policy space.[16]

More general is the problem that the General Affairs Council does not have the political authority to settle disputes among the different Council formations. At the national level the Minister of Foreign Affairs is usually not responsible for policy coordination. If the Foreign Affairs Minister attempts to coordinate at the EU level, he or she will likely come into conflict with the national ministers who have their own responsibilities, as well as with the prime minister who traditionally fulfills this coordinating role in national government. In its limited position the General Affairs Council is not able to ensure the coordination of policy in the European Union.

The European Parliament

The next possible coordination mechanism can be found in the European Parliament, which has substantial influence in the legislative process. The so-called co-decision procedure, introduced by the Maastricht Treaty (1992), has given Parliament far-reaching powers in legislative policy-making. Not only can Parliament block Council decisions, it can also initiate bargaining with the Council on proposals. The Treaty of Amsterdam (1997), and later the Nice Treaty (2000), extended the scope of co-decision to make it the most common procedure used in the Union. By its legislative power, Parliament can effect changes in legislation proposed by any Council formation to factor in concerns other than those represented by the sectoral Councils.

Parliament's coordinating abilities, however, are restricted. First, and unlike its national counterparts in the member states, the European Parliament does not have the power to initiate legislation. This right is reserved for the European Commission. So Parliament depends on the Commission for the timing and drafting of proposals. The Commission has then the opportunity to delay a proposal submission, to determine (in negotiations with Coreper) the relevant issues, or to alter the policy dimensions of the proposal. In other words, it is up to the Commission to determine whether a proposal has environmental dimension, as presented in figure 7.4, or energy dimension. Parliament does not have this power. Second, the internal structure of the European Parliament is based on a sectoral division of labor. Although I will not develop this point here, this structure does influence decision-making within Parliament and its weight in opposing any Council proposals that are tainted by sectoral interests.[17]

Parliament's impact on the decision-making process, and its role in policy coordination, can be represented by a game that resembles the models developed so far on EU legislation. In this model, and after the release of a policy initiative, Parliament can bargain on a proposal with the concerned sectoral Council.[18] If both agree on terms, the proposal is adopted. The outcome and possible influence of Parliament can be shown in a preference configuration with a status quo point as in figure 7.5. The figure is similar to figure 7.4, which was used to assess the impact of the General Affairs Council.

Should the Environment Council proposes a new policy, the outcome is found between y_{max} and y_{min} along the y dimension that

Environment

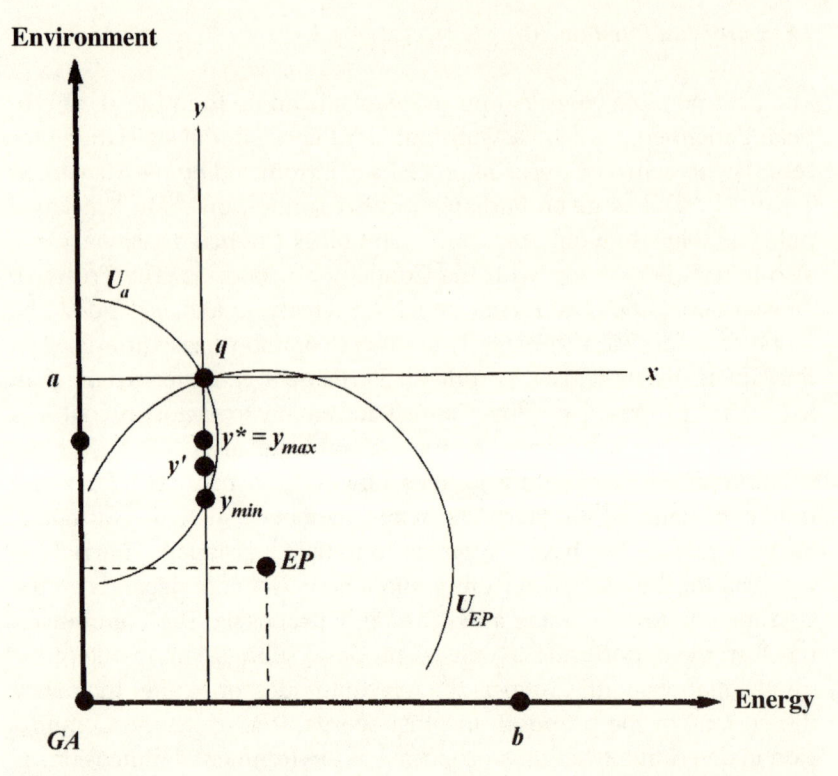

Figure 7.5
Decision-making by sectoral Council formations and the European Parliament

intersects the status quo. The points within this interval are the "negotiation set," which are new policies that are both feasible and Pareto optimal for the members of the two decision-making bodies. In applying a Nash bargaining solution, both Parliament and the Environment Council select a policy y' that maximizes their joint utility over all values in the negotiation set.[19] This policy is equivalent to y' in figure 7.5, where I assume that the Environment Council and Parliament each value a unit-distance change away from their ideal point in the same way.

The adopted policy based on Parliament's involvement hardly differs from policy y^* obtained in the previous analysis with the General Affairs Council. This is partly a consequence of Parliament's preferences versus the Environmental Council and the location of the status quo. If Parliament had extreme preferences on environmental issues (which can be associated with a change in the vertical dimension away from the origin), it could have blocked decision-making by rejecting any move away from the status quo. A second and more important observation is that Parliament's involvement does not lead to a two-dimensional change of policy. As shown in figure 7.5, policy-making is still restricted to the environmental dimension. Parliament's involvement does not allow the policy space to include the other policy dimension. Parliament is able to amend or reject a legislative proposal, but it cannot reformulate the proposal. It is not able to include new policy dimensions that are part of the jurisdiction of another sectoral Council.[20] Based on the analysis, Parliament's position can be characterized as having the possibility of ex post coordination, which is bound to the already initiated decision-making process.

Coreper

A third coordination mechanism is the Committee of Permanent Representatives (Coreper). All Commission proposals must pass Coreper before they are submitted to one of the various Council formations.[21] The permanent representatives negotiate at an early stage the proposals of the Commission. According to Martin Westlake, these diplomats can wield considerable power, as they study the purpose, the wording, the meaning, the interpretation, the loopholes, and a number of other implications of a proposal (Westlake 1999). If the permanent representatives reach agreement, the Council will adopt the proposal without further discussion.

An importance difference from the Council formations is that Coreper can review all aspects of policy proposals. Because its scope is not limited to one or more dimensions, it can consider all possible implications of a Commission proposal. In this way the committee is in a good position to make a balanced choice. In terms of the example presented earlier, Coreper is able to handle both energy and the environment policy, whereas these two Council formations are restricted to the one or the other.

Coreper's preparatory role in policy-making can be regarded in the following way: Coreper takes an initiative of the Commission and proposes new policy based on the agreement of its members.[22] Next the policy is submitted to one of the Council formations, which has to approve the proposal. The other Council has the possibility to object to the policy (as part of the opinion presented). Whether Council formations are able to approve or reject a proposal is not relevant to the

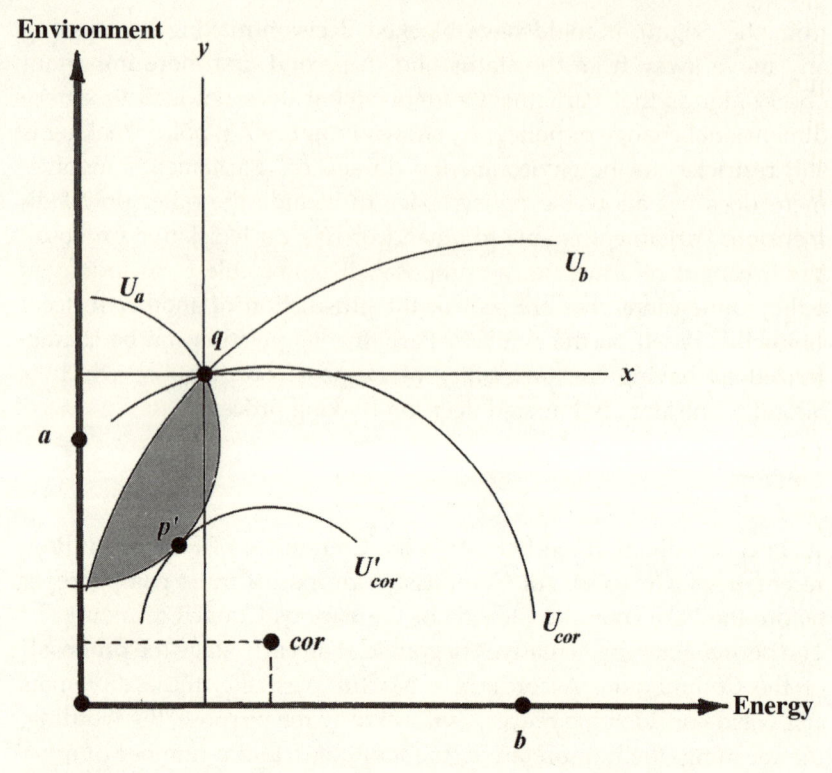

Figure 7.6
Decision-making by sectoral Council formations coordinated by Coreper

analysis, since this boils down to the veto of each formation. The process can now be represented by a two-stage game in which Coreper proposes a new (two-dimensional) policy that, in the second stage, has to be approved (not vetoed) by both Council formations.

The outcome of this process can be illustrated with the preferences as presented in figure 7.6. Coreper, denoted as *cor*, is assumed to have a moderate preference as the committee is composed of members who have to represent various national interests and not only the interests of specific policy sectors. Its ideal point is located in the area between both Council formations. The two Council formations—Environment and Energy—are at the same positions as before. The possibility of a veto implies that both Council formations only accept proposals that are found in the intersection of their win sets. The grey area in the figure indicates this intersection. Based on the preferences of the permanent representatives policy, p' is Coreper's best choice: this policy is closest to the preferences of the permanent members and located in the win sets of both Council formations.[23] Policy p' will be accepted by the Environmental and Energy Councils and forms the equilibrium outcome.

The analysis leads to several observations. First, the outcome differs from the one derived for the decision-making process in which the Council formations decide on only their policy dimension. In comparison to the outcome y^* that was produced by the game with the General Affairs Council, the new solution is shifted toward Coreper's most preferred policy. If sectoral preferences affect Coreper's preferences less, its involvement improves coordination and leads to more balanced policies. A second observation relates to the fact that the analysis thus far is based on homogeneous preferences. The ideal points of the permanent members are represented by only one position (i.e., the position cor). However, it is more likely that these members hold different views, which could be the result of differences in the extent to which member states depend on specific policy sectors. In those circumstances Coreper's involvement will become less effective. If the committee may not be able to reach agreement,[24] the policy is submitted to the Council, which then has to make a decision. Despite these limitations, the analysis indicates that Coreper, in contrast to the European Parliament, is able to engage in ex ante coordination by affecting the drafting of a new policy proposal.

The European Council

The last possible mechanism for increasing coordination is through the European Council—the meeting of European heads of state or government. The role of the European Council was extensively discussed in Helsinki. The Helsinki European Council approved "operational recommendations" on working methods that aimed to improve policy coordination (European Council, 1999, conclusion 20). The gist of these recommendations is to define "... a single chain of coordination capable of ensuring that Union action is consistent with the will of its political leaders. This chain of command starts in the Member States themselves with effective interdepartmental coordination and arbitration, and extends through Coreper, the General Affairs Council to the European Council."[25] So, from the perspective of the member states, the European Council is the last link in the Union's decision-making process that can secure the coordination of common policy.

Based on the views expressed by the member states at the Helsinki European Council, the Council could, first of all, decide on issues that have not been resolved by the General Affairs Council. When Council formations disagree on policy, and the General Affairs Council is not able to reach a solution, the issue can be brought before the European Council. Second, the Council discusses and decides on policy issues that have substantial political importance. Although the European Council does not have a formal position in most of the Union's legislative procedures, these informal accords, which are often based on a proposal made by the Commission, play an important role and bind the subsequent decision-making by the Council formations. An example is the agreement on combating mad cow disease in the United Kingdom during the BSE crisis. After months of deliberation, the Florence European Council (1996) finally settled the matter by reaching agreement on a Commission proposal for selective culling of British herds.

The European Council's coordinating role can be analyzed by the following sequential game, again using the environment-energy space as before: The Environment Council formation initiates the process by proposing a policy y. This policy is submitted to the Energy Council, which may provide its opinion on the proposal. If the Energy Council opposes the proposal, decision-making shifts to the European Council. In the last stage the European Council decides on a new policy p that covers *both* dimensions of the policy space.

This game can be resolved by backward induction. Starting from a policy that the European Council has concluded, the other actors plan their actions. So the European Council's preferred policy now forms a point of departure for possible deviations. If the Environment Council formulates its alternative policy along the y-dimension, which is supported by the Energy Council, this policy displaces the selected policy. If not, the Environment Council must concede to the policy of the European Council.

This dynamic can be translated into the preference configuration and status quo shown in figure 7.7. Since the European Council will set the policy at its ideal position of EC (i.e., (x_{EC}, y_{EC})), the Environment Council, which is at a, has to look for alternatives that are in the win set for the two Council formations based on the new reversion point EC *and* along the y-dimension that intersects EC. As such points do not exist, the Environment Council proposes $y'' = y_{EC}$ as its preferred policy.[26] Similarly, if the Energy Council initiates a proposal—which it

Coordinating Sectoral Policy-Making

Environment

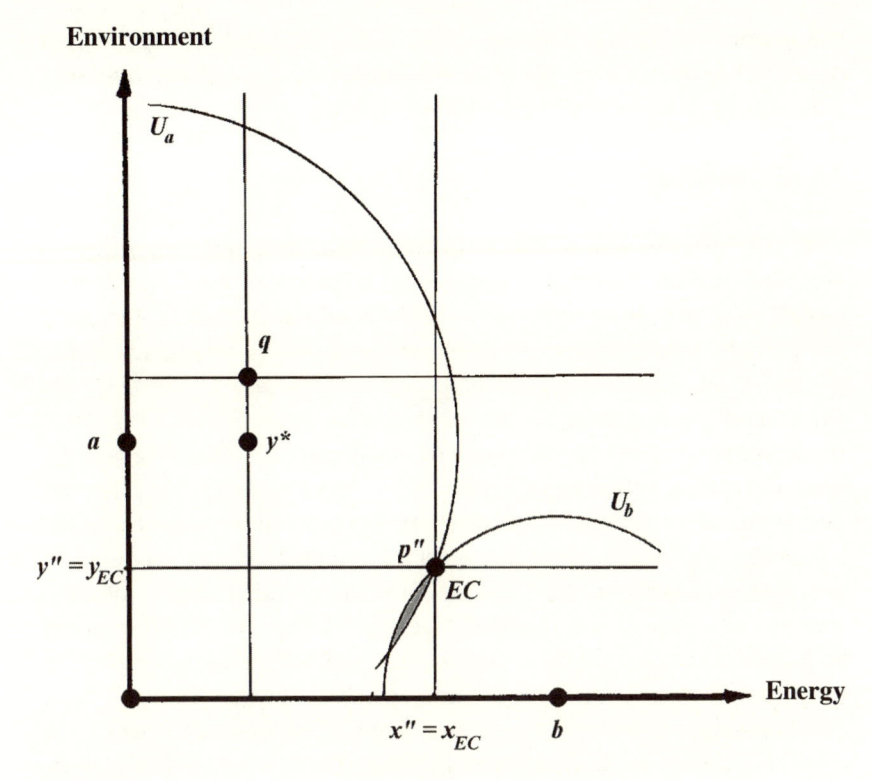

Figure 7.7
Decision-making by sectoral Council formations and the European Council

will do, as it has several alternatives including the European Council's most preferred position to the status quo—the new policy will be $x'' = x_{EC}$. In effect, both Council formations cannot deviate from the policy preferred by the European Council because of the preference configuration used in the figure. If the European Council showed less moderate preference in both dimensions, with its ideal position close to q or some other point farther away from the origin, the Council formations could have set a policy that differs from the European Council's preferred position.

The analysis shows, first of all, that by its decision-making power over two dimensions, the European Council can coordinate all relevant policy areas. Second, due to its political stature, the European Council forms the starting point for any decisions emanating from the Council formations. In this respect the EU legislative process is a two-level game in which the European Council can supersede policy-making by the sectoral Councils. The European Council's position can be best described as *hierarchical*, since its decisions take precedence over any decisions of the lower placed sectoral Councils.

7.5 Conclusions

The sectoral structure of the Council of Ministers has, according to observers, led to a loss of coherence, or in terms of the analysis presented here, to policies that only reflect the specific sectoral interests of the participating ministers. In contrast to cabinet government, where ministers responsible for *different* policy sectors seek to concede, the Council structure leaves EU policy decisions in the hands of national ministers with *similar* portfolios. The resulting EU policies reflect the specific sectoral interests represented by these ministers to a greater degree than in a national context where a policy has to be based on the balancing of different sectoral interests. This characteristic may explain why policy-making at the EU level has intensified. Further, interests that are not part of the ministers' portfolios, but are relevant to the problems addressed by these policies, are not sufficiently addressed in the Union's sectoral decision-making structure. In this chapter I have considered several mechanisms which can potentially counteract the consequences of sectoral decision-making. These mechanisms include the coordination by the General Affairs Council, joint policy-making with the European Parliament, the preparation of policy initiatives by Coreper, and the involvement of the European Council.

My analysis shows that ex ante coordination, which is possible during the stage of the drafting a proposal, is more effective than ex post coordination. Ex ante coordination allows political actors to influence the various issues that are part of a proposal, that is, the *dimensions* of the policy proposal. This possibility provides the actor who is engaged in ex ante coordination with the opportunity to include *all* dimensions regarded as relevant in a proposal. The Committee of Permanent Representatives (Coreper) has this possibility, since it negotiates at an early stage with Commission on proposals the Commission is considering to release. The European Parliament, on the other hand, can only maintain ex post coordinating power. Parliament does not have a hand in the drafting of a proposal; it is rather confronted with proposals as they are submitted to the Council. The best Parliament can do is amend existing proposals so that they reflect less the sectoral interests in different Council formations and more the interests of all members in Parliament.

An alternative mechanism discussed in this chapter is *hierarchical* coordination, which includes the European Council in the analysis. The European Council has different political stature than the different Council formations, and it is well placed to arbitrate between Councils in controversial issues, or to decide informally on matters of high political interest. Hierarchical policy coordination appears, in principle, to be effective because the European Council is not limited to a specific policy jurisdiction. *Any possible dimension* could be included in its decision.

Yet there are a number of negative aspects to endorsing for the European Council such a coordinating role. First, substantial policy coordination by the Council could overburden its agenda, and leave less time for other and perhaps politically more important issues. Second, the involvement of the European Council as an overarching political authority may lead to an erosion of procedural legitimacy in the Union, as it affects the legislative process in which Parliament is involved. Deal-making among the heads of state and government is not compatible with a democratic process in which decisions are based on legislative procedures specified by the treaties. Hierarchical coordination by a political actor other than Parliament would likewise be inconsistent with the aim of establishing the Union as a democratic political system.

A different approach would be to further merge the various Council formations as proposed by the Seville European Council. However, I showed in another paper (Steunenberg 2003), this requires a more radical reorganization of the Council structure than restricting the number of different Council formations to nine. Although the last merger can be regarded as an improvement, it nevertheless allows several Council formations to continue that set policies independently of the others.

Unfortunately, the discussion on EU policy coordination seems to suffer from the same problems as EU policy-making. Different possible solutions are discussed, while none seems to resolve fully the problem of fragmentation and a loss of coherence. The analysis here points to possible improvements but not to one solution. More discussion within the European Parliament or the European Council is needed, though this may not fully compensate for the problems that are caused by the sectoral division between Council formations. The main problem is that policy coordination is caught between two underlying and competing views on legislative policy-making in the European Union, as has become increasingly apparent over the past decade.

The first is the traditional community method in which EU policy is seen as the result of interactions between the member states and the Commission. In this view, Coreper, the General Affairs Council, and eventually the European Council all contribute in the coordination of common policy. The process is hierarchical and forms, as expressed by the member states, a chain of command (European Council, 1999, Annex III). *Hierarchical coordination* fits the conception of the Union as *confederation* in which the member states and thus the European Council is the most important political body.[27] In a confederation the legislative process may, for instance, be consultative, with the Council making the final decision. However, it does not fit a second view of decision-making in the Union, which was gradually introduced in the 1980s.

This view is based on the parliamentary method, whereby EU policy is seen as the result of interactions between the Council and Parliament. Policy coordination is now a function of the Council *and* Parliament, and it is no longer effected by a chain of command. In this view, each institution is responsible for the coordination of EU policy and possesses the legislative means to achieve it. In the case of Parliament this would imply that the Commission can no longer maintain the monopoly role in legislative initiatives. Parliament will also be able to initiate legislative proposals. The view of policy coordination is then *nonhierarchical*, and this fits the conception of the Union as *federation* in which the member states no longer are the most important actors. Legislative decision-making is the result of co-decision, or an amended version of this procedure in which Parliament and the Council are at equal footing.

The need for cohesion and coordination of policy thus requires a broader discussion on the institutional structure of the European Union. If the member states prefer to maintain the community method, policy coordination can only be improved by reinforcing the "chain of command" between the Union's traditional institutions. That would require substantial effort, especially on the part of the European Council, if the member states are not yet prepared to further merge the existing sectoral Council formations. An alternative way would be to follow the parliamentary method and focus on the possible coordinating role of Parliament in this process. As indicated in this chapter, Parliament's current position is not sufficient to take up the task of policy coordination. To be able to coordinate policy, the European Parliament and the Council should have full legislative power, and not be restricted by the Commission. The question is whether the member states, as well as the Commission, are prepared to provide Parliament with these powers. If they are not, the current way of allowing Parliament to participate in the legislative process, while maintaining the community method as much as possible, will not resolve the problem of policy coordination.

Appendix

Let a be a player who has simple Euclidean and separable preferences for the outcome space $R \times R$, which are defined by a utility function $U_a(p)$, $p \in R \times R$. Let q be the current state of affairs, $q \in R \times R$. $P_a(q)$, or simply P_a, is the preference set of player a with regard to q, that is, $P_a = \{p \mid U_a(p) > U_a(q)\}$. Let $W_M = \cap P_i$ be the win set of the group of ministers, $i \in M \subset N$, with regard to q and based on unanimity rule. A Council formation can be represented by a group of ministers, $a \in A \subset N$, responsible for policy dimension $Y(c) \subset R \times R$, with $Y(c) = \{(x, y) \mid x = c, y \in R\}$, with $c \in R$. To simplify the argument, assume that $U_i = U_j$ for all members $i, j \in A$, so that $W_A = P_a$. Similarly, a second Council formation can be defined as $B \subset N$, $B \cap A = \emptyset$, which is responsible for a policy dimension $X(c) \subset R \times R$, with $X(c) = \{(x, y) \mid x \in R, y = c\}$. For this Council B, as well as the General Affairs Council, GA, the European Parliament, EP, Coreper, cor, and the European Council, EC, I also assume equivalent ideal points for all the members of the same decision-making body.

A7.1 Policy-making with the General Affairs Council

The structure of the game is that (1) Council formation A initiates a policy-making process by proposing a policy $y \in Y(q)$; (2) the proposal is subject to submission to Council B by the General Affairs Council; and (3) if submitted, Council B decides whether or not it will veto the proposal. If vetoed, the proposal is rejected. Otherwise, it becomes common policy. Applying backward induction, Council B only accepts a proposal if $y \in W_B(q)$. Otherwise, Council B decides for q by using its veto. The General Affairs Council submits the proposal to Council B, when it prefers the outcome reached by Council B to the proposal made by Council A, that is,

- if $y \notin W_{GA}(q)$ and $y \notin W_B(q)$, the General Affairs Council submits the proposal to Council B;
- if $y \in W_{GA}(q)$ or $y \in W_B(q)$, the General Affairs Council will not submit the proposal to Council B.

Knowing this, Council A proposes the policy

$$y^* = \begin{cases} \max(U_a(y) \mid y \in W_A(q) \cap W_B(q) \\ \quad \cup W_A(q) \cap W_{GA}(q)) & \text{when } W_A(q) \cap W_B(q) \neq \emptyset \\ & \text{or } W_A(q) \cap W_{GA}(q) \neq \emptyset, \\ q & \text{when } W_A(q) \cap W_B(q) = \emptyset \\ & \text{or } W_A(q) \cap W_{GA}(q) = \emptyset. \end{cases}$$

This is the equilibrium outcome for policy dimension Y. Similarly one can derive the equilibrium outcome for the second and independent policy dimension X.

A7.2 Policy-making with the European Parliament

In this game one of the Council formations bargains with Parliament (denoted as EP) on a new policy $y \in Y(q)$. If $W_A(q) \cap W_{EP}(q) = \emptyset$, no agreement can be reached and the policy remains at status quo. If $W_A(q) \cap W_{EP}(q) \neq \emptyset$, agreement is possible if policies exist that are part of Y and Pareto preferred by both the Council and Parliament. Define $Z = \{z \in Y(q) \text{ and } z \in W_A(q) \cap W_{EP}(q) \mid W_A(z) \cap W_{EP}(z) = \emptyset\}$. Applying the Nash bargaining solution, Parliament and the Council select the following policy:

$$y' = \begin{cases} \max(U_a(z) \times U_{EP}(z)) & \text{when } Z \neq \emptyset, \\ q & \text{when } Z = \emptyset. \end{cases}$$

This is the equilibrium outcome for Y. Similarly one can derive the equilibrium outcome for dimension X.

A7.3 Policy-making with Coreper

The structure of the game is that (1) Coreper proposes a new policy, and (2) both Councils have to agree on the new policy. If one of the Councils disagrees, the proposal is rejected. Applying backward induction, we have Council A only accepting a proposal $p \in R \times R$ if $p \in W_A(q)$. Similarly Council B only accepts a proposal if $p \in W_B(q)$. Knowing this, the committee of permanent representatives, cor, proposes the policy

$$p' = \begin{cases} \max(U_{cor}(p) \mid p \in W_{cor}(q) & \text{when } W_{cor}(q) \cap W_A(q) \cap W_B(q) \neq \emptyset, \\ \quad \cap W_A(q) \cap W_B(q)) & \\ q & \text{when } W_{cor}(q) \cap W_A(q) \cap W_B(q) = \emptyset. \end{cases}$$

This is the two-dimensional equilibrium outcome.

A7.4 Policy-making with the European Council

The structure of the game is that (1) Council A initiates a policy-making process by a proposal submitted to Council B; (2) Council B decides whether or not it agrees with the proposal; if Council B disagrees with the proposal, the making of a new policy is shifted to the European Council, and (3) the European Council decides on a policy $p \in R \times R$, which includes both dimensions of the policy space. Applying backward induction, we have the European Council choosing its most preferred policy $p_{EC} = (x_{EC}, y_{EC})$ in the last stage. Knowing this, Council B only accepts a proposal if $y \in W_B(p_{EC})$, otherwise, this Council will use its veto and requests a decision from the European Council. Now define the new policy y, which Council A could propose as $y \in Y(x_{EC})$. In the first stage Council A proposes the policy:

$$y'' = \begin{cases} \max(U_a(y) \mid y \in Y(x_{EC}) \text{ and} & \text{when } Y(x_{EC}) \cap W_A(p_{EC}) \\ \quad y \in W_A(p_{EC}) \cap W_B(p_{EC})) & \quad \cap W_B(p_{EC}) \neq \emptyset, \\ y_{EC} & \text{when } Y(x_{EC}) \cap W_A(p_{EC}) \\ & \quad \cap W_B(p_{EC}) = \emptyset. \end{cases}$$

This is the equilibrium outcome for Y. Similarly one can derive the outcome for dimension X.

Notes

I would like to thank Paul 't Hart for his helpful comments and Dimiter Toshkov for his research assistance.

1. See European Council (1999: Annex III).

2. Council Decision of June 5, 2000, adopting the Council's Rules of Procedure, *Official Journal of the European Communities* L 149, 23.6.2000 (2000/396/EC, ECSC, Euratom). For the list of Council formations see Follow-up to the Helsinki Council Conclusions on December 10–11, 1999: Council formations, *Official Journal of the European Communities* C174/02, 23.6.2000.

3. Also see the Council Decision of July 22, 2002, adopting the Council's Rules of Procedure (2002/682/EC, Euratom), *Official Journal of the European Communities*, L230/20, 28.8.2002. Annex I of these rules presents the new list of Council formations, which

include Councils on Economic and Financial Affairs, Justice and Home Affairs, Competitiveness, Agriculture and Fisheries, and Environment.

4. In this chapter I focus on *horizontal* coordination, that is, the coordination of policy between different sectors at the EU level. A different perspective would be to concentrate on vertical coordination, that is, the coordination between the EU and the member states with regard to the further development and implementation of policy.

5. See, for instance, the models proposed by Crombez (1996, 1997), Steunenberg (1994), and Tsebelis (1994). Steunenberg and Selck (2002) present an overview of the various explanatory models of EU decision-making based on the spatial theory of voting and game theory.

6. See the debate between Crombez (2000b), Steunenberg (2000b), Tsebelis and Garrett (2000), and Garrett and Tsebelis (2001), and Corbett (2000, 2001). For the question on whether the Union is developing toward a parliamentary system, see also the contributions by Steunenberg and Thomassen (2002) and Crombez (2003).

7. In an earlier paper I showed how policy coordination could be improved by changes in the structure of the Council. These changes include the merger of Council formations, as proposed by the Seville European Council, and the strengthening of the Council presidency (Steunenberg 2003). In this chapter I will not discuss the Council's structure.

8. See also Westlake (1999, p. 59) and Nugent (1999, p. 143) for similar claims.

9. For the portfolios of Commissioners, see *http://europa.eu.int/comm/commissioners/ index_en.htm* (November 2002); for Parliamentary committees, see *http://www.europarl. eu.int/committees/home_en.htm#parliamentary* (November 2002).

10. This is the case for regulatory policies, which are a major part of EU policy-making, and to a less extent distributional policies. The assumption of having the same preferences can be relaxed, allowing ministers to have diverse preferences. This will complicate the analysis, but the main conclusions will not be affected as long as these preferences are found in an area around the ideal position used here.

11. The 2002 Council's rules of procedure renamed the General Affairs Council into the General Affairs and External Relations Council (see note 3). For convenience I will use the term General Affairs Council, since I focus on the coordinating task of this Council formation.

12. See for the Conclusions of the "Three Wise Men," Report on European Institutions, *Official Bulletin of the EC*, November 1979: 25–28.

13. See also Westlake (1999, pp. 166, 391–392) and the European Commission (2001, p. 29).

14. For this game I assume that the players have complete and perfect information. In addition no player prefers its decision to be overturned. This preference can be viewed as imposing some cost on a proposal that is not the final outcome of the decision-making process. See appendix A7.1 for the general solution of this game.

15. This outcome can be characterized as a structure-induced (Nash) equilibrium (Shepsle 1979; Shepsle and Weingast 1981), since it is a result of both the structure of the decision-making process and the preferences of the players.

16. The only possibility is to negotiate in the national political arena a compromise, or a national position, that will be represented by the minister in the main Council formation.

However, such a position does not guarantee a more favorable outcome as it depends on the positions taken by the other ministers in this Council formation. In addition the question arises whether, and to what extent, this minister will prefer the national position to his or her own sectoral position.

17. One way of approaching this is by assuming that Parliament (or its members) has "extreme" preferences with regard to policy issues. The results are presented in appendix A7.2, where these preferences are restricted to specific parts of the policy space so that all possible outcomes are no longer feasible.

18. See also Tsebelis and Garrett (2000). Their bargaining model differs from the models in which political actors choose their strategies sequentially. See Steunenberg (1994, 2000a), Garrett (1995), and Crombez (1997, 2000a) for sequential models of codecision. König and Pöter (2001) present some empirical evidence.

19. See appendix A7.2 for further details. See Calvert, McCubbins, and Weingast (1989, pp. 608–609) for a justification of the Nash bargaining model in the otherwise noncooperative context of this chapter.

20. There is also a germaneness rule, which does not allow Parliament to introduce an issue that is not related to the proposal (e.g., see Tsebelis and Kalandrakis 2002: 197). In this chapter this rule is interpreted as not being able to add a new dimension to a proposal. See, for instance, Hix (1999, p. 58) and Rasmussen (2000, p. 4) for this interpretation of the germaneness rule.

21. There are a few exceptions here, as the fragmentation of Coreper seems to follow the fragmentation of the Council. First, Coreper itself is split between Coreper I and Coreper II. The latter is composed of the permanent representatives and works mainly for Foreign Affairs ministers and the Economic and Financial Affairs Council (see Westlake 1999, p. 278). Second, and more important, there are several committees that work for specialized Councils besides Coreper. The Special Committee for Agriculture deals directly with the Agricultural Council. The meetings of the Justice and Home Affairs Council are prepared by the Article 36, Coordinating Committee.

22. The interactions between the Commission and Coreper can be treated as a bargaining problem. To keep my analysis simple, however, I will disregard this feature and focus on the consequences of Coreper's involvement for the coordination of policy.

23. See appendix A7.3 for further details.

24. Technically this situation occurs when the current state of affairs, or *status quo*, is found in the unanimity set of the committee members.

25. See European Council (1999, annex III) on "An Effective Council for an Enlarged Union: Guidelines for reform and operational recommendations."

26. See appendix A7.4 for further details. See also note 14 for some other assumptions that are used to solve this sequential game.

27. See Mueller (2002, pp. 41–46) for the distinction between confederation and federation.

References

Calvert, R. L., M. D. McCubbins, and B. R. Weingast. 1989. A theory of political control and agency discretion. *American Journal of Political Science* 33: 588–611.

Corbett, R. 2000. Academic modelling of the codecision procedure: A practitioner's puzzled reaction. *European Union Politics* 1: 373–81.

Corbett, R. 2001. A response to a reply to a reaction (I hope someone is still interested!). *European Union Politics* 2: 361–64.

Crombez, C. 1996. Legislative procedures in the European Community. *British Journal of Political Science* 26: 199–228.

Crombez, C. 1997. The co-decision procedure in the European Union. *Legislative Studies Quarterly* 22: 97–119.

Crombez, C. 2000a. Institutional reform and co-decision in the European Union. *Constitutional Political Economy* 11: 41–57.

Crombez, C. 2000b. Codecision: Towards a bicameral European Union. *European Union Politics* 1: 363–68.

Crombez, C. 2003. The democratic deficit in the European Union. *European Union Politics* 4: 101–20.

Dehaene, J.-L., R. von Weizsäcker, and D. Simon. 1999. The institutional implications of enlargement: Report to the European Commission. Brussels, October 18.

Edwards, G. 1996. National sovereignty vs integration? The Council of Ministers. In J. Richardson (ed.): *European Union: Power and Policy-Making*. London: Routlegde, pp. 127–47.

Enelow, J. M., and M. Hinich. 1984. *The Spatial Theory of Voting: An Introduction*. Cambridge: Cambridge University Press.

European Commission. 2001. European governance: A White Paper. Brussels, 25.7.2001 (COM(2001)428).

European Council. 1999. Presidency conclusions of the Helsinki European Council, 10–11 December 1999. Brussels, 11/12/1999 (Press release 00300/1/99): *http://ue.eu.int/ Newsroom/LoadDoc.asp?BID=76&DID=59750&LANG=1*.

European Council. 2002. Presidency conclusions of the Seville European Council, 21–22 June 2002 (SN 200/02): *http://ue.eu.int/en/summ.htm*.

Garrett, G. 1995. From the Luxembourg compromise to codecision: Decision making in the European Union, *Electoral Studies* 50: 289–308.

Garrett, G., and G. Tsebelis. 2001. Understanding better the EU legislative process. *European Union Politics* 2: 353–61.

Hayes-Renschaw, F., and H. Wallace. 1997. *The Council of Ministers*. Houndmills/London: Macmillan.

Hix, S. 1999. *The political system of the European Union*. Houndmills/London: Macmillan.

Konig, T., and M. Poter. 2001. Examining the EU legislative process: The relative importance of agenda and veto power. *European Union Politics* 2: 329–51.

Krehbiel, K. 1991. *Information and legislative organization*. Ann Arbor: University of Michigan Press.

Mueller, D. C. 1989. *Public Choice II: a revised edition of Public Choice*. Cambridge: Cambridge University Press.

Mueller, D. C. 2002. Constitutional issues regarding European Union expansion. In B. Steunenberg (ed.): *Widening the European Union: The Politics of Institutional Change and Reform*. London: Routledge, pp. 41–57.

Nugent, N. 1999. *The government and politics of the EU*, 4th ed. London: Macmillan.

Rasmussen, A. 2000. Institutional games rational actors play: The empowering of the European Parliament. *European Integration online Papers* 4(1): http://eiop.or.at/eiop/texte/2000-001a.htm.

Shepsle, K. A. 1979. Institutional arrangements and equilibrium in multidimensional voting models. *American Journal of Political Science* 23: 27–60.

Shepsle, K. A., and B. R. Weingast. 1981. Structure-induced equilibrium and legislative choice. *Public Choice* 37: 503–19.

Solana, J. 2002. Summary of the intervention by Javier Solana, High Representative of the European Union for the Common Foreign and Security Policy. Plenary Session of the European Parliament, Strasbourg. May 15 (S0090/02).

Steunenberg, B. 1994. Decision making under different institutional arrangements: Legislation by the European Community. *Journal of Theoretical and Institutional Economics* 150: 642–69.

Steunenberg, B. 2000a. Constitutional change in the European Union: Parliament's impact on the reform of the codecision procedure. In H. Wagenaar (ed.): *Government institutions: Effects, Changes and Normative Foundations*. Dordrecht: Kluwer, pp. 89–108.

Steunenberg, B. 2000b. Seeing what you want to see: the limits of current modelling on the European Union. *European Union Politics* 1: 368–73.

Steunenberg, B. 2003. Deciding among equals: The sectoral Councils of the European Union and their reform. In M. J. Holler, H. Klient, D. Schmidtchen, and M. E. Streit (eds.): *European Governance*. Tübingen: Mohr Siebeck (*Jahrbuch für Neue Politische Ökonomie* 22: 1–23).

Steunenberg, B., and T. Selck. 2002. The insignificance of the significance: a comparison of procedural models on EU decision making. Mimeo. Leiden University.

Steunenberg, B., and J. Thomassen (eds.). 2002. *The European Parliament: Moving toward Democracy in the EU*. Boulder: Rowman and Littlefield.

Tsebelis, G. 1994. The power of the European Parliament as a conditional agenda setter. *American Political Science Review* 88: 128–42.

Tsebelis, G., and G. Garrett. 2000. Legislative politics in the European Union. *European Union Politics* 1: 5–32.

Tsebelis, G., and A. Kalandrakis. 2002. The European Parliament and environmental legislation. In B. Steunenberg and J. Thomassen (eds.): *The European Parliament: Moving toward Democracy in the EU*. Boulder: Rowman and Littlefield, pp. 185–211.

Werts, J. 1992. *The European Council*. Amsterdam: North Holland.

Westlake, M. 1999. *The Council of the European Union*, 2nd ed. London: Harper.

8

How to Choose the European Executive: A Counterfactual Analysis, 1979–1999

Simon Hix, Abdul Noury, and Gérard Roland

8.1 Introduction

A key issue in the design of any constitution is how to (s)elect the executive. It is no surprise, then, that one of the most controversial issues in the Convention on the Future of Europe is how to elect the EU's executive: the European Commission. Several governments, such as the British and French, would like to maintain the institutional status quo as established by the Nice Treaty—whereby the Commission is elected by (a qualified-majority of) the EU heads of government (Blair 2002). Against the institutional status quo, the "parliamentary" model, where the executive is "fused" to a majority in the EU legislature, seems to be the most popular. For example, Germany and the Benelux have proposed that the Commission should be elected by the European Parliament (Fischer 2000; Brok 2002; Verhofstadt 2002). Also the Commission has proposed that it should be elected by a two-thirds majority in the European Parliament (Commission of the EU 2002). More recently the Chirac-Schroeder "compromise" proposal to have the Commission president elected by the European Parliament and a Council president elected by the Council has been gaining strong momentum. So far only the Irish government has considered a "presidential" model (Laver et al. 1995), where the Commission would be elected separately from the European Parliament—either directly by the voters or indirectly by an electoral college of national parliaments (see Hix 2002b; Berglöf et al. 2003). The first draft of the constitution, produced end of May 2003, favors the election of the president of the Commission by the European Parliament. The Commission president would be proposed by the Council, "following the results" of the elections to the European Parliament.[1] In any case, the debate over the choice of the European executive will be the most important decision to take in the coming stages before the European constitution takes its final shape.

The pros and cons of the parliamentary and presidential models of government are well rehearsed in the political science and political economy literature (e.g., Lijphart 1992). Essentially, presidential government allows for true separation of powers between the executive and legislative branch of government. With a formal separation of powers, the executive is unable to force the legislative majority to support its policy agenda (Shugart and Carey 1992), but the executive cannot be brought down by a vote of confidence in the legislature. In contrast, with a fusion of the legislative and executive majorities, the executive can force its parliamentary parties to support its policy agenda by threatening to resign, and hence risk a battle over the formation of a new executive (Huber 1996; Diermeier and Feddersen 1997). This often means less policy change with a separation of powers than with parliamentary government (Tsebelis 2002). Also parliamentary governments tend to produce more public goods but also a higher size of government and more rents to politicians than presidential government (see Persson, Roland, and Tabellini 1997, 2000). Parliamentary government also tends to lead more easily to creeping policy centralization (Bednar et al. 2001).

Rather than rehearse these theoretical debates in the EU context (see Crombez and Hix 2002), we do something completely different: we undertake a counterfactual analysis of how EU politics would have worked had different models of executive election been used in the EU since 1979. In this counterfactual analysis we use data from voting in the European Parliament. In previous research we have collected and analysed the total population of roll-call votes in the European Parliament between 1979 and 2001: approximately 12,000 votes by 2,000 MEPs (Hix, Noury, and Roland 2004). From these votes we calculate ideal point estimates for every member of the European Parliament (MEP) on the two main dimensions of EU politics (the left–right, and pro-/anti-integration), using the NOMINATE algorithm developed by Keith Poole and Howard Rosenthal (Poole and Rosenthal 1997).

We use the ideal points of the MEPs to model election of the Commission president by the European Parliament in each of the five directly elected parliaments. We calculate the partisan affiliation of the Commission president under several election procedures and different assumptions about MEPs' voting behavior. First, we allow each parliament to elect a single Commission president (who would then presumably put the rest of his/her team together in cooperation with the governments). This corresponds essentially to the federalist proposal for the Convention supported by Germany, the Benelux countries, and supporters of a federalist Europe. In one scenario, we assume that MEPs follow the "whip" of their party groups. In an alternative scenario, we assume that MEPs vote according to their individual policy position vis-à-vis the candidates.

Second, we model the process of government formation in each parliament. The purpose is to simulate what kinds of government a full-fledged parliamentary Europe would produce. While this scenario is not currently on the table, this is seen as a long-term desirable scenario by many. Here we either assume that a government requires the support of 50 percent plus one MEPs or that a government requires the support of two-thirds of MEPs, as in the proposal by the Commission to the Convention.

We then contrast the outcomes of these different parliamentary models of EU government with what would have happened had a presidential model existed. Here we assume that the Commission president is elected by an electoral college of national parliaments in the same year as a European Parliament election (Hix 2002b). This can be seen as a realistic scenario for a presidential model of Europe as the direct election of a European president is not being considered as a likely scenario in the current situation.[2] We compare these counterfactual parliamentary and presidential models with the real-world outcomes: the partisan makeup of the seven Commissions that were appointed between 1979 and 1999.

One must, of course, be cautious with such a counterfactual exercise, as it implicitly assumes that political agents (MEPs, members of national parliaments) behave the same way under a different institutional setup. We know this is not the case. Nevertheless, given the uncertainty surrounding the effects of any possible institutional change in the context of Europe, we consider it useful to use all the available data to shed light on the effects of various proposals for the selection of the European executive. Our database on roll-call votes in the European Parliament can serve exactly this purpose. We feel that such a counterfactual empirical analysis, which uses a comprehensive dataset of observed behavior, goes much further than mere speculation.

The main insights from this exercise are as follows: The composition of the Commission or the political color of its president would have been different under the different proposals before the Convention. If the Commission president had been elected by the national parliaments, a center–right politician would have been elected between 1979 and 1999, and a center–left politician in 1999. In contrast, a rather different Commission president would have been elected if a parliamentary model had been used. If the EP elected the Commission president directly, the 1994 center–right Santer Commission would have been presided over by a Socialist, and the 1999 center–left Prodi Commission would have been presided over by a Conservative (reflecting the new dominance of the European People's Party [EPP] in the European Parliament). But, if the Commission had been elected by a full-fledged parliamentary model, a "grand coalition" of Conservatives and Socialists would have resulted in all periods except 1999, which would have been a center–right coalition of Conservatives, Liberals, and Gaullists. Finally, with a two-thirds majority, the only feasible coalition in all periods would have been a grand coalition of Socialists and Conservatives, and in some cases other parties would also have been needed.

Basically any parliamentary model for electing the Commission would have resulted in a rather different Commission than those chosen by the governments, and rather different policy outcomes. For example, a parliamentary model would have meant that the single-market program would not have been supported so enthusiastically by the Commission, for throughout the 1980s the Commission would have been dominated by the center–left. In contrast, a quasi-presidential model, with the Commission president elected by national parliaments, would have produced an EU executive more similar to the majority in the Council yet independent from their direct influence because of the separation-of-powers system.

In section 8.2, we describe the current mechanism for the appointment of the Commission. In section 8.3, we describe the makeup of the European Parliament since 1979. In section 8.4, we explain our five scenarios for the election of the European executive. In section 8.5, we present and analyze the results obtained by our simulations. In section 8.6, we discuss and comment on the merits of the various proposals on the table in the light of our simulations. In section 8.7, we summarize the main findings.

8.2 How the Commission Is Currently Elected: Unanimity in the European Council

Under the Treaty of Rome, the Commission is chosen by "common accord" among the EU heads of government. In practice, this has meant that the Commission has been elected by unanimity among the EU governments. The governments appoint the Commission president by unanimity, each government then nominates its own Commissioners, the governments then formally adopt the College of Commissioners by unanimity.

In the 1993 Maastricht Treaty, the European Parliament was given the right to be "consulted" on the governments' nominee for Commission president—which the Parliament interpreted as a formal right to veto the proposed candidate (Hix 2002a). In the 1999 Amsterdam Treaty, the governments formally granted the Parliament a right to veto the governments' choice both of the Commission president and of the Commission as a whole. Finally, in the Nice Treaty, with the prospect of enlargement of the Union to twenty-five or more member states, the governments maintained their monopoly on the nomination of the Commission but agreed that the appointment should be made by a qualified-majority in the European Council rather than by unanimity.

However, as the Nice Treaty only entered into force in 2002, no Commission has been elected using the qualified-majority rule. The Santer Commission was the only executive to be elected under the Maastricht Treaty procedure, and the Prodi Commission was the only executive to be elected under the Amsterdam Treaty procedure. The next Commission, elected after the 2004 European elections will probably be the only executive elected under the Nice (qualified-majority) rules, as the next-but-one-Commission (probably in 2009) will be chosen under the rules established in the new EU constitution (assuming that the Nice status quo is changed).

The use of unanimity in the European Council has meant that the Commission has always reflected the partisan makeup of the governments at the time of the election of the Commission. The Commission is supposed to be politically neutral. But there have been political shifts in the composition of the Commission over time as the political composition of national governments has shifted. As table 8.1 shows, the center–right majority in the Council throughout the 1980s and early 1990s produced a center–right majority in the six Commissions in this period (Thorn, Jenkins, Delors I, Delors II, Delors III, and Santer). Even though Jenkins and Delors were Socialists, table 8.1 shows that their party only formed 38 percent of the Jenkins Commission, and respectively 43, 41 and 29 percent in the three Delors Commissions. All other Commissioners came from the center–right. Similarly the center–left majority in the Council in the late 1990s produced a center–left

Table 8.1
Partisan makeup of the European Commission, 1977–2004

Jenkins 1977–1980	Thorn 1981–1984	Delors I 1985–1988	Delors II 1989–1992	Delors III 1993–1994	Santer 1995–1999	Prodi 2000–2004
Socialist—38%	**Socialist—50%**	**Socialist—43%**	**Socialist—41%**	**Socialist—29%**	**Socialist—45%**	**Socialist—50%**
Cheysson (Fra)	Cheysson (Fra)	*Delors (Fra)*	Marin (Spa)	Millan (UK)	Bjerregaard (Den)	Busquin (Bel)
Davignon (Bel)	Contogeorgis (Gre)	Cheysson (Fra)	*Delors (Fra)*	*Delors (Fra)*	Cresson (Fra)	Diamantopoulou (Gre)
Giolitti (Ita)	Dalsager (Den)	Clinton Davis (UK)	Dondelinger (Lux)	Marin (Spa)	Gradin (Swe)	Kinnock (UK)
Jenkins (UK)	Davignon (Bel)	Narjes (Ger)	Millan (UK)	Ruberti (Ita)	Kinnock (UK)	Lamy (Fra)
Vredeling (Net)	Giolitti (Ita)	Ripa di Meana (Ita)	Papandreau (Gre)	Van Miert (Bel)	Liikanen (Fin)	Liikanen (Fin)
	Narjes (Ger)	Varfis (Gre)	Ripa di Meana (Ita)		Marin (Spa)	Nielson (Den)
	Richard (UK)		Van Miert (Bel)		Papoutsis (Gre)	Solbes Mira (Spa)
					Van Miert (Bel)	Verheugen (Ger)
					Wulf-Mathies (Ger)	Vitorino (Por)
						Wallstrom (Swe)
						Green—5%
						Schreyer (Ger)
Liberal—15%	**Liberal—7%**	**Liberal—14%**	**Liberal—18%**	**Liberal—18%**	**Liberal—10%**	**Liberal—10%**
Brunner (Ger)	*Thorn (Lux)*	Christophersen (Den)	Bangemann (Ger)	Bangemann (Ger)	Bangemann (Ger)	Blokestein (Net)
Gundelack (Den)		De Clercq (Bel)	Cardoso e Cunha (Por)	Christophersen (Den)	Bonino (Ita)	*Prodi (Ita)*
			Christophersen (Den)	Deus Pinhiero (Por)		

EPP—31%	EPP—21%	EPP—43%	EPP—35%	EPP—47%	EPP—30%	EPP—30%
Burke (Ire)	Andriessen (Net)	Andriessen (Net)	Andriessen (Net)	Brittan (UK)	Brittan (UK)	Barnier (Fra)
Haferkamp (Ger)	Haferkamp (Ger)	Cockfield (UK)	Brittan (UK)	Matutes (Spa)	Deus Pinhiero (Por)	de Palacio (Spa)
Natali (Ita)	Natali (Ita)	Mosar (Lux)	Matutes (Spa)	Paleokrassas (Gre)	Fischler (Aus)	Fischler (Aus)
Vouel (Lux)		Natali (Ita)	Pandolfi (Ita)	Schmidhuber (Ger)	Oreja (Spa)	Monti (Ita)
		Pfeiffer (Ger)	Schmidhuber (Ger)	Schrivener (Fra)	*Santer (Lux)*	Patten (UK)
		Sutherland (Ire)	Schrivener (Fra)	Steichen (Lux)	Van den Broek (Net)	Reding (Lux)
				Van den Broek (Net)		
				Vanni d'Archirafi (Ita)		
Other Right—15%	Other Right—21%	Other Right—0%	Other Right—6%	Other Right—6%	Other Right—15%	Other Right—5%
Ortoli (Fra)	O'Kenedy (Ire)		MacSharry (Ire)	Flynn (Ire)	de Silguy (Fra)	Byrne (Ire)
Tugendhart (UK)	Ortoli (Fra)				Flynn (Ire)	
	Tugendhart (UK)				Monti (Ita)	

majority in the Prodi Commission: which has 55 percent of Commissioners on the left (Socialist or Green), and 45 percent of Commission on the right (Liberal, EPP, or non-EPP Conservatives).

Also it should be pointed out that although the Commission seeks to reach consensus when proposing legislation, formally it can decide by a simple majority (with the Commission president casting the deciding vote). As a result the party-political makeup of the Commission does make a difference. For example, the single-market project of the late 1980s and early 1990s was driven by a center–right majority in the Council, supported by a center–right majority in the Commission—despite the existence of a Socialist (Delors) at the helm. Similarly in the late 1990s the drive to introduce a series of directives in the social affairs field (on working time, workers consultation, nondiscrimination on the grounds of race, etc.) was pursued by center–left majorities in the Commission and Council, against a center–right majority in the post-1999 European Parliament.

The question, then, is how would this have been different had the Commission been elected by the European Parliament rather than the Council? To do this, we first look at the evolution of the composition of the European Parliament since 1979.

8.3 The European Parliament since 1979

Table 8.2 shows the partisan makeup of the European Parliament just after each of the five direct elections. The first two parliaments had slight center–right majorities, with the European People's Party (EPP), the French Gaullists and their allies (GAU), the British Conservatives and their allies (CON), and the Liberals (LIB) together commanding 58 percent and 51 percent of the seats, respectively. The third parliament was evenly balanced, with the parties on the left—the Socialists (SOC), Greens (GRN), Radical Left (LEFT), and Regionalists (REG) (who were mostly on the left)—commanding 48 percent of the seats compared to 47 percent for the parties on the right. This was also the case in the fourth parliament, with both the left and right on 44 percent. Finally, in the fifth parliament, the center–right returned to the majority, with just over 50 percent of the seats.

On that arithmetic alone, it would be difficult to tell what majority would form in each parliament, especially in the evenly balanced third and fourth parliaments. Even when there seems to be a clear majority, as in the fifth parliament, one must be careful, however, since the left–

Table 8.2
Partisan makeup of the European Parliament, 1979–1999

Party	Abbr.	EP1—1979 N	%	EP2—1984 N	%	EP3—1989 N	%	EP4—1994 N	%	EP5—1999 N	%
Socialists	SOC	106	26.5	131	30.2	197	38.0	197	34.7	176	28.1
Christian Democrats/Conservatives	EPP	108	27.0	109	25.1	162	31.3	168	29.6	231	36.9
Liberals	LIB	40	10.0	32	7.4	46	8.9	31	5.5	51	8.1
French Gaullists and allies	GAU	22	5.5	30	6.9	21	4.1	29	5.1	32	5.1
Radical Left	LEFT	42	10.5	41	9.4	15	2.9	28	4.9	42	6.7
Regionalists	REG	13	3.3	19	4.4	13	2.5	21	3.7		
British Conservatives and allies	CON	62	15.5	49	11.3						
Radical Right	RIGHT			16	3.7	12	2.3				
Greens	GRN					26	5.0	22	3.9	48	7.7
Anti-Europeans	ANTI							15	2.6	17	2.7
Italian Conservatives	FE							24	4.2		
Nonaffiliated	NA	7	1.8	7	1.6	26	5.0	32	5.6	29	4.6
Total		410		434		518		567		626	

right dimension is not the only relevant dimension for the formation of political coalitions in EU politics. This is especially true in the European Parliament, where research on individual-level MEP voting behavior finds both the left–right and the pro- and anti-European integration dimensions to be prominent (e.g., Kreppel and Tsebelis 1999; Hix 2001; Noury 2002; Noury and Roland 2002). Consequently the individual level voting behavior in the parliament provides a more accurate picture on which to base a counterfactual analysis.

Figure 8.1 shows the result of applying the NOMINATE method of individual legislator ideal point estimate to all 2,124 roll-call votes in the first half (1999–2001) of the fifth parliament. Each letter in the figure represents the "revealed" ideal point of an individual MEP on the two main dimensions of EU politics: left–right (with −1.0 the farthest

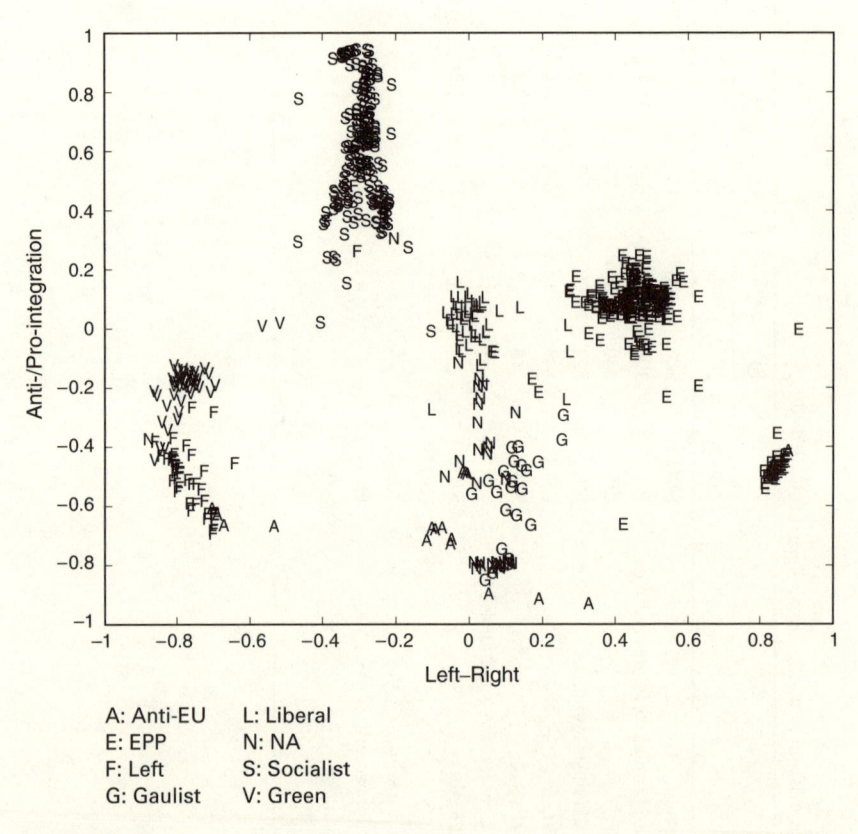

A: Anti-EU   L: Liberal
E: EPP   N: NA
F: Left   S: Socialist
G: Gaulist   V: Green

Figure 8.1
NOMINATE plot of MEP locations in the fifth European Parliament

left and +1.0 the farthest right) and pro-/anti-integration (with −1.0 the most anti-integration and +1.0 the most pro-integration). The distance between any two MEPs reveals the frequency with which these two legislators voted together. If two MEPs are in exactly the same point, they voted exactly the same way in every vote in this period; if the MEPs are at opposite ends on both dimensions, then they voted on different sides on every issue.

As the figure shows, most party groups in the fifth parliament where relatively cohesive, with the MEPs in these groups tightly clustered around a party median. The NOMINATE results clearly show the left–right spectrum on the first (horizontal) dimension: Green and Radical Left at the extreme left, the Socialists to the left, and the EPP to the right. Also the location of the Liberals approximately halfway between the two main groups reveals that these MEPs voted as much with the Socialists as with the European People's Party when issues split the parliament along left–right lines. Nonetheless, the MEPs' positions on the second dimension reveal that the three main groups (SOC, EPP, and LIB) have tended to vote together against the smaller groups of the extreme left and right as well as the Gaullists when issues split the parliament on pro-/anti-integration lines.

Table 8.3 shows the mean position of the party groups in all five parliaments. The position of the Liberals is particularly interesting. The distances between this group and the Socialists and EPP on the first dimension shows that the Liberals voted more with the right in the first three parliaments but voted more or less equally with the these two main parties in the fourth and fifth parliaments.

From the individual MEP (NOMINATE) scores we calculate the two-dimensional Euclidean distance between each MEP in each parliament. This information allows us to construct a series of counterfactual scenarios about who would have governed Europe had the European Parliament had the power to elect the EU executive.

8.4 Five Scenarios for Electing the EU Executive

Using the two-dimensional MEPs' NOMINATE scores we model four different scenarios of an election of the Commission by the European Parliament.

In the first scenario we assume that the parliament elects the Commission president (and that the Commission president is the agenda-setter when forming the College of Commissioners[3]), and that MEPs

Table 8.3
Mean party group NOMINATE scores, 1979–1999

Party (left to right)	EP1—1979 D1	EP1—1979 D2	EP2—1984 D1	EP2—1984 D2	EP3—1989 D1	EP3—1989 D2	EP4—1994 D1	EP4—1994 D2	EP5—1999 D1	EP5—1999 D2
GRN					−0.705	−0.674	−0.751	−0.530	−0.789	−0.195
LEFT	−0.318	−0.210	−0.385	−0.194	−0.361	−0.420	−0.605	−0.634	−0.749	−0.452
REG	−0.570	0.005	−0.652	−0.283	−0.404	−0.729	−0.283	−0.376		
SOC	−0.074	0.359	−0.373	0.172	−0.107	0.758	−0.301	0.709	−0.307	0.600
ANTI							0.361	−0.812	−0.090	−0.689
NA	0.167	−0.189	−0.061	−0.288	0.203	−0.392	0.564	−0.600	−0.005	−0.510
LIB	0.416	−0.338	0.398	0.023	0.280	−0.314	0.157	−0.253	0.016	0.014
EPP	0.518	−0.275	0.429	−0.102	0.483	0.214	0.537	0.420	0.494	−0.001
GAU	0.257	−0.824	0.542	−0.615	0.519	−0.764	0.684	−0.492	0.104	−0.562
FE							0.652	−0.224		
CON	0.808	0.533	0.524	0.796	0.813	−0.565				
RIGHT			0.847	−0.187						

follow the voting instructions of their European Parliament party groups. This is a reasonable approximation of how roll-call voting in the parliament works in practice. In roll-call votes, how each MEP has voted is recorded in the minutes, and can hence be monitored by the party group leaders. In previous research we found high levels of party group cohesion in roll-call votes in all five parliaments, and increased voting along party lines and decreased voting along national lines over time (Hix, Noury, and Roland 2004; Noury and Roland 2002).

To operationalize this, we assume that each party group nominates a candidate, and that the election of the Commission president is conducted as a multiple round contest in which, as the candidate with the lowest votes is eliminated in a round, the contest continues until one candidate has secured 50 percent plus one of the votes.[4] From the NOMINATE positions of the MEPs, we calculated the median position of each party group on each dimension, and chose the MEPs closest to these locations as the candidates of each group. We then calculated the two-dimensional Euclidean distance of each party group from these candidates, and assumed that each party group votes *en bloc* for the candidate closest to its two-dimensional median position.

In the second scenario the Parliament still elects the Commission president, but this time we assume that MEPs vote according to their personal ideological positions in the two-dimensional space of EU politics. This assumption can be justified as an approximation of what might happen if the vote were taken by secret ballot, which would free the MEPs from pressure from either their national party leaders or their European Parliament party groups.[5] For example, in implementing the Nice Treaty, the European Parliament changed its rules of procedure (in July 2002), so that the vote in the European Parliament on the nominee for Commission president (who would be chosen by a qualified-majority in the European Council) would be by secret ballot rather than by roll call.

To operationalize this, we again assume that each party group nominates a candidate, and that the election is conducted in multiple rounds. However, from the NOMINATE positions of the MEPs, we calculated the two-dimensional Euclidean distance of each MEP from these candidates, and assumed that each MEP votes for the candidate closest to his/her two-dimensional location.

Table 8.4 illustrates how these two scenarios play out in the fifth parliament. Interesting, if the MEPs follow party groups lines, the candidate

Table 8.4
Counterfactual election of the Commission president by the fifth Parliament, using NOMINATE scores, July 1999

Party	MEPs	Med.-D1	Med.-D2	Round 1	Round 2	Round 3	Round 4	Round 5
Scenario 1: MEPs voting along EP group lines (in two dimensions)								
EPP	231	0.494	−0.001	231	231	231	286	336
SOC	176	−0.307	0.600	176	176	176	176	176
LIB	51	0.016	0.014	59	61	61		
GRN	48	−0.789	−0.195	48	48	94	94	114
LEFT	42	−0.749	−0.452	46	46			
GAU	32	0.104	−0.562	32				
ANTI	17	−0.090	−0.684	34	64	64	70	
Nonaffiliated MEPs	29	—	—					

Party	MEPs	Round 1	Round 2	Round 3	Round 4	Round 5	Round 6
Scenario 2: MEPs voting according to their individual NOMINATE positions (in two dimensions)							
EPP	231	230	230	230	234	234	234
SOC	176	175	175	175	175	175	
LIB	51	64	113	65	113	217	392
GRN	48	47					
LEFT	42	48	48	94	104		
GAU	32	32	62	62			
ANTI	17	30					
Nonaffiliated MEPs	29						

of the EPP would win the contest. But, if the MEPs vote independently, the candidate of the Liberals would sneak through to beat the EPP candidate in the final round. These are not unreasonable outcomes if one considers that an EPP candidate (Nicole Fontaine) was elected president of the Parliament for the first half of this parliament's term and a Liberal candidate (Pat Cox) was elected president for the second half of the parliament's term. Looking more closely at table 8.4 allows us to understand the difference between both scenarios. In the first scenario, the Anti-Europeans (ANTI) get an important head start, as the Gaullists drop out and support the Anti-Europeans in round 2. In round 3, the Radical Left drop out in favor of the Greens. The Liberals are the smallest group in that round and drop out in favor of the EPP in round 4. The EPP in turn benefits in round 5 from support from the Gaullists to get an absolute majority against the Socialist and Green candidates. In the second scenario, the Liberals are able to exploit their pivotal position in the parliament to attract votes in successive rounds from the MEPs to their left against the EPP candidate.

In the third scenario, we assume that the parliament elects the Commission as a whole, through a process of "government formation" among the groups in the parliament—modeled on the classic parliamentary model of government formation in the domestic arena in Europe.

To operationalize this, we assume that only "connected" coalitions can form, where party groups prefer coalition partners that are closest to them over coalition partners that are further away. To work out which coalition is the most likely to form, we assume that each party group has a probability of being chosen as the coalition *formateur* in relation to their proportion of seats in the parliament. We then calculate the ideal "minimum-connected" winning coalition preference of each party. The *formateur* forms a coalition with the party closest to it first (in terms of a two-dimensional Euclidean distance), then the next closest second, and so on, until the coalition partners command 50 percent plus one of the seats. But, if adding a party group takes the coalition well over the 50 percent plus one threshold, and any parties in the coalition are in excess of the minimum winning majority, then these surplus parties are dropped, in order of the farthest away first. Finally, if two parties form the same winning coalition, we calculate the probability of this government forming as the combined probabilities of these parties being chosen as *formateurs* (i.e., the combined proportion of seats of these two parties).

Table 8.5 illustrates how this scenario works in the fifth parliament. If the EPP is the *formateur*, it chooses the Liberals (LIB) first, and then chooses the Gaullists (GAU) to bring the coalition over the 50 percent threshold. In contrast, the Socialists choose the Liberals first, next the Greens (GRN), and then the EPP. At this point the Liberals and Greens are surplus to a minimum winning coalition, so the preferred coalition of the Socialists is a SOC-EPP "grand coalition." However, because the Liberals and Gaullists prefer the same coalition as the EPP, the EPP-LIB-GAU is the most likely simple majority-winning government to be formed in the fifth parliament, with a probability of 50.4 percent.

In the fourth scenario, we assume an identical process of government formation (through a minimum-connected winning coalition), but that the coalition must command two-thirds support in the parliament, rather than a simple majority—in other words, as a way of operationalizing the Commission's proposal to the Convention.

Finally, in a fifth scenario, we assume a separation of powers between the Commission and the Parliament, and that the Commission president is elected via an electoral college of national parliaments in the same year as the European Parliament election (see Hix 2002b; Berglöf et al. 2003). To operationalize this, we assume that each European party (as constituted by the party groups in the parliament) proposes a candidate. National parties vote *en bloc* for the candidate that is put forward by the party group in which they sit in the European Parliament. We start from the number of MPs each national party had at the time of the European Parliament election (June 1979, June 1984, June 1989, June 1994, and June 1999). The votes of each national party are then weighted by the proportion of MEPs from their member state (in other words, each national party has a proportion of votes equal to their proportion of national MPs multiplied by the proportion of MEPs from their member state).

The contest is held over two rounds, with the two candidates winning the most votes in the first round going through to a runoff contest. In practice, this means a runoff between the Socialist and EPP candidates. In the second round we assume that the national parties to the left of the Liberals vote for the Socialist candidate and the national parties to the right of the Liberals vote for the EPP candidate. Where the Liberals are concerned, we assume that the "social liberal" parties (the British Liberal Democrats, Dutch D'66, Danish Radikale Venstre, Italian Radicals, Swedish Center Party, and Finnish KESK) vote for the

Table 8.5
Counterfactual coalition government formation in the fifth European Parliament, using NOMINATE scores, July 1999

Party	Two-dimensional Euclidean distance between the groups							MEPs (%)	Preferred minimal-winning coalition (>50%)
	EPP	SOC	LIB	GRN	LEFT	GAU	ANTI		
EPP	0	1.002	0.478	1.297	1.322	0.684	0.899	37.2	EPP-LIB-GAU
SOC	1.002	0	0.669	0.930	1.141	1.233	1.303	28.4	SOC-EPP
LIB	0.478	0.670	0	0.831	0.895	0.583	0.707	8.1	LIB-EPP-GAU
GRN	1.297	0.930	0.831	0	0.259	0.965	0.853	7.7	GRN-LEFT-LIB-SOC
LEFT	1.322	1.141	0.895	0.259	0	0.860	0.699	6.7	LEFT-GRN-ANTI-GAU-SOC
GAU	0.684	1.233	0.583	0.965	0.860	0	0.229	5.1	GAU-LIB-EPP
ANTI	0.899	1.303	0.707	0.853	0.699	0.229	0	2.7	ANTI-GAU-LEFT-EPP
Most probable winning coalition								50.4	EPP-LIB-GAU

Socialist candidate, while all the other Liberal parties vote for the EPP candidate.

Table 8.6 illustrates how such a "presidential" election among national MPs would have worked in July 1999. Table 8.7 illustrates the likely outcomes of such a contest in all five periods.

8.5 Results and Analysis

Table 8.8 gives the summary results for the five scenarios for each of the five parliaments elected since 1979. The first line shows the result of the election of the Commission president by the European Parliament assuming party group discipline. The Commission president would have been a Conservative in all parliaments except the 1994 Parliament, which would have elected a Socialist Commission president. Note that such predictions cannot be made readily from the arithmetic composition of the European Parliament. For example, the shift in the position of the Liberals to the left in the fourth Parliament is the key factor that would have led to the election of a Socialist Commission president in that period. Note also that for the fourth and fifth parliaments, the political color of the Commission president would have been different from the political color of the actual Commission. This is explained by the fact that the European Parliament elections are often protest votes against incumbent governments. Thus the fourth parliament was more to the left in the late 1980s and early 1990s when most European governments were on the center–right, and then the European Parliament shifted strongly to the center–right in the 1999 elections when Social Democrats where in government in most European countries.

The second line of the table shows the outcome of a European parliament election of the Commission president assuming no party group discipline (i.e., if a vote were taken by secret ballot). The main difference with the party discipline scenario is that in the third and fifth parliaments, a Liberal president would have been elected, as a result of the pivotal position of the Liberals in these parliaments (see Hix, Noury, and Roland 2004). Basically, if MEPs vote along party lines, the final round of the election is always likely to be between candidates from the Socialists and EPP groups. However, if the MEPs vote according to their personal policy preferences (or according to national party preferences rather than the preferences of their EP party groups), then a Liberal candidate has a better chance of picking up votes from the

How to Choose the European Executive 187

Table 8.6
Counterfactual national parliamentary election of a Commission president, 1999

National party	MPs	MPs (%)	*MEPs (%)	Equal votes	Support round 1	Support round 2
Germany						
SPD	298	44.5	15.8	7.04	SOC	SOC
CDU/CSU	245	36.6	15.8	5.79	EPP	EPP
Grune	47	7.0	15.8	1.11	GRN	SOC
FDP	43	6.4	15.8	1.02	LIB	EPP
PDS	36	5.4	15.8	0.85	LEFT	SOC
France						
PS+allies	283	49.4	13.9	6.86	SOC	SOC
RPR	140	24.4	13.9	3.40	GAU	EPP
PR+UDF	113	19.7	13.9	2.74	EPP	EPP
PCF	36	6.3	13.9	0.87	LEFT	SOC
NF	1	0.2	13.9	0.02	RIGHT	EPP
Italy						
DS+allies	172	27.3	13.9	3.79	SOC	SOC
PPI/CCD	123	19.5	13.9	2.71	EPP	EPP
FI	123	19.5	13.9	2.71	EPP	EPP
AN	93	14.8	13.9	2.05	GAU	EPP
LN	59	9.4	13.9	1.30	RIGHT	EPP
RC	35	5.6	13.9	0.77	LEFT	SOC
V	21	3.3	13.9	0.46	GRN	SOC
Reg-R	3	0.5	13.9	0.07	EPP	EPP
Reg-L	1	0.2	13.9	0.02	GRN	SOC
United Kingdom						
LAB	419	63.6	13.9	8.84	SOC	SOC
CON	165	25.0	13.9	3.48	EPP	EPP
LIB	47	7.1	13.9	0.99	LIB	SOC
UUP	10	1.5	13.9	0.21	ANTI	EPP
PC	6	0.9	13.9	0.13	GRN	SOC
SNP	4	0.6	13.9	0.08	GRN	SOC
DUP	3	0.5	13.9	0.06	ANTI	EPP
SDLP	3	0.5	13.9	0.06	SOC	SOC
SF	2	0.3	13.9	0.04	LEFT	SOC
Spain						
PP	156	44.6	10.2	4.56	EPP	EPP
PSOE	141	40.3	10.2	4.12	SOC	SOC
IU	21	6.0	10.2	0.61	LEFT	SOC
CiU	16	4.6	10.2	0.47	LIB	EPP
Reg-L	10	2.9	10.2	0.29	GRN	SOC
Reg-R	6	1.7	10.2	0.18	EPP	EPP

Table 8.6 (continued)

National party	MPs	MPs (%)	*MEPs (%)	Equal votes	Support round 1	Support round 2
Netherlands						
PvdA	45	30.0	5.0	1.49	SOC	SOC
VVD	39	26.0	5.0	1.29	LIB	EPP
CDA	28	18.7	5.0	0.92	EPP	EPP
D66	14	9.3	5.0	0.46	LIB	SOC
GL	11	7.3	5.0	0.36	GRN	SOC
SGP/G/R	8	5.3	5.0	0.26	ANTI	EPP
SP	5	3.3	5.0	0.17	LEFT	SOC
Belgium						
VLD	23	15.3	4.0	0.61	LIB	EPP
CVP	22	14.7	4.0	0.59	EPP	EPP
PS	19	12.7	4.0	0.51	SOC	SOC
PRL-FDF	18	12.0	4.0	0.48	LIB	EPP
VB	15	10.0	4.0	0.40	RIGHT	EPP
SP	14	9.3	4.0	0.37	SOC	SOC
ECOLO	11	7.3	4.0	0.29	GRN	SOC
PSC	10	6.7	4.0	0.27	EPP	EPP
AGALEV	9	6.0	4.0	0.24	GRN	SOC
VU	8	5.3	4.0	0.21	GRN	SOC
FN	1	0.7	4.0	0.03	RIGHT	EPP
Greece						
PASOK	162	54.0	4.0	2.16	SOC	SOC
ND	108	36.0	4.0	1.44	EPP	EPP
KKE/SYN	30	10.0	4.0	0.40	LEFT	SOC
Portugal						
PS	115	50.0	4.0	2.00	SOC	SOC
PSD	81	35.2	4.0	1.41	EPP	EPP
CDU/PRD	19	8.3	4.0	0.33	LEFT	SOC
PP	15	6.5	4.0	0.26	GAU	EPP
Sweden						
SAP	131	37.5	3.5	1.32	SOC	SOC
M	82	23.5	3.5	0.83	EPP	EPP
V	43	12.3	3.5	0.43	LEFT	SOC
KD	42	12.0	3.5	0.42	EPP	EPP
C	18	5.2	3.5	0.18	LIB	SOC
FP	17	4.9	3.5	0.17	LIB	EPP
MP	16	4.6	3.5	0.16	GRN	SOC
Austria						
SPO	65	35.5	3.4	1.19	SOC	SOC
OVP	52	28.4	3.4	0.95	EPP	EPP

How to Choose the European Executive 189

Table 8.6 (continued)

National party	MPs	MPs (%)	*MEPs (%)	Equal votes	Support round 1	Support round 2
FPO	52	28.4	3.4	0.95	RIGHT	EPP
GRUNE	14	7.7	3.4	0.26	GRN	SOC
Denmark						
S	63	36.0	2.6	0.92	SOC	SOC
V	42	24.0	2.6	0.61	LIB	EPP
KF	16	9.1	2.6	0.23	EPP	EPP
DF	13	7.4	2.6	0.19	ANTI	EPP
SF	13	7.4	2.6	0.19	LEFT	SOC
CD	8	4.6	2.6	0.12	EPP	EPP
RV	7	4.0	2.6	0.10	LIB	SOC
EL	5	2.9	2.6	0.07	LEFT	SOC
KRF	4	2.3	2.6	0.06	EPP	EPP
FRP	4	2.3	2.6	0.06	ANTI	EPP
Finland						
SDP	51	25.5	2.6	0.65	SOC	SOC
KESK	50	25.0	2.6	0.64	LIB	SOC
KOK	46	23.0	2.6	0.59	EPP	EPP
VAS	20	10.0	2.6	0.26	LEFT	SOC
SFP	12	6.0	2.6	0.15	LIB	EPP
VIHR	11	5.5	2.6	0.14	GRN	SOC
KD	10	5.0	2.6	0.13	EPP	EPP
Ireland						
FF	77	46.4	2.4	1.11	GAU	EPP
FG	54	32.5	2.4	0.78	EPP	EPP
LAB	17	10.2	2.4	0.25	SOC	SOC
IND	6	3.6	2.4	0.09	LIB	EPP
DL	5	3.0	2.4	0.07	LEFT	SOC
PD	4	2.4	2.4	0.06	LIB	EPP
GP	2	1.2	2.4	0.03	GRN	SOC
SF	1	0.6	2.4	0.01	LEFT	SOC
Luxembourg						
CSV	19	31.7	1.0	0.30	EPP	EPP
DP	15	25.0	1.0	0.24	LIB	EPP
LSAP	13	21.7	1.0	0.21	SOC	SOC
ADR	7	11.7	1.0	0.11	EPP	EPP
GRENG	5	8.3	1.0	0.08	GRN	SOC
LENK	1	1.7	1.0	0.02	LEFT	LEFT

Table 8.7
Counterfactual elections of the Commission president by national parliaments

Party	1979 Round 1	1979 Round 2	1984 Round 1	1984 Round 2	1989 Round 1	1989 Round 2	1994 Round 1	1994 Round 2	1999 Round 1	1999 Round 2
LEFT			15.1		2.9		4.2		5.1	
GRN					2.1		2.2		3.9	
SOC	30.3	43.3	28.3	47.0	41.4	48.4	31.3	41.1	41.8	53.1
REG	4.7		1.9		0.7		0.9			
ANTI							0.3		0.8	
LIB	10.8		9.6		10.6		8.1		7.6	
EPP	25.8	56.7	25.7	53.0	35.8	51.6	36.1	58.9	31.4	46.9
FE							2.4			
CON	11.3		12.3							
GAU	9.0		5.1		5.3		8.6		6.8	
RIGHT	1.4		2.0		1.3		5.9		2.7	

Note: The proportion of party seats in a national parliament is weighted by the proportion of MEPs from that member state.

Table 8.8
Summary of results

	EP1—1979	EP2—1984	EP3—1989	EP4—1994	EP5—1999
Real world	(Jenkins + Thorn)	(Delors I)	(Delors II + III)	(Santer)	(Prodi)
Commission majority	Right	Right	Right	Right	Left
Counterfactual analysis					
Election by EP of:...					
1. Commission president (EP group voting)	Right (EPP)	Right (EPP)	Right (EPP)	Left (SOC)	Right (EPP)
2. Commission president (individual MEP voting)	Right (EPP)	Right (EPP)	Center (LIB)	Left (SOC)	Center (LIB)
3. Coalition government (50%)	Grand coalition (SOC-EPP)	Center-Left (SOC-LIB-REG-LEFT)	Grand coalition (SOC-EPP)	Grand coalition (SOC-EPP)	Center-Right (EPP-LIB-GAU)
4. Coalition government (67%)	Center-Left (SOC-EPP-LEFT)	Center-Left (SOC-EPP-LEFT)	Grand coalition (SOC-EPP)	Grand coalition+ (SOC-EPP-LIB)	Grand coalition+ (EPP-LIB-SOC)
Election by national parliament of:...					
5. Commission president	Right (EPP)	Right (EPP)	Right (EPP)	Right (EPP)	Left (SOC)

smaller parties and making it into the final round ahead of either the Socialist or the EPP candidate.

The third line shows the most likely coalition if the Commission were a normal parliamentary government, in other words, a coalition enjoying a simple majority in the European Parliament. It is striking to see that in most parliaments there would have been a grand coalition between the Socialists and EPP. In the second parliament, however, the winning coalition would have been on the center–left: among the Socialists, Liberals, Radical Left, and Regionalists. Only the 1999 Commission would have been a right-wing coalition, of the Conservatives, Liberals, and Gaullists.

The fourth line shows the coalition outcome with a two-thirds majority rule. The Socialists and Conservatives would again have been part of all coalitions. However, because of the high threshold needed to form a coalition, the Radical Left would also have been part of the first two coalitions and the Liberals part of the last two. In other words, if a two-thirds majority is required to elect the Commission, there would be no possibility of a political contest for this post. The result would inevitably be a package deal of the biggest groups, where the party that is not awarded the Commission president would demand something else in return.

In sum, the parliamentary model of electing the Commission would have produced a European Union governed by the two big parties, and possibly joined by a third. This is not a terribly exciting prospect in terms of democratic competition for executive office and alternation of the executive. A parliamentary model in the European Union would not produce a clear opposition force, and this would not be good for the democratic accountability of the incumbents. Moreover, even with a 50 percent majority rule, the Radical Left would have been part of the 1984 Commission. In hindsight, this could have meant that the single-market program, pursued and implemented by the Commission in that period, would not have taken place!

The fifth line shows the result of the election of the Commission president in a two-round election by national parliaments. The Commission president would have been a member of the EPP in the first four periods and a Socialist in the fifth period. Note that this is the only scenario that follows closely the actual composition of the Commission. This is not surprising, since the composition of the Council that determined the composition of the actual Commission is based on governing majorities in national parliaments.

We believe the simulations above are the most accurate to date and utilize data on the composition of the European Parliament as well as the national parliaments at the time of the European Parliament elections. Table 8.8 shows that the various scenarios for appointment of the Commission do lead to different results. The main difference we observe in table 8.8 is between the parliamentary scenarios (rows 1 to 4) and the presidential scenario (row 5). This difference reflects the fact that elections to European parliaments are treated as "second-order national contests," so they tend to favor the opposition parties in the member states (van der Eijk and Franklin 1996). This means that a parliamentary mode of selection tends to lead to a political composition of the Commission that differs from the political composition of the Council at the same time. In our view, this built-in form of divided government would lead to unnecessary clashes between the Commission and the Council, which could be unproductive for the functioning of the European Union.

Our reasoning may nevertheless raise some objections. First, voters can change their behavior once the European Parliament, for which they voted, has appointed the European executive. Inertia in voting behavior may be expected, however, where the incentives of national political parties cause European elections to be used as national referendums on the performances of national governments (rather than that of the European government) regardless of the impact on the composition of the Commission. As elections to the European Parliament are likely to be second-order contests for some time, the effect of a divided government quite likely will not be felt in the first few decades of the EU Constitution.

Second, the division of government may not be particularly disturbing, since national elections take place frequently between the two elections for the European Parliament. It is thus not clear whether the division of government will be that apparent. The critical moment is at the inaugural point of each Commission, when a grace period is needed to allow the new Commission the chance to pass some legislation.

Third, the division of government could be limited if the rest of the Commission is appointed by the Council—as in our first scenario, where the European Parliament simply elects the Commission president, and the rest of the Commission is appointed according the current procedure, whereby each national government nominates a Commissioner, in consultation with the Commission president. However, even in this scenario, the Commission president may be viewed with suspicion by the Council in the beginning. It is important that the Commission and the Council work together toward a smooth functioning of the EU institutions.

8.6 How to Choose the European Executive?

The preceding analysis puts quantitative input to the debate on the question of how to choose the European executive, but it does not give the whole picture. Many other considerations are involved in determining a desirable way of choosing the executive.

If our analysis gives the impression that the European executive can continue to be elected by the Council, this is not our view. A main objective of the Convention is to make the Commission accountable (Berglöf et al. 2003; Hix 2002b). Steps to ensure a selection of the Commission president that cut away the layers between the electorate and the executive are important in raising the accountability of the Commission. Election of this president either by the European Parliament or by national parliaments implies the selection of an executive by the representatives of European citizens rather than by country governments. This means that compared to the current situation, the president of the Commission will have a democratic legitimacy that is independent from national governments; his accountability will be to European citizens. This will make the Commission stronger vis-à-vis national governments, which is desirable given the weakness of the current European executive. Departure from the status quo in the parliamentary or the presidential direction should thus strengthen the accountability, legitimacy, and authority of the European executive. Even though our preference goes toward the presidential route, we think a choice in the parliamentary direction would be better than the status quo.

This said, there are a number of arguments that favor the choice of a presidential rather than a parliamentary system for Europe in the long run (see Berglöf et al. 2003 for a thorough discussion). To be more explicit, the presidential system we have in mind is one with strong separation of powers between the executive and the legislative branches of government as in the US constitution. Many presidential systems, in Latin America but also in Russia, for example, concentrate the power in the hands of the president and leave very little to the legislature.

This kind of presidential system has been associated in practice with unstable democracies (Linz 1990; Mainwaring 1993, Lijphart 1999). This kind of presidency is less desirable than a parliamentary form of government.

The kind of presidentialism we have in mind is one that allows for a separation of powers between the executive branch and the legislative branch of government. In parliamentary government, the executive is supported by a majority in the legislature because the latter has the power to bring down the government by a vote of no confidence. There is a clear majority and a clear opposition, and the majority is fused with the executive. This is not the case under a presidential democracy with its decentralized form of legislation: issues are voted case by case rather than by majority and opposition. This way no group will systematically remain in the minority. This is important for Europe, as it could prevent situations where member states are systematically in the minority. As the independence of the Commission from a political majority in either EU legislative institution—the Council or the European Parliament—has been vital for the functioning of the Union so far, governments have been able to make credible commitments to each other by delegating agenda-setting and implementation to a political actor that is not controlled by a particular faction in the legislature (see Dehousse 1995; Majone 1996, 2002; Pollack 1997; Moravcsik 1999). Independence of the Commission was secured prior to the Nice Treaty, as its election was by unanimity rule in the Council (see Crombez and Hix 2002). The much larger majority required for electing the executive will mean a separation of powers in the European Union. If the same majorities are used for electing the Commission and for implementing its proposals—in accord with the Nice Treaty reform (where the Commission would be elected by a qualified-majority in the Council) or the notion of a majority in the European Parliament—there would be an end to the separation of powers. This would mean an end to the independence of the Commission, and an end to the ability of governments to delegate to an executive body that is not captured by a legislative majority.

Second, a presidential system has built-in strong accountability measures. The incumbent can be punished in elections and replaced by a challenger. In a parliamentary system, the Conservatives and Socialists would tend to be part of most coalitions. They would thus be less fearful of punishment by voters, which would make them less accountable.

Third, a presidential system would allow for more effective decision-making than a parliamentary system. A parliamentary government is essentially a coalition within which decisions must be continuously negotiated. More often than not, decisions are made too late.

While the presidential system may be not as desirable for global expenditure programs such as welfare programs (parliamentary systems tend to produce more economic redistribution and public goods), this is not a big disadvantage in the EU context. Strong welfare states already exist at the domestic level in Europe among the member states that have parliamentary models of government.

In sum, a presidential form of governance for Europe, whereby a president of the Commission elected by national parliaments, would be a good first step. The election of the president by national parliaments could be established through an electoral college system, where each member state has a particular number of electoral college votes, that would reflect state interests as well as population size. In such a system the votes in national parliaments could be replaced by universal suffrage by the countries that choose to do so (Hix 2002b; Berglöf et al. 2003). This could pave the way for the election of the president of the Commission by universal suffrage in the future. Each national parliament could have a number of electoral college votes equal to their representation in national parliaments, and these votes would be *proportional* to the ballot result in each national parliament. Such proportionality would avoid a winner-take-all outcome in certain countries. This detail of electoral law would avoid the flaws seen in the 2000 US presidential election where by a few thousand votes the electoral college vote for all Florida was given to George W. Bush and decided the outcome of the presidency. This way candidates for the presidency would have to campaign in each country to gain votes, and not slight any of the smaller countries. In this scenario, if votes are divided 51 to 49 percent in France between say a Socialist and a Conservative candidate, the electoral college votes of France would also be divided 51 to 49 percent among the two candidates.

8.7 Conclusion

In this chapter we used data from the European Parliament and national parliaments on the political compositions of the Commission in 1979, 1984, 1989, 1994, and 1999 and explored various scenarios being proposed in the Convention for the future of Europe. The main findings of this analysis can be summarized as follows.

First, the political character of the Commission can be changed if different rules are used to elect the EU executive. As we know from the political science and political economy literature, rules governing the election of the executive make a difference. These rules determine the political/partisan color of the executive and thus shape policy outcomes. Under the status quo procedures (pre-Nice), a center–right majority in the Council meant a center–right majority in the Commission, which in turn meant a liberal Single Market Program and monetarist plan for Economic and Monetary Union supported by these two institutions. A different executive-selection procedure could have produced a Commission with a different political orientation, and thus different EU policies and institutional relations among the Commission, the Council, and the European Parliament. Hence, when considering which selection procedure is best for the European Union, one needs to consider what policies one wants from the Union, and what types of relationships one wants between the Commission and the Council and European Parliament.

Second, if a Commission president had been elected by the national parliaments, he or she would have been a representative of the center–right alliance of Christian Democrats and Conservatives (the European People's Party [EPP]) in all periods except the present one (from 1999 on), as today he would have been a representative of the Socialists (SOC). Interestingly the presidential scenario closely follows the actual political composition of the Commission since 1979, since the Commission was dominated by the center–right until the current Prodi Commission.

Third, and in contrast, the color of the Commission president would have been very different if he/she had been elected by the European Parliament. For example, if MEPs had voted along party lines, the European Parliament would have elected a Socialist in 1994 instead of the center–right Jacques Santer, and a Conservative in 1999 instead of centrist Romano Prodi. But, if MEPs had followed their personal preferences, the European Parliament would have elected a Liberal Commission president in 1989 and 1999. If the Commission had been elected by a full-fledged parliamentary model, a "grand coalition" of Conservatives and Socialists would have been the most likely outcome, except in 1999, when a center–right coalition of Conservatives, Liberals, and

Gaullists (GAU) would have resulted. And, with a two-thirds majority, Socialists and Conservatives would have been part of all coalitions, though other parties would have to have been included in all parliaments except 1989 when the Liberals secured a large enough majority.

All in all, any form of parliamentary model for electing the Commission would have produced Commissions with very different partisan hues than those chosen by EU governments. This is because elections in the European Parliament are often protest votes against incumbent governments, and this ensures that the political majorities in the Council and the Parliament remain different. Any form of appointment of the European executive by the European Parliament would thus tend to have a built-in bias toward the political composition of the Commission that would be different from the political composition in the Council. This could create unnecessary conflicts between the Council and the Commission, which would be harmful for the EU, since one of the main objectives of the Convention is to make the Commission more accountable and to reduce the democratic deficit. Election of the Commission president by national parliaments could prevent this conflict, and enhance the democratic accountability of the Commission. The results of our simulations reinforce the case where the Commission president is elected by national parliaments rather than by the European Parliament.

One effect that would have systematically divided the government is that the composition of the European Parliament is determined by a protest vote. For example, the center–right dominated fifth parliament was elected at a time when most European governments were on the left. We suggest that the election of the Commission president by national parliaments will rather reflect the majorities in the national parliaments at the time of the vote. We see the election of the Commission president by national parliaments to offer the advantage of a clear separation of powers, and the European Parliament a clear autonomy with respect to the European executive. Our simulations show that the presidential model is less likely to lead to political clashes between the Council and the Commission, a clear danger with any appointment of the Commission by the European Parliament.

While we have emphasized the disadvantages of forms of appointment of the European executive by the European Parliament, the worst of all possible worlds would be the Chirac-Schroeder institutional compromise, where the Commission president is elected by the European Parliament and a new single Council president is elected by a majority in the Council. As has been pointed out by various commentators, this would create a dual executive with competing mandates, which could be disastrous for the European Union (see Berglöf et al. 2003). Further we show that the conflict between the two institutions would be exacerbated, since the presidents of the Commission and Council would in all likelihood be from opposite sides of the political divide.

Notes

We would like to thank Tapio Raunio, an anonymous referee, and participants at the February 2003 CESifo conference for comments on an earlier version of this chapter.

1. Although the wording is ambiguous, it goes clearly in the direction of a parliamentary model, where the prime minister is usually the head of the party that won the elections. Since the Nice Treaty, unanimity in the Council was replaced by a qualified majority in the Council proposing for the Commission president. Also the president must be approved by majority rule in the European Parliament. This way no single country will be able to veto a Commission president and the president proposed for the Commission will be chosen by a majority coming from the European Parliament elections. All this points in the direction of the parliamentary model.

2. The first American presidents were chosen by an electoral college constituted mostly of votes in the state legislatures. It is only later that universal suffrage became the norm for choosing the electoral college. Berglöf et al. (2003) argue that the Hix (2002b) proposal is the best suited for an evolutionary approach toward a presidential model of governance for Europe.

3. For example, the Commission president would nominate the members of the College of Commissioners, who would then be ratified by a qualified majority in the European Council and a simple majority in the European Parliament.

4. The European Parliament already uses a multiple-round contest for electing its senior offices and the president of the Parliament. Hence this is likely how the parliament will eventually chose to elect a Commission president.

5. Another assumption is that MEPs vote along national party lines. However, in practice, this is almost identical with MEPs' voting according to their personal preferences. This is because most national party delegations of MEPs are very collegial, and this implies that MEPs from the same national party will tend toward very similar NOMINATE scores.

References

Bednar, J., W. N. Eskeridge, and J. Ferejohn. 2001. A Political Theory of Federalism. In J. Ferejohn, J. N. Rakove, and J. Riley (eds.): *Constitutional Culture and Democratic Rule*. New York: Cambridge University Press.

Berglöf, E., B. Eichengreen, G. Roland, G. Tabellini, and C. Wyplosz. 2003. *Built to Last: A political Architecture for Europe*. London: CEPR.

Blair, A. 2002. A clear course for Europe. Speech at Cardiff. November 28.

Brok, E. 2002. *Constitution of the European Union*. Brussels: Convention on the Future of Europe.

Commission of the European Union. 2002. *For the European Union: Peace, Freedom, Solidarity—Communication of the Commission on the Institutional Architecture*. COM (2002) 728 final.

Crombez, C., and S. Hix. 2002. Unaccountable Brussels bureaucrats? Implications of constitutional reforms for the democratic accountability of the EU. Mimeo. London School of Economics.

Dehousse, R. 1995. Constitutional reform in the European Community: Are there alternatives to the majoritarian avenue? In J. Hayward (ed.): *The Crisis of Representation in Europe*. London: Frank Cass.

Diermeier, D., and T. J. Feddersen. 1998. Cohesion in Legislatures and the Vote of Confidence Procedure. *American Political Science Review* 92: 611–21.

van der Eijk, C., and M. Franklin (eds.). 1996. *Choosing Europe? The European Electorate and National Politics in the Face of Union*. Ann Arbor: University of Michigan Press.

Fischer, J. 2000. From Confederacy to Federation: Thoughts on the Finality of European Integration. Speech at Humboldt University, Berlin. May 12.

Hix, S. 2001. Legislative behaviour and party competition in the European Parliament: An application of nominate to the EU. *Journal of Common Market Studies* 39: 663–88.

Hix, S. 2002a. Constitutional agenda-setting through discretion in rule interpretation: Why the European Parliament won at Amsterdam. *British Journal of Political Science* 32: 259–80.

Hix, S. 2002b. *Linking National Politics to Europe*. London: Foreign Policy Centre.

Hix, S., A. Noury, and G. Roland. 2004. Power to the parties: Cohesion and competition in the European Parliament, 1979–2001. *British Journal of Political Science*, forthcoming.

Huber, J. 1996. The impact of confidence votes on legislative politics in parliamentary systems. *American Political Science Review* 90: 269–82.

Kreppel, A., and G. Tsebelis. 1999. Coalition Formation in the European Parliament. *Comparative Political Studies* 32: 933–66.

Laver, M., M. Gallagher, M. Marsh, R. Singh, and B. Tonra. 1995. *Electing the President of the European Commission*. Trinity Blue Papers in Public Policy: 1, Dublin: Trinity College, 1995.

Linz, Juan. 1990. The perils of presidentialism. *Journal of Democracy* 1(1): 51–69.

Lijphart, A. 1992. Introduction. In A. Lijphart (ed.): *Parliamentary Versus Presidential Government*. Oxford: Oxford University Press.

Lijphart, A. 1999. *Patterns of Democracy: Government Forms and Performance in Thirty-Six Countries*. New Haven: Yale University Press.

Mainwaring, S. 1993. Presidentialism, multipartism and democracy: The difficult combination. *Comparative Social Studies* 26(2): 198–228.

Majone, G. 1996. *Regulating Europe*. London: Routledge.

Majone, G. 2002. The European Commission: The limits of centralization and the perils of parliamentarization. *Governance* 15: 375–92.

Moravcsik, A. 1999. A new statecraft? Supranational entrepreneurs and international cooperation. *International Organization* 53: 267–306.

Noury, A. 2002. Ideology, nationality and Euro-parliamentarians. *European Union Politics* 3: 33–58.

Noury, A., and G. Roland. 2002. More power to the European Parliament? *Economic Policy* 34: 279–320.

Persson, T., G. Roland, and G. Tabellini. 1997. Separation of powers and political accountability. *Quarterly Journal of Economics* 112: 1163–1202.

Persson, T., G. Roland, and G. Tabellini. 2000. Comparative politics and public finance. *Journal of Political Economy* 108: 1121–61.

Pollack, M. A. 1997. Delegation, agency and agenda setting in the European Community. *International Organization* 51: 99–134.

Poole, K. T., and H. Rosenthal. 1997. *Congress: A Political-Economic History of Roll Call Voting*. Oxford: Oxford University Press.

Shugart, M. S., and J. M. Carey. 1992. *Presidents and Assemblies: Constitutional Design and Electoral Dynamics*. Cambridge: Cambridge University Press.

Tsebelis, G. 2002. *Veto Players: How Political Institutions Work*. Princeton: Princeton University Press.

Verhofstadt, G. 2002. Montesquieu and the European Union. Speech at the College of Europe, Bruges. November 18.

9 The Role of Direct Democracy in the European Union

Lars P. Feld and Gebhard Kirchgässner

9.1 Introduction

The democratic deficit of the European Union is legendary among legal scholars and political scientists.[1] In its decision on the EU Treaty's compatibility with the German Basic Law (GG) in 1993, the German Constitutional Court argued that the European Union lacks comparable democratic legitimacy to the principle of democracy as it is fixed in the German constitution. German citizens' civil rights as laid down in GG article 38 are not violated if the German Parliament (Bundestag) exerts substantial decision-making powers. As EU treaties explicitly sanction Community prerogatives that are in conflict with those of its member states, their democratic accountability is clearly compromised. In some member states—among them the "eurosceptics" Denmark, Sweden, and the United Kingdom, but also France—the EU's high handedness has already been criticized. The problem is that the EU is essentially organized as a supranational authority of European executives despite its far-ranging competencies in European legislation. The influence of the European Parliament (EP) or of national parliaments is quite small. Moreover, as Grande (2000) argues, the members of the EP are too far removed from European citizens as to follow citizen preferences or as to allow citizens to any effective control over the MEPs. Although the loss of democratic control with regard to international organizations or international treaties is a general feature of this modern form of governance, the unsettling effect of the EU on the balance of powers within the member states is of major importance (Abromeit 1998, p. 20).

There is besides the position of the German Constitutional Court to add to this argument, and Grimm (1994), a former judge of the Court, has argued that a fundamental condition for a treaty to be regarded as a Constitution is the existence of a European public. Abromeit (1998,

p. 32) calls this the *no-demos thesis*: a democracy can only be called such if it is based on a collective entity, the people or the nation, that is constituted by a common culture or common traditions and experiences. Since its creation, the EP faces the problem that the people of the member states have apparently not accepted it as the body that represents the interests of all EU citizens. If the democratic deficit of the EU could be improved by giving the EP more legislative power, a majoritarian decision in the EP would likely not be accepted by the losing minority, in particular, because the minority is concentrated in one or several member states (Hug 2002, p. 110).

Several scholars have proposed the instruments of direct democracy be introduced in EU decision-making to create such a European demos.[2] In his survey of the different policy proposals, Hug (2002, ch. 7) distinguishes among three: required referenda (mandatory referenda), nonrequired referenda on government proposals (optional referenda) and nonrequired referenda on opposition proposals (initiatives). However, these instruments are often discussed without specification of when and under what circumstances they should take place. Where specifications are given, required referenda are proposed for changes to the treaties. A referendum decision on Eastern enlargement, for example, would fall into this category. In these cases scholars agree on a "double" majority of voters and of states. Nonrequired referenda can be initiated apparently by voters or by the EP. Hug raises the problem they pose if the existing decision-making procedures are not considered when these proposals are made to determine the extent to which their introduction may affect EU-wide policy. Feld, Kirchgässner, and Weck-Hannemann (2002) introduce the idea of budget referenda in EU decision-making. Like Hug, they look closely at the impact of required referenda on budgetary outcomes in the European Union for the current budgetary process and the potential process after eastern enlargement. However, the authors are not realistic about what institutional provisions would shape the budget referendum. In the case of a general required referendum on the EU budget draft, they place it at the end of the current budgetary process with inputs from the Commission, the Council, and the EP, entirely neglecting the transaction costs that such a plan involves. Naturally, a required referendum on the whole budget draft would unduly increase the time needed to pass a budget.

In this chapter our aim is to analyze the extent to which the instruments of direct democracy may turn around the democratic deficit at the EU level and advance a European demos. We propose the introduction of referenda and initiatives in EU decision-making that go a step further toward a real solution. While we basically consider direct democratic decision-making in all EU decisions, we advance our proposals for circumstances where it does not prohibitively increase decision-making costs. In section 9.2, we discuss the constitution as a contract between citizens and a state, as it requires the explicit meeting of the minds of a majority of citizens. Our general interest is in the rationale of referenda and initiatives as instruments of citizen control in a representative democracy, and we summarize empirical results on the impact of direct democracy in the examples of Switzerland and the United States. The arguments lead to three specifications for the European Union in section 9.3: First, any European Constitution must be approved by the European citizens once it has been proposed by the Convention and the Intergovernmental Conference has agreed on the provisions of the Constitution; that is, a basic consent of the European people is required to found a new federation.[3] Second, any changes in the Constitution must be decided by citizens in European referenda. We see such referenda as *mandatory* (required and binding) *on total and partial revisions of the European Constitution*. Third, a pre-specified number of citizens from a pre-specified number of countries would have the right to initiate constitutional changes at the EU level, we hence consider the function of a *popular initiative on partial revisions* of the Constitution. In section 9.4, we discuss two additional institutional proposals. The first contains a statutory and a general initiative at the EU level. The second is a fiscal referendum for financially important EU projects. Concluding remarks follow in section 9.5.

9.2 Pros and Cons of Referenda and Initiatives at the EU Level

The Necessity for Controlling Representatives at the Constitutional Level

In *De republica*, one of his main political texts, Cicero (59 BC) defines three forms of government: democracy as the rule of the people or the "many," monarchy as the rule of a single principal, and aristocracy as the rule of an elite. By replicating the famous Aristotelian arguments (*Politika* III, 8, 1280a2), Cicero argues that aristocracy, which he called the rule of the "optimates," is the preferred way of government. Describing the time when Servius assumed power in Rome, he wrote that Servius "divided the people into property classes and constructed a voting system that gave the greatest number of votes to the rich and thus put into effect the principle which always ought to be adhered to in the commonwealth, that the greatest number should not have the greatest power" (Cicero 59 BC; quoted in Gordon 1999, p. 112). Government by the people in these days meant government by a minority of property owners. In contrast to that, Cicero defined "government by the masses" as an abortive development of the rule of the people, in the same way as dictatorship was defined being an unfavourable development of monarchy and oligarchy being a mutation of aristocracy. Government by the masses was called "ochlocracy."

The Aristotelian conception of government was already challenged in the ancient world, and later in the Middle Ages by a nascent philosophical contract theory. It took until the Enlightenment and the contributions by Hobbes, Locke, Rousseau, and Kant for contract theory to become fully developed as a justification for states (Höffe 1999, p. 48). Political legitimacy is no longer based on any organic normative justification of the state, like the divine right of kings or natural law, but on the contract between the individual and the state that is the foundation of law. In the contractarian conception of a constitution, the individual (*homo singularis*) is the fundamental point of reference: What set of political rules benefits the greatest number of individuals in a group?[4] In a Hobbesian initial situation, individuals are free to do what they want. They are not in any way coerced by other individuals or any state-like organization. In the absence of state-like organizations, selfish individuals do have, however, the incentive to expropriate possessions of others, and this can lead to open conflict. Buchanan (1975, p. 12) states the problem: "The issue is one of defining limits, and anarchy works only to the extent that limits among persons are either implicitly accepted by all or are imposed and enforced by some authority." In times of conflict, the rational individuals will work to subordinate conflict by means of a coercive power instituted by a state that recognizes the mutual benefits of order as opposed to anarchy. The state becomes an impartial mediator that can secure for individuals their property rights. In addition this newly created state can organize and enforce cooperative behavior among individuals in the provision of collective goods to the mutual benefit of a large number of the polity. It can work to prevent free-riding and to resolve other social dilemmas. The blueprint for such a voluntary agreement is found in a contract, in this case the basic initial contract.

The early contractarians, Hobbes, Locke, Rousseau, and Kant, and much later Rawls (1971), interpreted the contract-theoretic reconstruction of the state as a thought experiment to arrive at a set of polity rules on which individuals could potentially agree. In contrast, following Wicksell (1896), proponents of constitutional political economy, like Buchanan (1975, p. 147) and Buchanan and Tullock (1962, p. 96), emphasize the importance of real and practical agreement among citizens subordinating to a constitution. The coercive power of the state is, as such, legitimate only if agreement cannot be reasonably refused (Höffe 1999, p. 47), and the agreement to a constitution (and to a constitutional change) must be explicit (Buchanan 1975, p. 148). The importance of such individual explicit agreement becomes obvious from the following argument. Hobbes conducted a contractarian thought experiment to justify subordination to an absolute authority but underestimated to what extent absolute power can become corrupt. Because an authority has the incentive to exploit citizens and to behave like a Leviathan, *indispensable* to a constitution are rules that prevent the state, and the politicians, bureaucrats, and any interest groups from abusing their power. The design of the constitution must take into regard potentially disastrous political outcomes.[5] "The passions of men will not conform to the dictates of reason and justice without constraint" (Hamilton, Federalist 15, according to Hamilton, Madison, and Jay 1787/1788, p. 110). Just and reasonable government must thus subordinate itself to the rule of law. Checks and balances laid down in the constitution help create sufficient political competition so that dominant positions of specific centers of power in a polity cannot emerge.

Three basic institutions act to restrict state power and to ensure that basic individual rights are respected, to prevent illegitimate concentration of power, and to secure the interests of the largest number of individual citizens in a jurisdiction (Höffe 1999, ch. 4): First, the rule of law must be observed by strict protocol for amendments on basic rights and by an independent judiciary institution. Rights that can be arbitrarily altered cannot be regarded as basic rights (Buchanan 1975, p. 106). Basic freedoms should not be allowed easy changes by simple majorities in the legislature or by society at large. Any emendations should be only possible under unanimity rule to prevent suppression of structural (ethnic, linguistic, religious, or racial) minorities by a majority rule. The independent judiciary ensures that these basic rights are secured even against the access of the state. An independent judiciary also ensures that government authorities submit to the rule of law, and this helps make state commitment to private property credible. With secure property rights comes economic growth, through private investments in human and physical capital (Feld and Voigt 2003). An independent judiciary, as a component of the checks and balances in a democracy, also enhances political competition.

Second, the separation and division of powers means that political competition exists between centers of power. Since government is guided by humans who, by nature, are capable of surrender to the temptation of abusing power, a prudent division of powers into executive, legislative, and judiciary branches keeps each division in check and subordinates each to the other. Third, democracy is a way to have political preferences of individuals guide those who govern. To voluntarily accept a limitation of their liberty and tolerate the partial coercion by the state, citizens must have a voice in political decision-making and sufficient means to control and sanction their representatives.

Since the constitution is subject to the explicit consent of citizens, there is an inherent logic to direct democratic participation in constitutional changes. The rules of the political game in the form of a constitution are supposed to impose restrictions on the representatives. The prerogative to change the constitutional contract must be then with those voluntarily subordinating to it. The case for direct democratic decision-making follows from the need to control representatives in accord with the preferences of citizens. This is the eternal concern of political philosophers, and more recently arguments by rational choice theorists have provided the basic text on direct democracy. The logic holds with respect to the foundation of a new federation by a new constitution as is the case of the European Union. Presently the European Convention consists of an independent group of "wise men" who have an interest in the constitutional rules they propose. The Convention is comprised of MEPs, members from national executives and legislatures, and members of the Commission. In this situation, as Vaubel (2002) recently observed, it cannot be expected that these members of the Convention can decide by abstracting from their individual interests. So the final acceptance of the European constitution by the European people should be by a constitutional referendum if a European federation is to provide sufficient constitutional restrictions on EU representatives.

Information, Control, and Interest Groups

Proposals of direct democracy are challenged by several arguments on the importance of information and interest groups. Direct democracy is supposed to have an informational disadvantage compared to the representative democracy, which originates in a division of labor between ordinary citizens and politicians (Kirchgässner, Feld, and Savioz 1999; Feld and Kirchgässner 2000). Just as people may allow their investment consultant full discretion in financial decisions, they may delegate decision-making power on political issues to political specialists who have a comparative advantage in doing politics. Delegation to representatives in the public sector occurs in order to save information costs. However, representatives then have the leeway to act opportunistically or in the partial interest of narrowly defined groups. A trade-off between agency costs and information cost savings can occur, which might be resolved by organizing political decision-making in a representative democracy or by allowing citizens to intervene selectively in politics by referenda and initiatives when political outcomes deviate too unacceptably from their interests. Referenda and initiatives thus serve to selectively control representatives between election years in a representative democracy. Whereas a pure representative democracy has an informational advantage over direct democracy, referenda and initiatives allow public control of the representatives.

The referendum works as a veto of citizens against proposals from government and parliament,[6] and the initiative allows citizens to propose new policies that are neglected by the political establishment—mainly policies that are not in politicians' interest. Added to referenda, an initiative enables citizens to unbundle policy packages created in the parliament via log-rolling agreements. This way political outcomes that run contrary to the interests of a majority of citizens are declined (Besley and Coate 2000). However, initiatives entail additional costs for citizens, since they require the collection of signatures to bring an initiative to the ballot. Depending on the number of signatures required, the initiative will have a stronger or weaker impact on policy outcomes, and the more or less easily an issue unbundling can take place. Referenda and initiatives nevertheless can correct political outcomes in favor of the preferences of the median voter, even in the case of strategic manipulation or agenda setting.[7] Referenda and initiatives are particularly important as decision-making becomes more the domain of representatives and removed from citizen participation. While informal control instruments may exist at the lower local levels, they are replaced by formal institutions of control as political competencies are shifted to higher levels of government. At the EU level, elements of direct democracy can induce their most beneficial impact and force representatives to cede to citizens' preferences. Nevertheless, the first justification for proposing referenda and initiatives at the postconstitutional level in the European Union follows from the control argument.

The control argument invokes the idea of asymmetric information in politics because representatives are better informed than citizens. This is illustrated by Marino and Matsusaka (2000) who extend a model by Aghion and Tirole (1997) to study budget procedures used in private and public decision-making. They start from a situation where representatives have a bias toward higher spending and analyze their decision-making. They compare the results of a full delegation to representatives that have full discretion over spending with those of a partial delegation whose decisions on spending can be vetoed or overridden ex post by referenda. It is clear that in the partial delegation case, representatives have an incentive to supply biased information to citizens in order to obtain their approval for raising the spending levels. As Marino and Matsusaka show, these information biases can be so relentless that the full delegation will submit to the decisions of the partial delegation. It turns out that it is more difficult to distort information in large projects. Thus the optimal decision-making rule is that there should be a full delegation where routine projects with low spending threshold are exclusively to be decided by representatives, and partial delegation where larger projects with high spending thresholds can be vetoed by voters.[8]

Grillo (1997) argues against utilizing a partial delegation in polities of large scale and of uncertain federal/confederate nature such as the European Union. He sees decision-making and information costs to be large in larger polities, making direct democracy infeasible except at the local and regional levels. The costs of conducting referenda and initiatives turn out to outweigh the benefits of additional control. Direct democratic decision-making is said not to be useful at the supranational level of a confederation because of potential problems with the compromises involved. Binding compromises are nevertheless important in international organizations for mutual benefit of states on proposals of mutual interest. Referenda and initiatives do not allow for decisions on a supranational level because citizens rarely focus beyond their national interests.

However, in the small-scale argument, the benefits at stake can increase at least as much as the costs if direct democratic decision-making is introduced at higher levels of government. The agency problem becomes more serious at higher levels of decision-making in a federation. As decisions deviate from citizens' interests, higher costs can be expected for these citizens at the national level because political decisions have more impact compared to the local level. Most European countries in fact have a history of referenda for important constitutional changes. For example, the United Kingdom voted by referendum on their participation in the additional steps of political integration in the European Union. The legitimacy of such referenda was not challenged at all on grounds of a larger scale polity.

Likewise the point about higher organizational costs of conducting referenda and initiatives at the EU level, compared to the local level, is not convincing. Europe-wide referenda may pose some organizational difficulties, but they can be handled efficiently in today's information societies. Further the confederation argument does not hold because the EU Treaty already includes considerable features that pertain to the concept of a federation. The closer to a federation a polity is, the easier it is to argue for direct participation of citizens in political decision-making. From the perspective of optimal control by representatives, it may be necessary to introduce referenda and initiatives as control instruments as soon as the process of federation building starts.

Another sort of asymmetric information case can evolve if representatives are imperfectly informed about citizens' preferences. Matsusaka (1992) shows that under such circumstances even benevolent politicians may support policies that deviate from citizens' wishes. Hence they have incentives to propose a referendum whenever they are uncertain of citizens' wants as a way to avoid being punished at the polls for enacting the wrong policy. Matsusaka provides evidence that referenda in California are rather on distributive issues than efficiency/procedural issues. Referenda are also used in periods of political corruption to restrict government. The clear implications for the European Union are that as representatives are removed farther from citizens, the less informed they become about citizens' political preferences. Indeed, the EU redistributive politics are such that it will pay off for EU representatives to elicit citizens' preferences via referenda.

Another argument of opponents of direct democracy is that imperfect and asymmetric information can provide opportunities for interest groups to unduly influence political outcomes. Matsusaka and McCarty (2001) examine a case where interest groups might be able to fool representatives. The threat of an initiative is used whereby an interest group pretends that its position is close to citizens' preferences, although this moves the policy outcome farther away from the ideal point of the median voter. Gerber (1999) shows that interest groups can influence outcomes in direct democracies but that they also can affect policy outcomes in representative democracies. Theoretically, and on the basis of piecemeal evidence, it is still debatable whether interest group influence is stronger or weaker in the direct as opposed to the representative democracy. Given this ambiguity, it is worth noting that there is systematic evidence, from the United States and Switzerland, that political outcomes come closer to citizens' preferences under direct than under representative democracy. Using aggregate data on Swiss cities in 1970, Pommerehne (1978) found that the median voter model performed better in jurisdictions with referenda and initiatives. Gerber (1996, 1999) provides evidence for the United States that supports Pommerehne's finding. For two political issues, parental consent laws and capital punishment, she shows that initiatives corrected policy outcomes toward the preferences of the median voter. Gerber (1996a) traces the deviation of policy outcomes from citizens' preferences back to the influence of interest groups on representatives. Feld and Schaltegger (2002) provide evidence for Swiss cantons where the influence of the state administration on federal matching grants was reduced by a fiscal referendum. All this evidence supplements the argument in favor of including the instruments of direct democracy in the EU Constitution. There is good reason to think that referenda and initiatives can similarly bring EU policy close to the preferences of EU citizens.

Expressive Voting, Direct and Representative Democracy

The information problem in democracies is a fundamental one. It is not simply captured by asymmetric information between representatives and voters. The individual citizen has a low probability of influencing voting outcomes. Therefore an individual's instrumental benefit of participating in elections or referenda is much lower than the expected costs. From a rational choice perspective, this suggests that voter turnout should be low. The expected costs of participating in democratic decisions are high because citizens have to be better informed and provided facts on political issues. The information costs can be expected to be lower in representative than in direct democracy, although the incentives for supply and demand of information are higher in direct than in representative democracy (Kirchgässner, Feld, and Savioz 1999; Feld and Kirchgässner 2000).

Despite the lack of incentives to show up at the ballots, voter turnout is considerably high in direct and representative democracies. In Britain, voter turnout was on average 74.1 percent in the seven elections between 1970 and 1995 without showing any decreases until 1997. It was 70.9 percent in 1997, and then it fell sharply to 59.4 percent in 2001. In Germany, it was 77.8 percent in 1990, 79.0 in 1994, 82.2 percent in 1998, and 80.6 percent in 2002.[9] In Switzerland, turnout in referenda and initiatives has decreased since the 1950s when 51 percent of citizens participated. Since the 1970s, it appears to have stabilized at around 40 percent on average. Elections of representatives at the Swiss federal level were at a 46.3 percent turnout on average over the last twenty years.[10] In the United States, turnout was close to the Swiss level. In the seven presidential elections between 1972 and 1996 it was 48.1 percent on average and 51.3 percent in 2000. In midterm elections, it has averaged at 35.5 percent with a low of 33.1 percent in 1990.[11] These turnouts cannot be explained by rational actor theory if only instrumental voting is taken into account.

Brennan and Lomasky (1993) attempt to explain this paradox in terms of expressive voting. They suggest that voters use elections to express their discontent with specific policies of a government by showing solidarity with particular policy platforms or a specific position, ideology, or habit. Instead of being instrumental in the sense of an action to achieve a certain end as in the case of normal market transactions, voting is seen as an expressive means, like cheering a team at a football match (Brennan and Hamlin 2000, p. 130). If voting is expressive in this sense, there is a considerable concern that citizens vote irresponsibly along their political preferences for or against policies according to particular enthusiasms and prejudices. Brennan and Hamlin (2000, p. 176) thus question whether direct democracy can orient political decision-making in the public's interest. Rather, they argue for a pure representative democracy, which they see as better fitted to a world of expressive voting where the extent of irresponsible political outcomes may be reduced by a proper selection of representatives. Voters are naturally inclined to support candidates with relatively high civic virtue because of the general difficulty faced in discerning candidates' competences beyond political style. Their opinions may be informed by societal codes of ethics. By a basically Madisonian argument, representatives would hence be regarded as more public spirited, conscientious, and knowledgeable about issues than those they represent (Brennan and Hamlin 2000, p. 180). As a result voters are inclined to judge the people rather than the competing policy options they represent.

The Brennan and Lomasky (1993) and Brennan and Hamlin (2000) conception of direct democracy is flawed for several reasons. First, the authors fully neglect the discussion process that precedes direct democratic decisions, and also elections. From their arguments it appears as if citizens decide at the ballots after they have reflected on different issues in isolation. Decisions in referenda and initiatives actually take place in an entirely different environment. Frey and Kirchgässner (1993), Kirchgässner, Feld, and Savioz (1999), and Feld and Kirchgässner (2000) analyze the deliberation process in direct democracy and characterize it as a relatively rational one with an intensity that depends on how important is a political decision, and how informed are the different positions of political parties, interest groups, but also by experts and less organized individuals. In the course of discussion, a learning process occurs at least for part of the citizenry. Since many citizens are confronted with the arguments from two sides, those opposing and those favoring a certain policy outcome, they are induced to consider each proposal anew. So discussion can lead to a revision of their individual position. Therefore the possibility also emerges that citizens examine the extent to which their preferences might generalize. In addition it can be presumed that citizens' willingness to bear costs of information acquisition is higher in direct legislation than in representative democracies. The reason for this is that it can become privately important for citizens to be well informed about political issues. Such a situation emerges if members of a social network are expected to be well informed on political issues and at the ballots to vote sincerely. Being politically uninformed leads to loss of esteem. These private costs may arise with respect to single political decisions but not with respect to political parties. Private costs of political participation in direct democracy increase the individuals' incentives to vote according to their own interests, such that the extent of expressive motivation is lower in direct than in representative democracy.

Second, the hypothesis that representatives have higher civic virtue than those whom they represent can be fairly well challenged on the basis of the experiences with most democratically elected governments and assemblies in OECD countries. Brennan and Hamlin (2000, p. 178) may be right in asserting that the relevant virtues need not coincide with prejudices. It is perhaps more important that representatives behave virtuously in the sense of not exploiting citizens, instead of subscribing to a certain morally informed sexual behavior. However, cases of political corruption in France, Germany, the United Kingdom, and Italy in the last two decades compared with those in Switzerland and United States well illustrate that representative democracies are not able to select the more virtuous among their citizenry as representatives, so the degree of corruption does not seem to correspond to whether or not the citizenry has direct political rights. Somehow the authors seem to hang onto the old dream of selecting statesmen instead of politicians. German-speaking economists still lament that a statesman like Ludwig Erhard, the first German Minister of Economics after the Second World War, has not been seen for years in Germany.[12] That voters fail to select virtuous representatives may result from the false assumption that a person's moral character reflects his or her policies. A candidate's attractive appearance can have more appeal than his or her positions on policy. Physical appearances matters as much in the election of representatives as it does in the labor market, where physical beauty, ceteris paribus, has the capacity to extract rents.

Third, in regard to Brennan and Hamlin's expressive voting argument, it is not entirely convincing that citizens use the ballot in the same way they cheer at a football match. Mueller (2003, p. 321) notes that it is at least just as likely that citizens at the ballots take the opportunity to express basic noble sentiments on the "norms that govern conduct toward others." Kirchgässner (1992, 1996) argues that voting is a low-cost way for citizens to effect collective well-being but neither their own instrumental well-being nor that of immediate others. It is therefore cheaper to follow moral sentiment than to invest in market-like decisions where moral behavior may be punished by utility maximizing individuals. The theory of low-cost decision-making hence provides a competing argument for why people vote and why their voting is guided by moral code. This is where the discourse preceding a referendum decision at the ballots should help inform the public of policy issues. Citizens may act more altruistically in referenda and initiatives than in economic decisions. For example, Pommerehne and

Schneider (1985) presented empirical evidence that Swiss people vote for redistributional programs despite the losses they entail in their own wealth. At the ballots voters will often take a more ethical position than might be expected from their behavior in the market place. This result can be traced to the discourse that precedes the vote, which increases the probability that common interests will guide social choice. Direct democracy may in this way provide a better chance for the development of civic virtues than representative democracy.

Direct Democracy and the European Demos

As mentioned at the start of this chapter, an often criticized aspect of EU decision-making is the lack of a common European political conscience of the citizens in the individual member states.[13] All the while elements of direct democracy at the EU level are expected to form a European *demos* and develop common understanding of policy. Again, Switzerland is an inspiring example. After the Swiss civil war in 1847, a federal state was created that could not depend on a national *demos*: a Swiss *demos* did not exist then, only cantonal *demoi* could be observed. According to Hug (2000), it was the elements of direct democracy in the Swiss Constitution that contributed to the development of a Swiss *demos*.

Hug (2000) argues that the hopes of an EU-wide referendum forming an EU *demos* should not be exaggerated. There are two caveats to observe in drawing an analogy between nineteenth-century Switzerland and the European Union. First, the elements of direct democracy, though helpful, are neither necessary nor sufficient for a European *demos*. Too little is known about the mechanisms that lead citizens to overthrow positions that are based on their narrow (national or cantonal) interests and instead adopt more general positions (Cederman and Kraus 2003). For Switzerland, the empirical evidence on the differences in tax evasion among cantons with and without referenda indicate that a referendum could transform such shortsighted interests. Nevertheless, national interests may prevail and be exacerbated by EU-wide referenda if, for instance, referenda outcomes follow along the lines of distinction between poor and rich member countries. Second, it is obvious that at least in some member countries citizens are not yet ready to accept majority decisions at the EU level. Consider the case of an increase in tax rates in order to finance additional programs for Eastern European countries on a larger scale. Within the single member states, such a regional redistribution from northern Italy to the Mezzogiorno, may be more or less accepted by the citizens paying for it because a national feeling of solidarity exists. At the European level, a corresponding consciousness is still lacking. Thus at the moment any such proposal would probably be rejected by the member states.

As in nineteenth-century Switzerland the introduction of referenda might help develop a public consciousness that would accept in the long run redistributional measures at the European level. Just as central bank independence is neither necessary nor sufficient but helpful for price stability, the discourse among citizenry that precedes referenda or initiatives at the EU level could shift individual self-interest to public interest and national to European public interest. The nationally informed positions of citizens may be pushed to the extent they can be generalized to the European level. In order to make thoughtful political decisions at the EU level, citizens need the incentive to discuss the broader European issues. Referenda and initiatives at the EU level are a good way to provide these incentives.

The Wicksellian Connection between Public Services and Tax Prices

The most convincing argument for the introduction of instruments of direct democracy at the EU level stems from the fact that referenda and initiatives allow the conduct of public policy on the linkages between the taxes citizens pay for public goods and services and the benefits they obtain from these public goods and services. Breton (1996) calls this the Wicksellian (1896) connection. Side by side analyses of the impacts of referenda and initiatives on economic policy for Switzerland and the United States provide strong support for the Wicksellian hypothesis on this connection for direct rather than in representative democracy.[14] These studies showed that public spending,[15] revenue,[16] and debt[17] are significantly lower in jurisdictions with direct democracies than in those with pure representative democracies. With respect to spending structure, the fiscal referendum mainly restricts welfare and administrative spending according to Schaltegger (2001) and Vatter and Freitag (2002). With respect to revenue structure, both the United States with its initiatives and the Swiss cantons with their fiscal referenda depend more on user charges than on broad-based taxes.[18] Moreover Matsusaka (1995, 2002) and Schaltegger and Feld (2001) provide evidence that centralization of spending and revenue is reduced by the referendum.

The question remains, however, whether the lower level of public spending also leads to a more efficient public sector. Pommerehne (1983) analyzed costs and prices of local garbage collection in 103 Swiss cities in 1970. He found that average refuse collection costs (per household) were, ceteris paribus, lowest in cities with direct legislation and private garbage collection. For a panel of Swiss cantons Barankay (2002) reports that from 1970 to 1996 there were significantly lower infant mortality rates and a greater share of college degree holders in more direct democratic cantons, indicating a higher quality of public goods in the cantons. Pommerehne and Weck-Hannemann (1996) show that in Swiss cantons where citizens have a voice in budgetary policy through direct legislation, tax evasion is, ceteris paribus, lower as compared, on average, with cantons without such direct citizen participation.[19] These results are corroborated by Feld and Frey (2002a) and by Torgler (2002) using different data sets. Apparently, if a citizen's willingness to pay taxes is higher the more satisfied that citizen is with the public services supplied, these results are good evidence for relatively high satisfaction of citizens and consequently for a relatively efficient provision of public services. Indeed, Frey and Stutzer (2000, 2002) find that people in Switzerland even perceive themselves as more satisfied with their lives overall in the direct democracy cantons, with income levels and other controls held constant. As the link between tax rates and public services in direct democracy indicates, Swiss citizens appear to act more responsibly toward their communities. They appear to be more accepting of decisions that take a bite out of their income or wealth than citizens of representative democracies.

If, as these studies show, direct democratic systems are more efficient than representative democratic ones, we might expect more efficient political systems also to lead to better economic performances. Feld and Savioz (1997) study the relationship between budgetary referenda and economic performance of Swiss cantons measured by GDP per employee. Using annual panel data from 1984 to 1993 for the 26 Swiss cantons, they arrive at the conclusion that GDP per employee is, ceteris paribus, higher by about 5 percent in those cantons with budgetary referenda compared to cantons without such referenda. Corroborating evidence comes from Freitag and Vatter (2000) for Switzerland and by Blomberg, Hess, and Weerapana (2004) for the United States. The evidence from the United States and Switzerland lends further support to the idea that (economic) policy outcomes in jurisdictions with referenda and initiatives are relatively closely orientated in terms of the Wicksellian connection of public spending to tax rate. This evidence speaks strongly for the value of introducing direct democracy in the future EU constitution.

9.3 A Mandatory Referendum on the European Constitution

The successes of referenda and initiatives in the United States and Switzerland, and the necessity to control the political game at the EU level, lead us to propose that provision for *mandatory constitutional referenda* be made in the EU constitution. We propose that it include two components: first, the basic document, the founding Treaty that comprises the EU constitution, which should be adopted by a mandatory referendum; second, provision for changes to the EU constitution such as may in time be adopted by European citizenry by a mandatory referendum as well. These referenda would be binding and required. The EU institutions involved in the decisions on the EU constitution—the Commission, the Council, and the EP—should not be able to abrogate nor overrule referenda decisions other than propose any amendments to the constitution or prepare a draft of the new constitution in the first place. The EU citizenry as defined in Article 8 of the current Draft constitution are to be empowered to decide on EU constitutional issues.

Both constitutional referenda, the first founding referendum and the second referendum on constitutional changes, can be adopted if a simple majority of citizens and a qualified (two-thirds) majority of countries accept the constitution or any constitutional amendments, respectively. We follow Frey (1995), Schneider (1996), Epiney (1997), and Papadopoulos (2002) and propose that the vote be by a double majority in the member countries.[20] Although Frey and Schneider do not call for required majorities, Epiney recommends the majority of voters and the qualified majority of at least ten member states. Papadopoulos' suggestion corresponds to ours. While Epiney's proposal is also close to ours, we have adapted our proposal to eastern and any further enlargements. Our proposal is also close to that of Abromeit (1998), but it is less restrictive. Abromeit suggests a majority of voters in all states, and she sees the parliaments of the representative democratic EU member states as the EU decision-making structure within a direct democracy. This would, however, give every member state extreme veto power, provide incentives for strategic behavior and therefore make changes nearly impossible.[21] For these reasons we think that the quorum with respect to the member states should be reduced to two-thirds. No other restriction with respect to the majority requirement should be imposed. In particular, there does not seem to be need for a requirement that the referendum be adopted if the turnout exceeds a certain threshold of the EU citizenry. Such a quorum would also invite strategic behavior, as it is actually a quorum on the share of approval votes.[22] No such quorum should indeed be considered.

We envision the first founding referendum to be on the entire new Treaty, as it already contains three sections of an actual constitution, on policy areas, and on general and concluding provisions. The mandatory referendum should not extend to the normal statutes of the EU; it should only be on constitutional changes. In the current Draft, prepared by the Convention, the mandatory constitutional referendum would apply to title III of part one on the assignment of powers of the EU, title IV on EU institutions, title V on procedures to decide EU policy measures, title VI on the democratic principle, title VII on the finances of the EU, titles VIII on EU foreign policy, and title IX on entry to and exit from the EU. In addition the mandatory constitutional referendum should be used for changes to the second and third parts of the constitution. Of course, no mandatory constitutional referendum would be appropriate for title I of part one on the structure of the constitution or title II of part one and the entire part two on EU citizenship and basic rights. The substances of both titles are further to be protected by an eternity clause. The mandatory referendum on the adoption of a constitution is to be included in the final part of the Draft Article IV-8. The mandatory constitutional referendum should be added in Article IV-7 on the procedures for changes in the constitution of that same section.

If the European Court becomes a constitutional court, it will be obligated to evaluate the compatibility of any proposed changes of the constitution with the substance of title II of part one and the entire second part.[23] On extending a mandatory constitutional referendum to *all* constitutional provisions, we follow Buchanan (2001) who objects against this because of the potential conflict between the rule of law and the principle of democracy to protect basic human and civil rights. Buchanan (2001) acknowledges, however, the usefulness of a mandatory constitutional referendum in preserving property rights granted by the constitution. The referendum allows European citizens to participate as additional veto players in the EU decision-making game. Thus, once agreed upon, constitutional outcomes should reflect the document's stability. Constitutional changes should be more difficult to enact, though not impossible. Moser (1996, 1996a) shows how this stability factor might figure theoretically in spatial voting models. It is particularly important with respect to the assignment of competencies to the EU. The creeping centralization dreaded by Vaubel (1994) and Blankart (2000) might thus be less probable.[24]

9.4 Constitutional/Statutory Initiatives and a Fiscal Referendum at the EU Level

Constitutional and Statutory Initiatives at the EU Level

While the institution of referendum enhances the stability of constitutional and policy outcomes, it is a relatively conservative practice. The use of popular initiative offers citizens the possibility of introducing political legislation or unbundling of unfavorable policies. Either way the initiative is a means of creating or modifying policy. The initiative in EU decision-making would, in addition to the mandatory constitutional referendum, help facilitate the launching of policies neglected by the political elite. The initiative accomplishes this goal at relatively low cost; it does not involve the foundation of new parties, and it can serve as a valve for political protest. In a direct democracy citizens who oppose the established politics can thus use these political instruments instead of taking themselves to riot in the streets.

We propose that a constitutional and statutory initiative be introduced in the EU constitution. The constitutional initiative would serve the purpose of bringing additional institutional innovation to the EU level. If the European Union develops into a federation it will in time acquire broader strength in policy areas than it does today. The use of mandatory referenda may check some of this power, but it cannot (and should not) challenge it if it reasonably serves the interests of a majority of EU citizens and a qualified majority of the member states. A more powerful Union can be expected to need more funds, find more ways to spend them, and pass more legislation and more frequently than what we see today. In that political climate citizens may find the necessity to create additional instruments, such as optional statutory referenda, to control EU legislation. Naturally the constitutional initiative can also be a means of broadening the scope of EU polices or launching policy as the Union enlarges to embrace new member states.

Unlike Schneider (1996), Epiney (1997) and Abromeit (1998), we dismiss the idea of including an optional statutory referendum in the EU constitution. Our reason is mainly pragmatic: The presence of an optional referendum would unduly reduce the efficiency and extremely raise the cost of EU decision-making. On the one hand, the optional referendum, because it would be relatively easily accessible to a small number of citizens with their special interests, could considerably slow down EU decision-making. On the other hand, access to the optional referendum could be so prohibitively high that it would be declined anyway. Abromeit (1998) recommends a type of optional referendum on regional (sectoral) objectives that could be triggered by 5 percent of the voters of a region (50,000 voters in a sector) and would come into force if a simple majority of voters in that region (in that state) adopts it. This scheme, however, gives strong veto power to regional or sectoral interests that might run contrary to the interests of a majority of EU citizens. Epiney (1997) enlarges a proposal made by Zürn (1996, 2000) whereby the European Parliament would be able to trigger an optional referendum. According to this proposal, it would be triggered by an absolute majority of MEPs representing at least five member states. It would conform to all directives and regulations and be accepted if a simple majority of voters in member states adopts it. By this scheme, the EP would be unduly strengthened in the balance of EU powers and encourage the use of plebiscites in EU decision-making. Plebiscites can be used by the legislature or the executive and would thus be at their disposal. In the past they were often used strategically by the French and by the Germans, in particular. Plebiscites should not have a place in EU decision-making. Last there is Schneider's (1996) proposal that an optional constitutional referendum could be initiated by 5 million EU citizens and adopted by majorities of voters and states if a turnout of 30 percent is reached. The problem is that the turnout quorum in this scheme also invites strategic behavior of opponents of a particular constitutional proposal.[25] The need for any optional constitutional referendum, of course, would not exist if there is provision made for mandatory constitutional referenda: Because any change to the constitution would have to be decided by EU citizens, the selective use of constitutional veto would become obsolete.

We see the constitutional initiative as a more cautious means than the optional (statutory) referendum in terms of both efficiency for the EU decision-making and the openness to special interests. It is a more practical instrument than referenda at the EU level, in general. The only objection comes from Abromeit (2002, p. 201), who uses the same argument against the EU initiative as is used here to reject the optional statutory referendum: initiatives allow special interest groups undue influence. An additional problem the initiative poses is the question of having a proper formulation of constitutional amendments and legal statutes in the first place.

Abromeit's basic argument against the initiative is unconvincing, however. An initiative is necessarily intensively discussed before it is launched. During the collection of signatures, many people have to be convinced of an initiative's validity in order to subscribe to it. Then, after the signatures are successfully collected, the legislature (EP and Council) and the executive (Commission and Council) are given ample time to discuss and evaluate its substance. They can even make a counterproposal that includes useful parts of the initiative or provides a more reasoned alternative for the citizens. It should be noted that any innovative policy or institutional innovation resulting from a constitutional initiative is more difficult to enact than a veto on a proposal by the legislature or the executive. Risk-averse people are status quo oriented. Such inclination plays against the initiative, but for the veto via an optional referendum. Empirical evidence from the United States and Switzerland well supports this argument. As mentioned in section 9.2, special interests, in particular, financially important groups in the United States, face difficulties in succeeding with an initiative compared to citizen groups, whereas money is influential in stopping policies by using a referendum. The experience with initiatives in Switzerland has hinted the same: Most federal initiatives are rejected but will influence policy even when declined if the political elite realizes that it has neglected some political issue to an unjustified extent and corrects this.

All in all, the provision for a constitutional and statutory initiative in the European constitution may help develop the EU institutionally and politically. With respect to the constitutional initiative we propose that this be an option open to EU citizens as defined in the constitution as well as to official authorities like the EP, the Commission, or special groups that are able to collect signatures of 5 percent of the electorate. According to Matsusaka's (1995) study in the United States a signature requirement of 10 percent of the electorate or more prevents the initiative from having a significant impact on (fiscal) policy outcomes. The median signature requirement for the popular initiative at the US state level is 5 percent. When Switzerland included a constitutional initiative in 1891, the signature requirement for it was 5 percent of the electorate as well. Because it was fixed at the absolute number of 50,000 signatures and only once increased to 100,000 after the women obtained their voting rights, the signature requirement for an initiative is much lower today in relative terms. Alternatively, this requirement could be adapted to reflect the representation of member states more fully by a signature quota of 15 percent of the electorate in five countries, but 2 percent of the electorate at least.[26]

There is much less research on the time allowed to collect signatures. Even a low signature requirement of 2 percent of the EU electorate might be unduly restrictive if merely a month were allowed to collect them. A look at the Swiss cantonal level might be helpful. With the exception of the canton of St. Gallen, no difference in collection time is made with respect to constitutional and statutory initiatives. While citizens have two months to collect signatures in Nidwalden and the Ticino, they have eighteen months in Solothurn. St. Gallen allows three months for signature collection in the case of the statutory initiative and six months for the constitutional initiative. Nine cantons have no time restrictions. At the EU level more time to collect signatures would of course be needed than at the Swiss cantonal level. The collection time might be from eighteen months to two years so that the initiative committee can have sufficient time to collect a fair share of signatures representing citizen support from different member states. The EU constitution must also find ways to ensure that collection of signatures is not locally concentrated or corrupted by organized groups that pressure people to sign. The German experience with direct democracy during the Weimar Republic teaches us that signature collection should not be concentrated in officially fixed administrative buildings. It appears to be better for signatures to be collected in public places as in most US states and in Switzerland.

The constitutional initiative is adopted if a majority of citizens and a qualified (two thirds) majority of countries is reached. Unlike the mandatory referendum, the jurisdiction of a constitutional initiative is not a priori restricted to basic human and civil rights. However, both the constitutional and statutory initiative are subject to judicial control ex ante. Constitutional amendments and laws resulting from the initiative can be abrogated when they contradict basic human and civil rights. Like the mandatory constitutional referendum, the protocol for constitutional initiatives should be laid down in Article IV-7, which pertains to procedures for instituting changes to the constitution.

The provisions for the statutory initiative are the same as those for the constitutional initiative as regards who can propose an initiative and the signature requirement. However, the statutory initiative can be accepted if only a majority of the citizenry adopts it. Again, the Parliament or the Council is allowed to formulate a counterproposal to a statutory initiative ex ante. The European Court has further the obligation to check the compatibility of the statutory initiative with constitutional provisions before the ballot takes place. Moreover it should also be possible to make a "general initiative" for a specific political objective, and it would be the role of the (Council and/or the) Parliament to formulate the corresponding law. The statutory as well as the general initiative should be included under title VI of the constitution on the democratic "life" of the Union. Article II-46, (4) should by extended such that a binding referendum decision is required to conclude this procedure.

Two detailed proposals for an EU initiative exist. Although constitutional and statutory initiatives are not distinguished, but instead formulated for abstract general rules, Epiney (1997) proposes that 10 percent of the citizens in at least five states or the governments of five states can trigger an initiative that is adopted by the double majority of voters and countries. Weiler (1997, 1999) proposes a statutory initiative that is triggered by citizens in at least five member states (without specifying how many citizens) and is adopted as well by the double majority. Compared to the form of constitutional initiative we propose here, both have relatively low signature and majority requirements. In our proposal, the majority requirement for the statutory initiative is with a simple majority of citizens, relatively low.

A Fiscal Referendum at the EU Level

Despite the instruments of mandatory constitutional referenda, and the constitutional and the statutory initiatives, the question arises whether the EU constitution contains sufficient safeguards to bind EU representatives to the preferences of EU citizens. In the United States and the Swiss cantons, the response to this question is in the negative. Mostly the Americans and the Swiss have additional provisions for the direct influence of citizens on public spending. As our survey in section 9.2 indicates, the empirical results generally pertain to fiscal referenda. Does the EU constitution need a fiscal referendum as well? To begin to answer that question, we should consider two things. First, a fiscal referendum, in accord with the most common Swiss definition, could consist of an optional or mandatory fiscal referendum or a combination of them all. If government and parliament propose a spending project that exceeds a certain spending threshold, an optional or mandatory fiscal referendum is triggered. In addition specific fiscal referenda may relate to changes in taxation or new bonds that are used to finance the spending project.

Second, there is the matter of how European policy domains should be financed. In Kirchgässner (1994) it is argued that EU spending should be financed by proportional (indirect) taxes, but not by (progressive) personal income taxes. The rationale behind this proposal lies in the different control possibilities that exist at different governmental levels. Any government will act more in accordance with the preferences of the individuals if more citizens make an effort to control it. At the lower levels, in smaller jurisdictions, the citizens are better able to force the government to act according to their preferences. In this respect there exists a significant difference between progressive (direct) and proportional (indirect) taxes. If tax rates can only be changed by changing a law, which is the usual way for indirect taxes, a relative increase of the government share has to be decided by parliamentary process or referendum. This ensures a public discussion, and at least as long as a government seeks re-election, it will hesitate to increase taxes. Thus increases of indirect tax rates are rather rare events, even for quantity taxes, whose real yield is eroded by inflation. Such proportional taxes leave relatively narrow leeway for Leviathan behavior of a government. Progressive direct taxes, on the other hand, create larger revenue not only whenever private economic activity and—consequently—private income increases but also as long as inflation prevails, if there is no corresponding indexation. Thus there is seldom a need for a change of the tax law if the government wants to collect higher revenue: it gets it automatically. Therefore progressive taxes provide a comparatively wide leeway for a government to behave as a Leviathan.

For taxes whose revenue rises (nearly) automatically, there is need of more controllability compared to (indirect) taxes that cannot be easily increased by politicians. Citizen control is more needed to keep down direct taxes than to restrict indirect taxes, especially general sales taxes like the VAT. At the European level it appears that only the revenues from indirect taxes will be available. We believe that in the EU constitution there should be a fixed surcharge on national VAT revenue that is equivalent to the revenue the European Union now gets from its VAT resource. This surcharge should already be included in the proposed EU constitution that is to be decided in the founding mandatory constitutional referendum. Just as there should be a mandatory constitutional referendum on each constitutional change, each change of the surcharge rate should be decided by referendum as well. When there are no constitutional changes that degrade financial constitutional provisions to mere statutes, no tax referendum is needed. Similarly no referendum on new bonds is needed as long as the principle of a balanced budget is fixed as in Article 52 of the Draft constitution. If there are changes in both constitutional provisions, for whatever reason, specific fiscal referenda on tax changes and the issuing of new bonds should be introduced in the EU constitution. The majority requirement should then be the same as for the mandatory constitutional referendum.

The Draft constitution does not contain any specific provisions with respect to EU spending. Indirectly, however, spending is predetermined by the assignment of tasks to the EU level. The current EU budget, though following the principle of unity, can be (politically) divided in different funds, the agricultural and the structural funds. Again, the mandatory constitutional referendum suffices as long as the assignment of new responsibilities is as closely attached to spending as it currently is at the EU level. If, again, for whatever reason the EU should adopt more competencies and power and thus also have increased spending needs, a fiscal referendum for new spending projects would be useful. In that case we propose to have an optional and a mandatory fiscal referendum on new spending projects with different spending thresholds. The thresholds could be in absolute or relative terms. Moreover the spending threshold should also differ depending on whether it is a one-time or a recurring expenditure, but it does not make sense to specify exactly these four different thresholds. The majority requirement could be a simple majority of EU citizens. It must be noted that such a fiscal referendum would be useful if the European Union should acquire more power. Because constitutional provisions are created for a longer time horizon, a fiscal referendum may even be considered to be included today. We believe, however, that the current EU financial structure and the constitutional provisions considered in the Draft constitution of the Convention do not necessarily need to be restricted additionally by a fiscal referendum. Given the current state of the discussion, a mandatory constitutional referendum as well as a constitutional and statutory and general initiatives appear to be sufficient to bind EU policy outcomes to the preferences of EU citizens.

9.5 Concluding Remarks

In this chapter we considered the introduction of direct democratic decision-making in all EU decisions when it is feasible and does not prohibitively increase decision-making costs. We discussed the role of a constitution as a contract joining the citizens of a state and the pros and cons of direct democracy from theoretical and empirical perspectives. We showed that citizens have better control in direct rather than in representatives democracies, and this provides the strongest argument for the introduction of direct democracy in the European constitution. We considered the argument that citizens may vote expressively in a direct democracy. In comparing US and Swiss evidence, we found that expressive voting can be expected to lead citizens to express moral sentiments rather than narrow self-interests at the ballots. Taking this perspective, we recommended that referenda and initiatives be institutionalized in order to shape a European *demos*. Our final strong argument for direct democracy was based on the comparative empirical evidence on economic policy outcomes in direct and representative democratic jurisdictions. The evidence shows that policies in direct democracy more strongly follow the Wicksellian connection of tax prices and spending.

From these arguments we were led to propose the introduction of elements of direct democracy in the new European constitution. We feel that European citizens should be able to shape the future European constitution as well as be able to make any future changes to it. Thus we propose a *mandatory*, required and binding, *referendum on total and partial revisions of the European constitution*. We also propose that the European Union have its own value added tax revenue, whose rate would be fixed in the constitution, and any tax increases would be subject to mandatory referendum. In addition we propose that there be included a *constitutional initiative*, a *statutory* as well as a *general initiative*. Finally, in the event that the European Union should assume broader policy power and therefore increase its spending needs, we propose a *fiscal referendum* for controlling expenditures on financially critical projects.

Notes

We gratefully acknowledge financial support from the Swiss National Science Foundation (Grant 5004-58524). We would like to thank Beat Blankart, Giuseppe Eusepi, Gianluigi Galeotti, Simon Hug, Dennis Mueller, and two anonymous referees for very valuable comments and suggestions.

1. See Boyce (1993), Abromeit (1998, p. 4), Hug (2002, p. 8), and for the following, *BVerfG* 89 (1993): 155–213.

2. See Bogdanor (1989), Opp (1994), Christiansen (1995), Körkemeyer (1995), Frey (1995), Schneider (1996), Zürn (1996, 2000), Epiney (1997), Weiler (1997, 1999), Abromeit (1998), and Papadopoulos (2002).

3. See also Let the people vote, *The Economist* 367 (May 24, 2003): 10.

4. For a comprehensive analysis of the contractarian approach to constitutions, see Buchanan (1975, p. 5).

5. See Hume (1741), Popper (1945), and Buchanan (1975).

6. Citizens can use (binding) referenda to reject government statutes or constitutional amendments. These can be mandatory or optional. An optional referendum is used if a certain number of citizens desire it.

7. For the first rigorous analysis of referenda, see Romer and Rosenthal (1979); for a comprehensive analysis under perfect information, see Steunenberg (1992). Other good analyses are presented in Mueller (1996, p. 183), Feld and Kirchgässner (2001), Matsusaka (2002), and Feld and Matsusaka (2003).

8. See Kessler (2003) for such a summary of the Marino and Matsusaka model.

9. In the 1970s voter turnout was even higher than 90 percent in Germany, in the 1980s, it was more than 80 percent. See *Statistisches Jahrbuch 1997 für die Bundesrepublik Deutschland*, p. 90. For the British data, see *Annual Abstract of Statistics*, 1997, p. 75.

10. The exact figures are 1979, 48.0; 1983: 48.9; 1987: 46.5; 1991: 46.0; 1995: 42.2. Source of the data: *Schweizerisches Bundesamt für Statistik*, and W. Seitz, *Nationalratswahlen 1995: Übersicht und Analyse*, Bundesamt für Statistik, Bern 1997, p. 115.

11. See *Statistical Abstract of the United States*, 1997, p. 289.

12. See, for example, Vaubel (1988).

13. See the more recent discussions in several European newspapers on the development of a European demos in light of the geopolitical developments after the second Iraq war: J. Derrida and J. Habermas, Unsere Erneuerung, *Frankfurter Allgemeine Zeitung* 125 (May 31, 2003): 33.

14. For earlier descriptions of these studies, see Kirchgässner, Feld, and Savioz (1999, ch. 5), Feld and Kirchgässner (2000, 2001), and Matsusaka (2002).

15. See Matsusaka (1995, 2000, 2002) for the United States and Feld and Kirchgässner (1999, 2001), Feld and Matsusaka (2003), Schaltegger (2001), and Vatter and Freitag (2002) for Switzerland.

16. See Matsusaka (1995, 2000, 2002) for the United States and Feld and Kirchgässner (2001) for Switzerland.

17. See Kiewiet and Szakaly (1996) for the United States and Feld and Kirchgässner (1999, 2001, 2001a) for Switzerland.

18. See Matsusaka (1995) for the US states and Feld and Matsusaka (2003a) for the Swiss cantons.

19. There are also theoretical arguments why citizens in direct democracies evade taxes less than those in representative democracies. See Pommerehne, Hart, and Feld (1997) and Feld and Frey (2002).

20. For a useful summary of the different proposals for direct democracy in the EU, see again Hug (2002, p. 102). Our comparisons of proposals in sections 9.3 and 9.4 are based on his summary.

21. In current circumstances log-rolling could help overcome such blocking but not if the final decisions are taken by popular referenda.

22. The experiences in the Weimar Republic, in the Bundesland Hamburg, as well as in Italy are discussed by Kirchgässner, Feld, and Savioz (1999, pp. 6, 38f, 161).

23. This check should only occur with respect to the Bill of Rights of the European constitution. In addition there must be a way to ensure that there is accord on the contents of any proposed changes to the European constitution. This means that no disparate issues should be allowed to be combined in order to succeed at the ballots. See also Papadopoulos (2002). The role of the constitutional court should not be as active as that of the US Supreme Court or the German Constitutional Court.

24. Unlike Vaubel (1996), we place more trust in centralization reducing impact of the constitutional referendum. In this we follow the arguments of Blankart (2000) and the empirical results of Schaltegger and Feld (2001).

25. Papadopoulos (2002) also proposes a participation requirement that has the same problems.

26. Papadopoulos (2002) proposes similar provisions for an EU initiative. He suggests a signature requirement of 5 percent of the electorate in at least five member countries.

References

Abromeit, H. 1998. *Democracy in Europe: Legitimizing Politics in a Non-state Polity*. New York: Berghahn.

Abromeit, H. 2002. *Wozu braucht man Demokratie? Die postnationale Herausforderung der Demokratietheorie*. Opladen: Leske and Budrich.

Aghion, Ph., and J. Tirole. 1997. Formal and real authority in organizations. *Journal of Political Economy* 105: 1–29.

Aristotle. *Politika*, ed. by H. Flashar. Berlin: Akademie Verlag, 1879.

Barankay, I. 2002. Referendums, citizens' initiatives and the quality of public goods: Theory and evidence. Mimeo. University of Warwick.

Besley, T., and St. Coate. 2000. Issue unbundling via citizens' initiatives. Mimeo. London School of Economics.

Blankart, C. B. 2000. The process of government centralization: A constitutional view, *Constitutional Political Economy* 11: 27–39.

Blomberg, S. B., G. D. Hess, and A. Weerapana 2004. The impact of voter activity on economic activity. *European Journal of Political Economy* 20: 207–26.

Bogdanor, V. 1989. Direct elections, representative democracy and European integration. *Electoral Studies* 8: 205–16.

Boyce, B. 1993. The democratic deficit of the European Community. *Parliamentary Affairs* 46: 458–77.

Brennan, G., and A. Hamlin. 2000. *Democratic Devices and Desires*. Cambridge: Cambridge University Press.

Brennan, G., and L. Lomasky. 1993. *Democracy and Decision: The Pure Theory of Electoral Preference*. Cambridge: Cambridge University Press.

Breton, A. 1996. *Competitive Governments: An Economic Theory of Politics and Public Finance*. Cambridge: Cambridge University Press.

Buchanan, J. M. 1975. *The Limits of Liberty: Between Anarchy and Leviathan*. Chicago: University of Chicago Press.

Buchanan, J. M. 2001. Direct democracy, classical liberalism, and constitutional strategy. *Kyklos* 54: 235–42.

Buchanan, J. M., and G. Tullock. 1962. *The Calculus of Consent: Logical Foundations of Constitutional Democracy*. Ann Arbor: University of Michigan Press.

Cederman, L.-E., and P. A. Kraus. 2003. Transnational communication and the European demos. Mimeo, Harvard University.

Christiansen, T. 1995. Gemeinsinn und Europäische Integration: Strategien zur Optimierung von Demokratie- und Integrationsziel. In W. Steffani and U. Thaysen (eds.): *Demokratie in Europa: Zur Rolle der Parlamente*. Opladen: Westdeutscher Verlag, pp. 50–64.

Cicero. [59 BC] 1988. *De re publica and De legibus*, trans. by C. W. Keyes. Cambridge: Harvard University Press.

Epiney, A. 1997. Le référendum européen. In A. Auer and J.-F. Flauss (eds.): *Le référendum européen*. Brussels: Bruylant, pp. 287–315.

Feld, L. P., and B. S. Frey. 2002. Trust breeds trust: How taxpayers are treated. *Economics of Governance* 3: 87–99.

Feld, L. P., and B. S. Frey. 2002a. The tax authority and the taxpayer: An exploratory analysis. Mimeo. University of St. Gallen.

Feld, L. P., and G. Kirchgässner. 1999. Public debt and budgetary procedures: Top down or bottom up? Some evidence from Swiss municipalities. In J. M. Poterba and J. von Hagen (eds.): *Fiscal Institutions and Fiscal Performance*. Chicago: Chicago University Press, 151–79.

Feld, L. P., and G. Kirchgässner. 2000. Direct democracy, political culture and the outcome of economic policy: A report on the Swiss experience. *European Journal of Political Economy* 16: 287–306.

Feld, L. P., and G. Kirchgässner. 2001. The political economy of direct legislation: Direct democracy and local decision-making. *Economic Policy* 16 (33): 329–67.

Feld, L. P., and G. Kirchgässner. 2001a. Does direct democracy reduce public debt? Evidence from Swiss municipalities. *Public Choice* 109: 347–70.

Feld, L. P., and J. G. Matsusaka. 2003. Budget referendums and government spending: Evidence from Swiss cantons. *Journal of Public Economics* 87: 2703–24.

Feld, L. P., and J. G. Matsusaka. 2003a. The political economy of tax structure: Some panel evidence for Swiss cantons. Mimeo, University of St. Gallen.

Feld, L. P., and M. R. Savioz. 1997. Direct democracy matters for economic performance: An empirical investigation. *Kyklos* 50: 507–38.

Feld, L. P., and Ch. A. Schaltegger. 2002. Voters as hard budget constraints: On the determination of intergovernmental grants. Mimeo, Philipps-University of Marburg.

Feld, L. P., and S. Voigt. 2003. Economic growth and judicial independence: Cross country evidence using a new set of indicators. *European Journal of Political Economy* 19: 497–527.

Feld, L. P., G. Kirchgässner, and H. Weck-Hannemann. 2002. Enlargement and the European budget: Budgetary decision-making and fiscal constraints. In B. Steunenberg (ed.): *Widening the European Union: The Politics of Institutional Change and Reform*. London: Routledge, pp. 144–62.

Freitag, M., and A. Vatter. 2000. Direkte Demokratie, Konkordanz und Wirtschaftsleistung: Ein Vergleich der Schweizer Kantone. *Schweizerische Zeitschrift für Volkswirtschaft und Statistik* 136: 579–606.

Frey, B. S. 1995. A directly democratic and federal Europe. *Constitutional Political Economy* 7: 267–79.

Frey, B. S., and G. Kirchgässner. 1993. Diskursethik, Politische Ökonomie und Volksabstimmungen. *Analyse und Kritik* 15: 129–49.

Frey, B. S., and A. Stutzer. 2000. Happiness, economy and institutions. *Economic Journal* 110: 918–38.

Frey, B. S., and A. Stutzer. 2002. *Happiness and Economics*. Princeton: Princeton University Press.

Gerber, E. R. 1996. Legislative response to the threat of initiatives. *American Journal of Political Science* 40: 99–128.

Gerber, E. R. 1996a. Legislatures, initiatives, and representation: The effects of state legislative institutions on policy. *Political Research Quarterly* 49: 263–86.

Gerber, E. R. 1999. *The Populist Paradox: Interest Group Influence and the Promise of Direct Legislation*. Princeton: Princeton University Press.

Gordon, S. 1999. *Controlling the State: Constitutionalism from Ancient Athens to Today*. Cambridge: Harvard University Press.

Grande, E. 2000. Post-national democracy in Europe. In M. T. Greven and L. W. Pauly (eds.): *Democracy beyond the State? The European Dilemma and the Emerging Global Order.* Lanham: Rowman and Littlefield, pp. 115–38.

Grillo, M. 1997. Democracy, competition and the principle of Isonomia: An economic analysis pf the political exchange as an incomplete contract. In A. Breton, G. Galeotti, P. Salmon, and R. Wintrobe (eds.): *Understanding Democracy: Economic and Political Perspectives.* New York: Cambridge University Press, pp. 47–63.

Grimm, D. 1994. *Braucht Europa eine Verfassung?* Munich: Olzog.

Hamilton, A., J. Madison, and J. Jay. [1787–88] 1982. *The Federalist Papers.* New York: Bantam Books.

Hobbes, Th. [1651, 1991] 1991. *Leviathan or the Matter, Form and Power of a Commonwealth, Ecclesiastical and Civil.* Cambridge: Cambridge University Press.

Höffe, O. 1999. *Demokratie im Zeitalter der Globalisierung.* Munich: Beck.

Hug, S. 2002. *Voices of Europe: Citizens, Referendums and European Integration.* Lanham: Rowman and Littlefield.

Hume, D. [1741] 1985. That politics may be reduced to a science. In *Essays: Moral, Political and Literary.* Indianapolis: Liberty Classics, pp. 14–31.

Kant, I. [1985] 1902. Grundlegung zur Metaphysik der Sitten. In Königlich-Preussische Akademie der Wissenschaften: *Gesammelte Schriften.* Berlin, pp. 385–463.

Kessler, A. 2003. Representative versus direct democracy: The role of informational asymmetries. CEPR Discussion Paper 3944. *Public Choice,* forthcoming.

Kiewiet, D. R., and K. Szakaly. 1996. Constitutional limitations on borrowing: An analysis of state bonded indebtedness. *Journal of Law, Economics and Organization* 12: 62–97.

Kirchgässner, G. 1992. Towards a theory of low-cost decisions. *European Journal of Political Economy* 8: 305–20.

Kirchgässner, G. 1994. Constitutional economics and its relevance for the evolution of rules. *Kyklos* 47: 321–39.

Kirchgässner, G. 1996. Bemerkungen zur Minimalmoral. *Zeitschrift für Wirtschafts- und Sozialwissenschaften* 116, 223–51.

Kirchgässner, G., L. P., Feld, and M. R. Savioz. 1999. *Die direkte Demokratie: Modern, Erfolgreich, Entwicklungs- und Exportfähig.* Basel: Helbing and Lichtenhahn.

Körkemeyer, S. 1995. *Direkte Demokratie und Europäische Integration: Zu den Möglichkeiten und Grenzen unmittelbarer Volksbeteiligung an der staatlichen Willensbildung in der Europäischen Union, dargestellt am Beispiel der Schweiz, unter Berücksichtigung der Rechtslage in den derzeitigen EU-Mitgliedstaaten.* Bern: Stämpfli.

Locke, J. [1689] 1970. *Two Treatises of Government.* Cambridge: Cambridge University Press.

Marino, A. M., and J. G. Matsusaka. 2000. Decision processes, agency problems, and information: An economic analysis of budget procedures. Mimeo. University of Southern California, Los Angeles.

Matsusaka, J. G. 1992. Economics of direct legislation. *Quarterly Journal of Economics* 107: 541–71.

Matsusaka, J. G. 1995. Fiscal effects of the voter initiative: Evidence from the last 30 years. *Journal of Political Economy* 103: 587–623.

Matsusaka, J. G. 2000. Fiscal effects of the voter initiative in the first half of the twentieth century. *Journal of Law and Economics* 43: 619–50.

Matsusaka, J. G. 2002. *For the Many or the Few: How the Initiative Process Changes American Government*. Chicago: University of Chicago Press, forthcoming.

Matsusaka, J. G., and N. M. McCarty. 2001. Political resource allocation: Benefits and costs of voter initiatives. *Journal of Law, Economics, and Organization* 17: 413–48.

Moser, P. 1996. Why is Swiss politics so stable? *Schweizerische Zeitschrift für Volkswirtschaft und Statistik* 132: 31–60.

Moser, P. 1996a. Zwischen Immobilität und Instabilität: Auswirkungen der Einführung der allgemeinen Volksinitiative und der Verfassungsgerichtsbarkeit in der Schweiz. *Schweizerische Zeitschrift für Politische Wissenschaft* 2: 233–55.

Mueller, D. C. 1996. *Constitutional Democracy*. Oxford: Oxford University Press.

Mueller, D. C. 2003. *Public Choice III*. Cambridge: Cambridge University Press.

Opp, K.-D. 1994. The role of voice in a future Europe. *Kyklos* 47: 385–402.

Papadopoulos, Y. 2002. Peut-on imaginer d'organiser des référendums à l'échelle Européenne et à quelles conditions? Mimeo. University of Lausanne.

Pommerehne, W. W. 1978. Institutional approaches to public expenditure: Empirical evidence from Swiss municipalities. *Journal of Public Economics* 9: 255–80.

Pommerehne, W. W. 1983. Private versus öffentliche Müllabfuhr—Nochmals betrachtet. *Finanzarchiv* 41: 466–75.

Pommerehne, W. W., and F. Schneider. 1985. Politisch-ökonomische Überprüfung des Kaufkraftinzidenzkonzepts: Eine Analyse der AHV-Abstimmungen von 1972 und 1978. In E. A. Brugger and R. L. Frey (eds.): *Sektoralpolitik vs. Regionalpolitik*. Rüegger: Diessenhofen, pp. 75–100.

Pommerehne, W. W., and H. Weck-Hannemann. 1996. Tax rates, tax administration and income tax evasion in Switzerland. *Public Choice* 88: 161–70.

Pommerehne, W. W., A. Hart, and L. P. Feld. 1997. Steuerhinterziehung und ihre Kontrolle in unterschiedlichen politischen Systemen. *Homo oeconomicus* 14: 469–87.

Popper, K. 1945. *The Open Society and Its Enemies, Vol. I: The Spell of Plato*. London: Routledge.

Rawls, J. A. 1971. *A Theory of Justice*. Cambridge: Harvard University Press.

Romer, Th., and H. Rosenthal. 1979. Bureaucrats versus voters: On the political economy of resource allocation by direct democracies. *Quarterly Journal of Economics* 93: 563–87.

Rousseau, J.-J. [1762] 1959. Du contrat social ou principes du droit politique. In *Œuvres complètes, Vol. 3*, Paris: Gallimard, pp. 349–470.

Schaltegger, Ch. A. 2001. The effects of federalism and democracy on the size of government: Evidence from Swiss sub-national jurisdictions. *ifo Studien* 47: 145–62.

Schaltegger, Ch. A., and L. P. Feld. 2001. On government centralization and budget referendums: Evidence from Switzerland. CESifo Working Paper 615.

Schneider, F. 1996. The design of a minimal European Federal Union: Some ideas using the Public Choice approach. In J. C. Pardo and F. Schneider (eds.): *Current Issues in Public Choice*. Cheltenham: Edward Elgar, pp. 203–20.

Steunenberg, B. 1992. Referendum, initiative and veto power: Budgetary decision-making in local government. *Kyklos* 45: 501–29.

Torgler, B. 2002. Tax morale and institutions. *European Journal of Political Economy*, forthcoming.

Vatter, A., and M. Freitag. 2002. Die Janusköpfigkeit von Verhandlungsdemokratien: Zur Wirkung von Konkordanz, direkter Demokratie und dezentraler Entscheidungsstrukturen auf den öffentlichen Sektor der Schweizer Kantone. *Swiss Political Science Review* 8: 53–80.

Vaubel, R. 1988. Möglichkeiten einer erfolgreichen Beschäftigungspolitik. In H. Scherf (ed.): *Beschäftigungsprobleme hochentwickelter Volkswirtschaften*. Berlin: Duncker und Humblot, pp. 17–35.

Vaubel, R. 1994. The political economy of centralization and the European Community. *Public Choice* 81: 151–190.

Vaubel, R. 1996. Constitutional safeguards against centralization in federal states: An international cross-section analysis. *Constitutional Political Economy* 7: 79–102.

Vaubel, R. 2002. Die Politische Ökonomie des Europäischen Verfassungskonvents. *Wirtschaftsdienst* 82: 636–40.

Weiler, J. H. H. 1997. The European Union belongs to its citizens: Three immodest proposals. *European Law Review* 22: 150–56.

Weiler, J. H. H. 1999. *The Constitution of Europe: "Do the New Clothes Have an Emperor?" and Other Essays on European Integration*. Cambridge: Cambridge University Press.

Wicksell, J. 1896. *Finanztheoretische Untersuchungen nebst Darstellung und Kritik des Steuerwesens Schwedens*. Jena: Gustav Fischer.

Zürn, M. 1996. Über den Staat und die Demokratie im europäischen Mehrebenensystem. *Politische Vierteljahresschrift* 37: 27–55.

Zürn, M. 2000. Democratic governance beyond the nation-state: The EU and other international institutions. *European Journal of International Relations* 6: 183–221.

10 Bringing the European Union Closer to Its Citizens: Conclusions from the Conference

Charles B. Blankart and
Dennis C. Mueller

10.1 Introduction

What are the institutional requirements for an European Union that will serve the interests of its citizens? What has to be done so that the claim of the Declaration of Laeken of 2001 that "European institutions must be brought closer to its citizens" can be fulfilled? Some answers have been given in the preceding chapters of this book. Others will be advanced in this chapter, with the goal of highlighting the main issues that emerged out of the discussion of the European constitution in Munich.

The chapter is organized as follows: We start with a discussion of the common goals that underlie the creation of the European Union as we see them, and as proclaimed in the Draft of the first six articles of the constitution. Section 10.3 takes up the central issue of whether the Union is best organized as a confederation, a federation or some hybrid of the two. Sections 10.4 to 10.6 deal with the rules of collective decision making in the ongoing political process. The key issue to be resolved is how an open political process can be organized so that all citizens can contribute their views and participate in the collective decisions. We propose a bottom-up democratic process with authority extending from the wine grower on a distant island in the Aegean Sea up to Brussels and not from an autonomous center in Brussels down to the Aegean islands. Only such an approach can achieve the proclaimed goal of the new constitution as declared at Laeken of bringing the European institutions "closer to its citizens." In the concluding section 10.8 our findings will be compared with the emerging constitution as proposed by the Convention and the question will be asked as to how likely it is that the political process in the European Union achieves this attractive goal.

10.2 The Goals of European Union

In chapter 1 Brennan and Hamlin correctly emphasize, that the original purpose in founding the European Union was to prevent future wars among the member countries. This objective has been achieved, and consequently the European Union must be regarded as a resounding success regardless of its other achievements and failures. Appropriately, the first entry of the draft of Article 3: The Union's objectives, begins: "The Union's aim is to promote peace...."[1]

Other entries of Article 3 are more problematic, however. We select but three examples:

• The third entry of Article I-3 presents as an EU goal "aiming at full employment." Of course, the use of the word "aiming" leaves open the possibility that the goal is never achieved or even approached, but it also creates the impression that the Union will be responsible for achieving this goal and that it will try to achieve it by monetary policy, presumably. Article I-29 makes clear, however, that the goal of European Central Bank is to maintain price stability and that other goals such as full employment must not be pursued at the costs of this primary goal.[2]

• Article I-3 goes on to proclaim several additional goals for forming the Union including "social justice and protection." As with aiming at full employment, one can argue that the goal of social protection is so vague that it does not actually commit the Union to any specific actions. Why list it as a goal then? To do so runs the danger of creating future tensions within the Union, if some groups complain that the Union has not provided them with social protection.

• Article I-3 also states as goals of the EU "solidarity between generations and protection of children's rights." The former presumably implies some redistribution from the young to the older people, usually through a pay-as-you-go pension system, implying that the children are to be burdened with a substantial tax since the population is not growing.

To avoid creating false expectations about the purpose and potential of the European Union by setting conflicting or ambiguous goals, we thus favor a simpler and shorter statement of goals for the Union:

Article 3 (according to our formulation): The Union's aim is to promote peace and the well-being of its citizens through the creation of a free single market, and an economic, monetary, and political union.

10.3 The Structure of the European Union: Confederation or Federation?

In several chapters and during the discussions, the issue came up as to whether the EU should be organized as a confederation of autonomous states, a federation with a central level of government at the EU level and the nation states serving as "regional governments," or as some hybrid of the two. In addition the issue was addressed, most directly in chapter 8 by Hix, Noury, and Roland, as to whether there should be one or more presidents of the European Union.

Currently the European Union is a hybrid of the two alternative forms of representation, with the Commission and Council appearing as if they belong in a confederate state, and the Parliament having the structure that one might find in a federation. This structure has evolved from the various treaty changes that have characterized the European Union's history. We know of no theoretical demonstration nor empirical evidence that suggests this structure to be the best of all possible structures for revealing Europeans' preferences for the goods and services that should be supplied at the EU level. Indeed, this structure undoubtedly contributes to the paradox that the EU does not provide the many public goods that it should, and yet engages in numerous policies, like the CAP, that actually harm a vast majority of Europeans (see Blankart and Kirchner, chapter 6 in this volume; Mueller 1997). An important step toward improving the quality of collective decision-making in the European Union would be to choose a suitable structure of government. We review the three options.

Confederation

A confederation is the optimal structure for making democratic collective decisions in the European Union, if the preferences of EU citizens for EU policies are homogeneous within countries and heterogeneous across them. The elected government of a member country can then speak with one voice for all of its citizens. In fact the members of a confederation *are* the governments representing their citizens and not the citizens themselves. The system is characterized as one of "intergovernmental cooperation." During the first quarter century of its existence, the European Union essentially functioned as a confederation, with the European Council, to which the member countries' governments send delegates, serving as the legislature and the Commission serving as an executive branch administration. De facto the European

Union still largely functions as a confederation, with the heads of state playing the leading role in deciding major policy questions and the Council and Parliament falling into line once they have. Once Schröder and Chirac agreed at the end of 2002 that the CAP should be extended to 2006, the issue was decided. If the constellation of citizen preferences on EU-level issues is such as to make a confederation the optimal structure, then it can easily be achieved by abolishing the EU Parliament.

Citizens are able to exercise control over collective decisions at the Union level mainly through national elections but also through popular vote where referenda exist. It may, however, be argued that this is insufficient, since many member states lack the check of referenda. The European Constitutional Group (2003) has proposed therefore that a Chamber of Parliamentarians be created, consisting of a sample of national parliamentarians. The members of this chamber would have veto power over EU legislation, if they believed that it would contradict their voters' preferences (see section 10.6).

A Federation

The members of a federation are the citizens, not national states. A federalist governmental structure is optimal if Europeans' preferences for EU-level goods and services are heterogeneous within countries. Greens exist in all countries and a Green party wins votes in all countries. In this situation there should be EU-wide parties competing for votes in all countries, with each citizen's vote getting the same weight regardless of her country of residence. Such a situation would eliminate the overrepresentation of the smaller countries in the Parliament, a feature that violates the one-man, one-vote principle, and that is incompatible with the notion that a federalist structure is optimal. In addition to modifying the way in which seats in the Parliament are filled, a move to a federation would entail shifting decision-making authority from the Council to the Parliament.

A Hybrid

It is possible that *some* of the decisions that have to be made at the EU level fulfill the criteria that make a confederation optimal, and others fulfill the criteria for federation. If this is the case, then it may be optimal to retain both the Council and the Parliament in the optimal structure, *but not under the present procedural rules*. Rather a constitutional bifurcation of issues that are to be decided at the EU level should be made with those issues that suit a confederate mode of decision-making assigned to the Council and the rest going to the Parliament.

A Presidential System

Most countries have a president of one form or another, but in many cases they play little role in the country's collective-decision process. In a strong presidential system, the president can both propose legislation and veto legislation passed by the legislature. The more difficult it is for the legislature to override a president's veto, the stronger is the president. Strong presidential systems are favored by those who wish to have checks and balances in the governmental structure.

In chapter 8 Hix, Noury, and Roland showed that the party identification of a president of the European Union is dependent on the way in which this person is elected. The chapter leaves open to some extent, however, the issue of whether or not the European Union should have a strong president. Currently there is a proposal for an elected president of the Commission, and a second proposal to elect a president of the Council. In both cases it appears that the presidents would not be strong in the sense of having strong veto powers, but rather would have some strength through their agenda-setting roles. With respect to the proposal for an elected president of the Council, the major advantage of the proposal seems to be to do away with the present rotating presidency.

Although some alternative to the rotating presidency must be found, we do not see a significant improvement arising from introducing a presidency with strong veto powers. Rather, if the European Union remains effectively a confederation, the EU central government will continue to be kept in check by the national governments, who control its sources of revenue. This brings us to the assignment problem.

10.4 The Assignment Problem

EU Level and Member State Provision of Public Services

Regardless of whether the EU is organized as a confederation or a federation it faces the assignment problem. Which public goods and services are supplied at the EU level, and which are left to the states? This question is addressed in chapter 3 by Salmon. The answer given in the economics literature depends on the extent of spillover from the goods and services provided. When these spillovers span the entire Union, it should be responsible for providing the good or service. Goods or services with narrower spillovers should be supplied by subsets of the nation states, the individual states acting alone, or regional and municipal governments within the nation states. A large fraction of the public services that are of most interest to citizens, such as education, streets and highways, police and fire protection, and sanitation, are best supplied at the nation state or lower local levels. The number of public goods with spillover across the entire European Union is small, and will even shrink as the EU expands geographically.

A standard claim of the fiscal federalism literature is that redistribution activities should be assigned to the central government. There are both normative and positive justifications for this assignment. The two strongest normative arguments for redistribution rest on the existence of either altruism or uncertainty over future incomes within the population. If a Dane gets displeasure from seeing or contemplating another Dane living in poverty, she may obtain utility from transferring part of her income to the poor person. If this altruistic satisfaction is present for transfers to all Danes, and not just those in the contributor's local community, redistribution at the national level is justified.

Uncertainty over future incomes can be real or self-imposed. If a Dane is uncertain about whether she might fall into poverty at some place and some time within Denmark in the future, she may out of pure self-interest favor national redistribution programs. Alternatively, she may impose uncertainty over future positions upon herself as an ethical act. If from behind the veil of ignorance she contemplates being a Dane anywhere in Denmark, she will favor national redistribution programs.

The positive case for redistribution at the national level rests on the assumption that poor individuals will respond to differences in welfare payments across local communities by moving to the communities with the highest benefits. If it is technically or legally impossible to discriminate between local residents and immigrants into a local community, communities with generous redistribution programs will be overwhelmed with poor immigrants and will be forced to cut their transfers offered to the poor.

The normative and positive arguments for the centralization of redistribution seem quite compelling for a highly mobile and homogeneous country like the United States. Most Americans can realistically contemplate living in other cities or states over their lifetime, and identify with their "fellow Americans," even when they are not mobile. The arguments for centralization seem less compelling when applied to the European Union. Does a Dane get as much utility from seeing the income of a poor Greek raised as she does for a poor Dane? Does she identify with other Europeans as readily as she does with other Danes? If the answers to these questions are no, then there is no normative case for shifting redistribution programs to the EU level. Nor is there a positive case. Everyone living in the EU carries a passport from a nation state. It is technically simple to base eligibility for transfers within a country on the possession of citizenship in that country or perhaps proof of permanent residence. The redistribution programs of nation states need not be overwhelmed by poor migrants, *if their benefits are restricted to their own citizens.*

Hans-Werner Sinn, however, pointed out in his introductory statement to the Conference that some elements in the proposed constitution could easily lead to precisely the sort of destructive migration just described. Article I-8 of the Draft proclaims "the right to move and reside freely within the territory of the Member States," and makes all citizens of Member States "citizens of the Union." The Charter of Fundamental Rights, which the Draft proposes to make part of the constitution, guarantees all Union citizens a plethora of economic and social rights. If these various elements of the proposed constitution were interpreted by the courts in such a way that migrants from poor members of the EU could quickly have claims on the same unemployment, pension, and welfare benefits in rich countries as their own citizens have, the welfare states of the Union, indeed perhaps the Union itself, would quickly become undone.

EU Level and National Taxation

In addition to assigning authority for making expenditures and transfers, the constitution should assign authority for raising revenues. In most nation states taxation authority is concentrated at the central level, while much spending authority is assigned to lower levels. This arrangement gives rise to "the common pool problem" of local authorities' overspending.

Fortunately in the EU, taxation authority is concentrated at the nation state level with the central, EU-level government having almost no independent authority. Thus no common pool problems exist other than those arising within the nation states. Common pool problems at the EU level can be avoided, if new EU-level revenue sources are tied to new expenditure programs. Indeed, because EU expenditures have been largely financed up until now through contributions from the member states, the possibility exists at the EU level to establish "the Wicksellian connection" to combine each new expenditure program with a proposed revenue source to finance it. As chapter 6 by Blankart and Kirchner makes clear, all EU expenditure programs other than the CAP have initially been financed by set formulas, and this largely explains why outlays on these other programs have remained in bounds, while the CAP has escalated out of control. Indeed, the early budgetary regime with earmarked budgets and earmarked contributions per member state made budgetary decisions much more transparent compared to the general fund financing introduced in 1971. Each finance minister and, indeed, each citizen could easily see how much she had to pay, for what, and for whom, if expenditure programs were closely tied to sources of finance.

The Convention also examined whether the European Union should have its own taxes. Several proposals have been made in recent years. A CO_2 tax, for example, could be designed exclusively for the European Union and raised by the member states' according to an EU regulation, and then transferred directly to the EU. In such a way, already now, net revenues of customs duties are levied and transferred to the European Union. What other EU taxes there should be is not so easy to see, for most tax bases are already utilized by the member states. Of course, the European Union could raise a second tax according to its own rules on a base already taxed by member states. Such a tax would obviously interfere into the tax authority of the member states whose tax power on the particular tax would be impaired. Moreover such double taxation tends to increase the deadweight costs of taxation dramatically.[3]

Most of these problems could be avoided by tax sharing. The European Union would receive a percentage of a tax already levied by the member states. Such a solution is much simpler, though it would require some tax harmonization among member states. The revenues of that tax would, however, enter into the pool of revenues of the general budget of the member state from which a part would be withdrawn to pay for EU programs. Rather than adopting this form of earmarked tax to finance the EU, it would be preferable to stay with the current practice of having member states make contributions to the EU.

Within a regime of contributions, three alternatives have been discussed: Contributions attached to the population, to GNP, and to global tax revenue. Population might be preferable from an enforcement standpoint. For the national authorities cannot disguise the base so easily. GNP may be attractive from an equity standpoint. For larger countries would, ceteris paribus, pay more than smaller countries, and high-income countries would, ceteris paribus, pay more than low-income countries. Basing contributions on published GNP figures, however, excludes the shadow economy. Tax revenue as a base, in contrast, would exclude tax evasion. It would, however, generate incentives for the national authorities to hold the tax burden down to economize on own contributions to the EU, and for the EU administration not to overcentralize its activities.[4]

What is important, however, is that the decisions on contribution rates remain tied to the unanimous agreement of the member states. For as long as the expenditure side is institutionally separated from the revenue side, and earmarking of particular contributions to particular purposes cannot take place, large payers with relatively little voting power can hardly escape their exploitation by smaller member states with relatively larger voting power (but see section 10.5).

The Subsidiarity Principle

The purpose of amending the subsidiarity principle to the Maastricht Treaty of 1992 (e.g., Article 3b, Article 5 EC) was to put a brake on the ever-increasing centralization of competences in the European Union. The principle has been of little relevance, however, for it has lacked institutional procedures to enforce it. The Draft of a European Constitution makes some progress insofar as it delineates a procedure attached in a protocol to Article I-9 (par. 3) by which one-quarter or one-third of all the votes allocated to the national parliaments can submit their "reasoned opinion" of why they consider that a proposal of the Commission does not comply with the principle of subsidiarity. It is certainly a good idea to entrust the national parliaments with the task of watching over centralization in the European Union, because neither the Commission, nor the Council, nor the EU Parliament, has an interest in stopping the process of centralization, which has contributed so much to their power. The Convention and its Presidium have, however, only gone half way. They have not dared to grant decision-making power on subsidiarity to an institution such as the "Chamber of Parliamentarians," as proposed by the European Constitutional Group

(2003). Merely creating a consultative procedure as laid down in a protocol is not enough (see section 10.3).

10.5 Parliamentary Voting Rules in the Council and in the Parliament

Qualified Majorities

Chapters 5 and 6 by Widgrén and Blankart and Kirchner discuss the problem of choosing a voting rule for making collective decisions. The voting rule appropriate for a confederation is the unanimity rule, since membership is voluntary and exit costs may be low, particularly when the confederation is young. Any attempt to enforce a non-unanimity rule in these early stages, would lead to outvoted minorities and possibly to the breaking apart of the confederation. In fact the unanimity rule has been used in the Council, particularly during the Union's first decades. With the growing integration of the member countries' relationships, however, exit costs have risen and the Union has gradually shifted toward making more decisions with qualified majorities, which is fully in accordance with the lessons from public choice (Buchanan and Tullock 1962, pp. 63–91).

In chapter 5 Widgrén adds to a large literature illustrating the consequences of choosing different qualified majorities. We have nothing to add to this discussion other than to point out that the logic behind the choice of a qualified majority, like 72 percent, to reduce the number of issues passing that harm European citizens, applies equally to both the Council and the Parliament. Thus a federalist EU with all decision-making authority concentrated in the Parliament might well function better under a super-qualified majority rule.

A qualified majority rule is halfway between simple majority rule and unanimity rule. On the one hand, it reduces the probability of minorities being outvoted without, however, eliminating it. On the other hand, small minorities are able to block an issue strategically. Their veto implies no costs to themselves. They may simply say "no" and are not motivated to make a constructive proposal how to solve the issue.

Voting by Veto and Other Options

Such obstructive behavior can be overcome by the voting by veto procedure as developed by Mueller (1978) and proposed by Blankart and Kirchner in chapter 6 for collective decisions in the Council. Under the procedure each minister submits one proposal. An additional, status quo proposal is added to form the proposal set. An order of veto-voting is determined by lot, after which each Council member eliminates one proposal from the proposal set. The proposal that is not vetoed wins. Voting by veto has several attractive properties as a procedure for the EU Council. First, it always produces an outcome. Second, it provides an incentive to cooperate—a veto cannot be exercised unless a member has contributed to the solution of a problem by submitting a proposal—abstainers have no veto (see above). Third, its use should eliminate the tensions that arise because some countries are large net losers from certain programs, since these countries will be able to veto such discriminatory programs. More generally, voting by veto gives each country an incentive to increase the attractiveness of its proposals by adding programs to them that benefit all countries. Thus, over time, one would expect the proportion of the EU budget devoted to public-good-like programs to expand relative to that devoted to pure redistribution programs.

As each minister in the Council would be forced to openly make a proposal to settle a common issue, voters at home would learn more about their politicians' behavior in Brussels.

Up until today, the decision process in the Council has been opaque with few, if any, citizens knowing what their government's role has been in reaching the final outcome. Accordingly party positions on EU matters seldom play an important role in national elections, and these elections cannot be interpreted as referenda on member country actions in the Council. By forcing each country's representatives to make specific proposals, the use of voting by veto would provide EU citizens with the information needed to judge their government's actions at the EU level, and would make these actions a part of a voter's calculus in national elections, thus helping to close the "democratic deficit" at the EU level.

The same normative arguments, which make voting by veto attractive over a qualified majority rule in the Council, apply to its use in the Parliament. As a parliamentary voting rule, it would work as follows: Each party caucuses and agrees on its proposal for the resolution of a particular question, say, an expenditures tax package. If there are seven parties in the parliament this produces seven proposals with the status quo making the eighth proposal. If the Commission remained the de facto executive branch of the EU, it could be given the right to submit the eighth proposal leaving it to the other parties to propose the status quo if they so chose.[5] Each party then meets a second time and ranks the eight proposals and announces its rankings. A computer can then randomly order the members of the parliament and use the announced rankings to determine a winner under the assumption that each member's ranking of the proposals corresponds to that of her party. The voting stage can be over in a minute. When used in a parliament, voting by veto would supply two pieces of information to citizens, which they could use to evaluate the different parties—the proposals each made and how they ranked them.

Voting by veto is but one of several voting procedures that public choice scholars have invented, which improve upon the class of qualified majority rules.[6] The objection that they are too complicated to be employed in real world situations does not seem defensible, particularly in the context of the European Union. First of all, in any context, voting by veto is not that difficult to understand. Second, the *normative* logic underpinning the voting rule presently in use in the Council must be abstruse to the citizen in the street. The allocation of votes across countries violates the basic principle of one person, one vote, and the required majority of 71.264 percent to pass an issue seems like a number picked out of the air. To the extent that this particular choice of majority has a normative underpinning, it rests on calculations of voting power indexes and simulation results that no citizen can understand. In comparison, voting by veto's normative properties are relatively transparent.

10.6 Direct Democracy

Chapter 9 by Feld and Kirchgässner makes a convincing argument for the inclusion of referenda in the set of institutions for revealing individual preferences in the EU. Four different settings can be envisaged for employing referenda in the EU: EU-wide referenda on EU policies, national referenda on EU-policies, ex ante EU-wide referenda on constitutional questions, and ex post referenda on "urgent" constitutional issues.

EU-wide Referenda

Allowing citizens the possibility of calling EU-wide referenda on EU decisions can serve to correct both errors of commission and errors of omission by EU authorities. The justification for referenda is straightforward if the Union is regarded as a federation, whose citizens want to check the decisions made by their representatives in the European Parliament, whenever the latter deviate in a particular case too far from their voters' preferences. Hence an EU-wide referendum may be regarded as an institution contributing to the solution of the principal-agent problem. The relevance of the referendum lies not in the fact that a vote might take place on every issue, but rather as a potential safeguard for citizens, ensuring them that their representatives do not choose outcomes too far from the citizens' preferences.

If the Union is considered as a confederation whose members are the governments, the case for referenda is less obvious. Governments can, however, agree on the European level to have referenda for major changes (see Declaration of Laeken 2001).

Referenda are most relevant, in our view, if the Union is a type of a *hybrid system* as it appears today: a system situated somewhere between a confederation and a federation in which the Council as well as the European Parliament both have responsibilities, but none has full responsibility (the worst of all cases), and neither the elections to the member states' Parliaments nor those to the EU Parliament serve as effective checks on EU policy, not to speak of them as vehicles for revealing citizens' preferences. Under such circumstances EU-wide referenda would be very useful to bind political actions closer to voters' preferences, be it for introducing a policy or for negating an enacted policy.

The technical obstacles to initiating such referenda are, on the other hand, formidable. If the same practices are used in the EU as in nation states, namely petitions signed by X percent of the population, even an X of 5 percent would necessitate obtaining some 20,000,000 or so signatures in an expanded Union. The fact that it will be more difficult to introduce referenda at the EU level than in individual countries does not imply, however, that this option should be ignored.

Referenda on EU Policies at the National Level

A case for referenda can also be made if the Union is regarded as a *confederacy* consisting of a voluntary association of sovereign states. Each state enters the agreement expecting to be better off within the confederacy than outside of it. Each state should be free to exit—perhaps subject to certain conditions—should it find that it is not better off in the confederacy. A right to secede is a logical component of any confederate agreement. Indeed, the Convention has endorsed this view in Artical I-59 of the Draft.

So long as collective decisions in a confederacy are made by unanimity, a member can protect itself from adverse decisions by exercising the veto right inherent in the use of the unanimity rule. The secession option is not needed. Once the confederacy begins making decisions using a less-than-unanimity rule, however, as is now the case in the European Union, a member state can be harmed by collective decisions, and the secession option may help guarantee that its net benefits from participation in the confederacy remain positive over time. A secession clause is a desirable element in any agreement establishing a confederation of states.

Secession is, however, an extreme and costly way to express disagreement with a decision taken at the EU level. A less costly alternative would be to allow a member state to nullify the decision within its own borders. Such a nullification option might impose costs on the other members of the confederation and, if too frequently exercised, could lead to the complete unravelling of the confederation. Thus an opt-out option for member countries should require a substantial consensus in any country exercising the option. Here a compulsory national referendum might play a useful role. One possibility would be to require only a national referendum with, say, a 75 percent majority needed to nullify a policy of the confederation in the member country. A second option might be requiring a 75 percent majority in the parliament of the member country, and a simple majority in a national referendum.[7]

Referenda on Constitutional Amendments

The case for referenda is strongest when the constitution itself, namely the document that delineates the rules of the political game, is at stake. In a *federation*, whose members are the citizens, an explicit endorsement by the citizens would seem to be a necessity to establish the legitimacy of the constitutional contract. If the citizens have not participated directly in the writing of the contract, then such an endorsement can only be obtained through a referendum.

A *confederation*, in contrast, is *a contractual joining of states*, not of citizens, and logically does not require a separate endorsement by the citizens, once their representative governments have agreed to the terms of the contract. As shown in the introduction to this chapter, however, a central objective in creating the convention has been to close the democratic deficit by bringing the institutions closer to its citizens. Up until now, the citizens have played only a passive role in the constitution drafting process. The political elite of the Union created the convention and filled it with its own members. If final ratification of the document emerging from this process requires only the endorsement of the same political elite, it is difficult to see in what way the exercise has brought the citizens of Europe in closer touch with European Union political institutions. Requiring the ratification of a new European Union constitution in all member countries would be a desirable first step in introducing direct democracy into the Union.

Urgent Constitutional Amendments

The European Union's authority to act is constrained by the principle of the conferral of competences of Article I-9 of the Draft. Therefore the Union can assume new competencies only if the constitution is amended which requires basically the same procedure as that of a reform of the constitution (see above). The Draft envisages, however, a flexibility clause Article I-17: "If action by the Union should prove necessary ... and the Constitution has not provided the necessary powers, the Council, acting unanimously on a proposal of the Commission and after obtaining consent of the European Parliament, shall take appropriate measures." This article may open the door to discretionary action. It is true that unforeseen circumstances may require a quick reaction, even if the EU has no competence to take action in the particular field. Therefore a simplified procedure without (immediate) ratification seems to be necessary. But it is not evident why the usual ratification procedure cannot be resumed ex post. The Union competences under discussion would simply expire if ratification by national parliaments (and, as we suggest, by the voters in a referendum) had not been reached within, say, one year's time.

The Views of the Convention

It seems that the members of the Convention were not willing to allow popular votes in the Union neither for adoption of the constitution nor for constitutional changes. Rather the traditional ratification procedures known from the Treaties are to be applied when the constitution is adopted or revised (Articles IV-7 and IV-6, par. 3, respectively).

10.7 Citizenship and Rights

As the Draft makes each citizen of a member state a "citizen of the Union," and confers upon each Union citizen a long and broad set of rights, there are two dangers in this feature of the proposed constitution. They relate in particular to the Charter of Fundamental Rights included in part II of the Draft.

The first danger is that many rights proclaimed in the Charter, like that offering families "social protection," will prove to be unenforceable in the courts. Instead of the constitution becoming a contract among the citizens of Europe bestowing meaningful rights and liberties on all citizens, it becomes a vacuous list of the kinds of platitudes that politicians utter during elections but fail to deliver when in office—full employment, social protection of families, consumer protection, and so on. Once European citizens realize that the much of the constitution offers them no meaningful rights but is instead merely a list of "European values" as defined by its drafters, the gap between the citizens and the political elite who governs it may grow even wider.

The second danger is that some provisions of the constitution, which threaten to overturn national laws and programs, will be enforced, and will produce bitter conflicts between member states and the European Union and its Court of Justice. Mueller's chapter 4 gives several examples of rights contained in the Charter, which, if vigorously enforced, would strike down laws and constitutional articles of some of the member states. We have also noted above, that a liberal interpretation of rights to migration, residency, and economic security could tremendously overburden the welfare systems of the richer member states, again leading to tensions between their citizens and the Union. Thus the first danger is that the new constitution becomes a meaningless addition to the list of treaties that delineate the EU's institutional structure. The second danger is that it undoes that structure.

Our reading of the situation in Europe today is that there exists considerable heterogeneity across its nation states with respect to not only income and state of economic development, but also with respect to the basic views of citizens regarding rights and freedoms and the historical context that shapes these views. This underlying heterogeneity argues for having *no set of rights defined in the EU constitution*, with all EU citizens' rights being provided by the constitutions of their nation states and the European Convention for the Protection of Human Rights and Fundamental Freedoms, which all member countries have accepted. The constitution of the European Union should contain only a short statement of the goals of the Union, as given above, a description of its institutions for making collective decisions, and a description of the process for adoption and amendment of the constitution. Should the cultural and economic differences that divide Europe today eventually disappear, the assumptions that justify defining rights and citizenship at the level of the Union will hold, and a new constitution containing a new set of rights can be written. If and when that day comes, we hope that the citizens will be given a greater opportunity than in the present case to express their views on what should go into the constitution.

10.8 Conclusion: Values or Rules?

All constitutions contain both an expression of the values of the polity and a statement of the institutions and rules under which it will operate in the future. Our view is that the rules portion of a new EU constitution should dominate over a list of values. All Europeans wish to have peace, prosperity, and freedom, and favor the rule of law and tolerance of opposing opinions and life styles. Greatly extending this list of shared values, as has been proposed in the Draft constitution, risks imposing definitions of values held by the political elite on the citizens of all member states. Such proclamations of collective values by "supreme authorities" we tend to associate with totalitarian regimes. They have no place in a constitution that is supposed to enhance the role of EU citizens in its democratic process. Thus we favor leaving the more elaborate statements of values and rights to the national levels.

In contrast, we feel that considerable attention should be given by those drafting the new constitution to writing a new set of rules for the EU's collective decision process. A fundamental question to be decided is whether the European Union should be organized as a confederation or a federation. The answer to this question depends on the distribution of individual preferences across Europe. If the future distribution of preferences for EU policies will be characterized by homogeneity within countries and differences across them, a confederation is appropriate. If, however, differences of preferences prevail intra-regionally as well as inter-regionally, a federation is justified.

If one decides that a confederation is the optimal structure, then something like the Council should be the locus of legislative power and the Parliament should be abolished. If a federation is optimal, then the Council should be abolished and the locus of legislative power placed in the Parliament. In either case, a system of checks and balances through a Chamber of Parliamentarians and/or through direct democracy would protect against excessive centralization of power. Alternatively, one might decide that some EU-level decisions lend themselves to a confederate structure, others to a federate structure, and retain both legislative bodies with each responsible for different sets of decisions.

Traditionally changes or amendments of the Treaty had been ratified following Article 313 of the EC Treaty, that is, by a decision of the Council with later ratification by the member states' parliaments. We proposed for the new constitution that the final confirmation should be made by a referendum in all member states. So politicians, in the Convention, would anticipate citizens' opinions, and the preceding discussion would be more bottom up than top down. As the new EU constitution, however, will be ratified in the traditional way, clearly not much will have changed, and the constitution-making process will continue to be the top-down now and in the future. The hope that a bottom-up process will evolve and, following the Declaration of Laeken, "the European institutions [will] be brought closer to its citizens" will be in vain.

To put it differently, if a referendum were to take place, and the proposed new constitution contains most of the elements that we have criticized above, we suspect that it would be rejected by the citizens of several member states. A rejection of the new constitution would be a bitter pill for its drafters and many others of the political elite in Europe to swallow. But perhaps it would also lead to a period of self-reflection by the elite over why the constitution was rejected. Perhaps it would lead to the recognition that an open debate about the content of a new constitution involving both the citizens and members of the elite should take place *before* a constitutional convention is called, and the citizens should play a direct role in its convening. Eventually perhaps such a convention might actually be convened, and European citizens would get a new constitution that serves their interests and receives their overwhelming endorsement.

Notes

1. All references to articles of the EU constitution in this chapter are to the draft of the Convention released on June 27, 2003, and will be referred to simply as "Draft."

2. "The primary objective of the Bank shall be to maintain price stability. Without prejudice to the objective of price stability, it shall support the general economic policies in the Union with a view to contributing to the achievement of the Union's objectives."

3. See Sobel (1997).

4. See Buchanan and Lee (1994).

5. If the Commission is to have a popularly elected president, one might argue that he—like the US president—speaks for all of Europe. Allowing him to make a proposal would make the position of the president of more interest to the European citizen.

6. See Mueller (2003, chs. 7 and 8).

7. In addition, to allowing a country to opt out of a decision of the confederation, one could allow it to nullify the decision across the entire confederation. These two options along with secession are discussed further in Mueller (1996, ch. 21).

References

Buchanan, J. M., and Lee, D. R. 1994. On a fiscal constitution for the European Union. *Journal des économistes et des études humaines* 5 (2–3): 219–32.

Buchanan, J. M., and Tullock, G. 1962. *The Calculus of Consent*. Ann Arbor: University of Michigan Press.

European Council. 2001. *The Future of the EU: Declaration of Laeken*. Brussels: EU.

European Constitutional Group. 2003. A Basic "Constitutional Treaty" for the European Union. London: *http://www.european-constitutional-group.org/*.

Mueller, D. C. 1978. Voting by veto. *Journal of Public Economics*, 10 (1), pp. 57–75.

Mueller, D. C. 1996. *Constitutional Democracy*. Oxford: Oxford University Press.

Mueller, D. C. 1997. Federalism and the European Union: A constitutional perspective. *Public Choice* 90: 255–80.

Mueller, D. C. 2003. *Public Choice III*. Cambridge: Cambridge University Press.

Sobel, Russell S. 1997. Optimal taxation in a federal system of governments. *Southern Economic Journal* 64: 468–85.

Index

Accession treaty, as contract, 44
Accountability, of European Commission or European Union, 194, 198, 203
Ackerman, Bruce, 45
Acquis communautaire principle, 41, 43–44, 46, 56
  and Britain's acceptance of Community's own resources, 123
  entrenchment of, 48–49
Agenda-setting game, 88
Aggregate uncertainty, in European integration, 37–38, 40, 55, 59n.15
Agricultural Fund, 119, 120–22, 127
Agriculture Council, 139
Aid policies, 10. *See also* Agricultural Fund; Common Agricultural Policy; Redistribution; Social Fund
Ambiguities, in relationship between constitutions, 2
Amsterdam Treaty, 125, 129, 151, 173
Aristotle, 205
Assignment problem, 241–46
Assumption, about rationality and goals, xvi
Assurance Game, and war, 6
Austria
  and EU budget incidence, 115
  threat position of, 124
Autonomy, popular desire for, 20

Banzhaf index or measure, 87–88, 100, 105n.9
Bargaining
  and constraints on moving ahead, 51
  under rule of unanimity, 46–48
Benelux states
  and EU budget incidence, 115
  threat position of, 124

Berlin summit (1999), 127
Big bang strategy, 53
Britain. *See* United Kingdom
"Bruges group," 25
Buchanan, J. M., 206, 207, 220
Budget of European Union, 133–34
  incidence of, 113–17
  and incomplete contracts, 111 (*see also* Theory of incomplete contracts)
  literature on, 112–13
  projections for future of, 128–30
  and redistribution, 109–10, 111–12, 113, 117–28, 134–35
  way out of deadlock on, 130–33
Budget referenda, 204
Bush, George, Jr., 9
Bush, George, Sr., 9

California, referenda in, 211
CAP. *See* Common Agricultural Policy
Centralization, of EU institutions, 27–28, 42, 245
Chamber of Parliamentarians, 240, 245–46, 254
Charter of Fundamental Rights of the European Union, 62, 77, 78, 252
  citizen rights under, 78–79, 80, 243
  and Convention, 79–80
  preamble to, 81
Checks and balances, 19–20, 241, 254
Chicken Game, and war, 6
Chirac, Jacques, 169, 198, 240
Cicero, 205–206
Citizen rights within European Union, 77–80. *See also* Rights
Citizenship, 61, 62, 253
  in European Union, 67–70
  and European Union structure, 61

Citizenship (cont.)
  and immigration, 63, 83n.4
  optimal with dispersed populations and heterogeneous preferences, 66–67
  optimal with heterogeneous preferences, 63–65
  optimal with heterogeneous preferences and separated communities, 65–66
  optimal with homogeneous preference, 62–63
Civil Protection Council, 143
Clausewitz, Carl von, 19
Coalition, formation of, 183
Codecision procedure, 89, 90–91, 92, 94, 96, 97, 99–100, 139, 140, 151
  inefficiency of, 97–99
  and USC principle, 103
Collective choice procedures, xv
Collective decision-making, external costs of, 64
College of Commissioners, 179, 199n.3
Cologne European Council (1999), 16
Committee of Permanent Representatives. *See* Coreper
Common Agricultural Policy (CAP), 69, 239, 240
  and EU budget, 114, 119–22
  expenditures on, 244
Common Foreign and Security Policy, 44
Common Market, 118
  and EU budget incidence, 115, 119
"Common pool problem," 243–44
Community method, of legislative policy-making, 160
"Community's own resources," 122
Competitive federalism, 25–26, 34, 39–40. *See also* Federalism
  vs. competition within single-market nexus, 30–31
  and efficiency, 31–34
  and minimax criterion, 31
  opposition to, 25
Compromises, and direct democratic decision-making, 210
Conciliation Committee, 91, 96, 97–99, 103
Confederation
  and citizenship, 66, 66–67
  and European Council, 141
  European Union as, 68–69, 70, 239–40, 241, 253–54
  and hierarchical coordination, 160
  and principles of constitutional design, 86
  and referenda, 240, 249, 249–50, 250–51
  and rights, 80
  as support for peace, 11–15
  and unanimity rule, 246
Constitution, US
  and homogeneity, 81
  and state sovereignty, 82
Constitutional changes, budgetary impact of, 129–30
Constitutional constraints
  on form of gradualism in integration process, 52–56
  on moving ahead, 49–52
  on reversal, 46–49
Constitutional Convention, US (1787), 34
  selection of delegates for, 82
Constitutional entrenchment, of goal-oriented evolution, 41–45, 49
Constitutional political economy, 61
Constitutional rights. *See* Rights
Constitutional rules
  principles for, 86
  vs. values, 253
Constitutional and statutory initiatives at EU level, 221–25
"Constitution for Europe," 38, 41. *See also* European Constitution
Constitution-making, and evolving nature of European Union, 39–41
Consultation procedure, 89, 93, 94, 96, 97, 99, 102–103, 105n.15, 139
Contract, constitution as, 205
Contractarian political philosophy, 32, 206–207
Contracts, incomplete, 110–11, 120
Convention of EU members (2002, 2003), xv, xvi
Convention on the Future of Europe, and election of
European Commission, 169
Convention for the Protection of Human Rights and
Fundamental Freedoms, 62, 77, 252–53
  and Charter, 79–80
  citizen rights under, 77–78, 80
Coordination
  cross-Council, 143, 147
  horizontal vs. vertical, 164n.4
  ex post vs. ex ante, 140, 158
Coreper (Committee of Permanent Representatives), 141, 153–55, 158, 160, 162–63

Index

and European Council, 155
"Correlates of war" program research, 12
Council formations, 139
  sectoral, 141, 143
Council of Ministers. *See* European Council
Cox, Pat, 183

Decentralized federations, 39
Decision-making procedures of EU, 101–104. *See also* Sectoral policy-making in EU; Voting rules
  analysis of, 87–89
  bargaining in, 46–48, 51
  constitutional rules for, 253
  and direct democracy, 204–205 (*see also* Direct democracy in EU decision-making)
  and distribution of preferences, 70
  and enlargement, 85–86
  and equal representation of EU citizens, 99–101
  and inefficiency of co-decision, 97–99
  and institutional structure of EU, 89–97
  sectoral structure of, 139–140 (*see also* Sectoral policy-making in EU)
  unanimous, 44–45, 93 (*see also* Unanimous decision making)
Declaration of Laeken, xv, 237, 254
Defense issues, 16–17
de Gaulle, Charles, 121
Deliberation process, in direct democracy, 214
Deliberative democracy, 14
Delors Commissions, 173
Democracy. See also Majoritarian democracy; Majority-voting
  deliberative, 14
  and design of federal system, 13–14
  and European Constitution 18
  and war-making, 7–9, 19–20
Democratic deficit, 81–82, 198, 203–204, 247
Denmark, as "eurosceptic," 203
Direct democracy in EU decision-making, 204–205, 228, 248–51
  and Aristotelian conception of aristocracy, 205–206
  vs. centralization of power, 254
  for constitutional changes, 208
  constitutional and statutory initiatives at EU level, 221–25

and contract theory, 206–207
and expressive vs. instrumental voting, 212–16
and European *demos* (public), 203–204, 216–17
fiscal referendum at EU level, 225–28
and information as control, 209–11
and institutional foundation, 207–208
and interest groups, 212
and mandatory referenda on European Constitution, 219–21
and Wicksellian connection between public services and tax prices, 217–19
Discount rates, 55
Discretionary action, 251
Divided government, in parliamentary mode of selection, 193–94
Double-hat scheme, 97, 103
Dual executive, 199

Economic integration, as reducing probability of war, 11–12
Economic and Monetary Union, 197
Economic nationalism, 28
EC Treaty
  Article 269 of, 133
  Article 313 of, 254
Electoral college system, 196
Energy Council, 148, 149–50, 154, 156
Engrenage (spillover) principle, 52–53
Enlargement of EU
  and decision-making procedures, 85–86, 93–96, 102
  and EU budget debates, 109, 128–29
Environment Council, 148, 149, 150, 151–52, 154, 156
Erhard, Ludwig, 215
European Central Bank, 238
European Coal and Steel Community
  and *acquis communautaire*, 43
  budget of, 136n.21
European Commission, 58–59n.11
  accountability of, 194, 198
  in decision-making, 89–91, 93, 97, 97–98, 99, 102–103, 105n.15, 127
  and democratic pressures, 13–14
  election of, 169–76 (*see also* Executive election for EU)
  and entrenchment of *acquis communautaire*, 48
  initiation of legislation reserved to, 151
  majority vote in, 176

European Commission (cont.)
  in policy coordination, 160, 161
  and sectoral division, 143
  and taxation power, 134
European Community, 43
European Constitution
  Bill of Rights of, 230n.23
  and Charter, 79–80
  and competitive federalism, 25–26 (*see also* Competitive federalism)
  democratic approval of, 205
  as emergent structure, 26–27, 34–35
  and evolving nature of EU, 39–41
  fiscal referenda in, 227
  goals proclaimed in, 238
  and institutionalizing peace, 18
  issues arising in, xv–xvi
  and liberal interpretation of rights, 252
  mandatory referenda on, 219–21
  and nation-state sovereignties, 82–83
  as outcome of dynamic two-player game, 27–29
  planned division of, 129–30
  purpose of, 1
  referendum on, 208, 251, 254
  and subsidiarity, 245
  values vs. rules in, 253–54
European Constitutional Convention
  debate preceding, 254
  and direct democracy, 208, 251
  and institutionalization of peace, 3–4
  and taxation, 134, 244
European Constitutional Group, 240, 245–46
European Convention for the Protection of Human Rights and Fundamental Freedoms. *See* Convention for the Protection of Human Rights and Fundamental Freedoms Protection of Human Rights and Fundamental Freedoms
European Council (Council of Ministers), 58n.11, 141
  changes in structure of, 164n.7
  and confederation, 253–54
  as coordination mechanism, 155–58, 158, 159, 160, 161, 163
  and Council formations, 139, 158 (*see also* Sectoral policy-making in EU)
  and decision-making, 89–90, 91, 93, 96, 97, 99, 102, 103, 105n.15, 127
  and European Commission election, 173

and federation, 254
majority-voting within, 52
opaque decision process in, 247
qualified majority in, 199n.1, 246
and voting by veto, 133, 247–48
European Court of Human Rights, 78
European Court of Justice, 44
  British proposal to increase powers of, 52
  and changes in Constitution, 220
  and conflicts over rights, 252
  and entrenchment of *acquis communautaire*, 48
European Economic Community
  budget of, 113
  and Common Market, 118
European identity, 18, 20, 77
European Investment Bank, 129
European Parliament, 70
  and budget initiative, 128
  composition of determined by protest vote, 198
  and confederation, 240, 253–54
  as coordination mechanism, 151–53, 158–59, 160–61, 162
  and decision-making, 89, 90, 91, 96, 99, 102, 103
  elections to as "second-order national contests," 193
  and federation, 254
  makeup of (since 1979), 176–79
  multiple-round elections in, 199n.4
  and optional referendum, 222
  in plans for election of Commission, 169
  and referenda, 249
  in scenarios on election of Commission, 179–94, 197
  secret ballot for, 181
  and sectoral division, 143, 159
  slight influence of, 203
  and taxation, 134
  and Wicksellian unanimity, 131
European public (*demos*), 203–204
  and direct democracy, 216–17, 228
European Social Fund. *See* Social Fund
European Union
  accountability of, 203
  allocation of responsibility in, 13
  and assignment problem, 241–46 (*see also* Confederation; Federation)
  budget of, 109–10, 113–35 (*see also* Budget of European Union)

Index

citizenship in, 61, 67–70 (*see also* Citizenship)
"closer to citizens" as goal of, xv, 237, 254
as confederation, 68–69, 239–40, 241 (*see also* Confederation)
decision-making in, 87–97, 101–104 (*see also* Decision-making procedures of EU; Voting rules)
democratic deficit in, 81–82, 198, 203–204, 247
electing executive for, 169–76, 179–98 (*see also* Executive election for EU)
enlargement of, 85–86, 93–96, 102, 109, 128–29
ever-closer union as objective of, 42–43, 51, 56
evolving nature of, 39–41, 49
and external wars, 20
institutional structure of, 89–97, 239–41 (*see also* Confederation; Federation)
as open-ended, 37–38, 40, 41
and original six members, 43, 45
purpose or goals of, 1–5, 16–19, 238
questions on, 10
rights in, 61, 74–80 (*see also* Rights)
and sectoral Council formations, 139 (*see also* Sectoral policy-making in EU)
as solution to yesterday's problem, 10
and strong president, 241
and taxation power, 134, 226 (*see also* Taxation)
"Europe's Constitutional Opportunity" (Buchanan), 25
Europe vs. United States, in relationship between politicians and citizens, 81
Europhiles, 50, 51, 52, 57
Europhobes, 50, 51, 52
Euroscepticism, 40, 50, 203
and feeling of inexorability, 49
Executive election for EU, 169–70
conclusions on, 196–99
counterfactual analysis of, 170–72
and election of current Commission, 172–76
proposed method of, 194–96
scenarios for, 179–94, 197–98
Executive model, 91
Exit right, and referenda, 249–50
Exit threats, and financial arrangements, 124, 128
Expressive voting, 8–9, 13, 17, 21n.8, 213, 228

External costs of collective decision-making, 64
Externalities
from migration, 67–68
negative, 4, 72, 73

Fair (Banzhaf) index of power, 100. *See also* Banzhaf index or measure
Falklands war, 9
Federalism (federation). *See also* Competitive federalism
autonomy from, 20
and citizenship, 67
and co-decision procedure, 92
and constitutional activity, 39–41
and constitution-making, 39–40
and direct participation of citizens, 211
and EU decision-making, 99
and EU, 70, 240, 253, 254
and executive election proposal, 170–71
fiscal, 58n.8, 242
and nonhierarchical coordination, 160
and principles of constitutional design, 86
and referendum, 249, 250
and rights, 76
rightist opponents of, 25
as support for peace, 11–15
Firm, purpose of, 1–2
Fiscal federalism, 58n.8, 242
Fiscal referendum at EU level, 225–28
Flexibility clause, 251
Florence European Council (1996), 156
Fontaine, Nicole, 183
France
and Common Market, 118
and EU budget incidence, 115
as "eurosceptic," 203
and financing of CAP, 119–22
political corruption in, 215
and redistribution, 117
Free-rider problem
and state, 206
and war-making, 9–10
Free trade, benefits of, 21
Free-trade area in Europe, 3
Functional overlapping competing jurisdictions (FOCJ), 22n.10

Game theory
cooperative vs. noncooperative, 87
and European Constitution as outcome of two-player game, 27–29

Game theory (cont.)
  and minimax criterion, 31
  in sectoral policy-making, 140, 148, 151–52, 156, 161–63
  and war, 6
General Affairs Council, 139, 140, 140–41, 148–50, 158, 160, 161–62
  and European Council, 155, 156
German Basic Law (GG), and EU Treaty, 203
Germaneness rule, 165n.20
Germany
  and Common Market, 118
  and EU budget incidence, 115
  political corruption in, 215
  and redistribution, 117, 127
  threats not feasible for, 124
  voter turnout in, 213
Goal-oriented evolution, constitutional entrenchment of, 41–45, 49
Goals of European Union. *See* Purpose or goals of European Union
Gradualism, 52, 53–54
  and limitations on size of each step, 56
  without reversals, 55–56
  apparent unforeseen implications of, 54–55
Great Britain. *See* United Kingdom
Greece, and redistribution, 122, 123–24

Habeas corpus protections, 75
Hamilton, Alexander, 207
Hayek, Friedrich von, 26
Hayes-Renshaw, Fiona, 141, 143
Helsinki European Council (1999), 16, 139, 147, 155, 156
Heterogeneity of preferences
  costs of, 68–70
  optimal citizenship with, 63–67
  and rights, 74
  and rights (EU), 80, 81
Hierarchical policy coordination, 158, 159, 160
High Representative for the Common Foreign and Security Policy, 16–17, 140
Hobbes, Thomas, 206
Hybrid (federation-confederation) structure, 240–41, 249

Ideologues, 50
Ifo Institute, xv
Immigration. *See also* Migration
  and citizenship, 63, 83n.4
  and EU decline in population, 67
  European political leaders vs. voters on, 81
Incomplete contracts, theory of, 110–11, 120
India, partitioning of from Pakistan, 11
Initiatives, 204. *See also* Direct democracy in EU decision-making
  in European Union, 210–12, 221–25
  and representative democracy, 209
Institutional design, analysis of, 87–89
Institutionalization of peace, 4, 13, 15–19, 20
Institutional structure of EU, 89–97
Integration, negative and positive, 54
Interest groups, 212
Intergovernmental Conference, 205
Ionnina compromise, 104n.2, 125
Iraq war, 9
Ireland, partition of, 11
Iron and Steel Council, 143
Italy
  and Common Market, 118
  political corruption in, 215

Jenkins Commission, 173
Justice and Home Affairs Council, 143

Kant, Immanuel
  and contract theory, 206, 207
  on democracy and "perpetual peace," 7

Laeken, Declaration of, xv, 237, 254
Locke, John, 206, 207
Log-rolling, 46, 47, 209
Luxembourg compromise (1966), 93, 121, 122, 124
Maastricht Treaty (Treaty of the European Union), 28, 46, 151, 173, 245
  preamble of, 42
  and resistance of status quo, 49
Mad cow disease, agreement on combating, 156
Madison, James, 34, 207, 214
Majoritarian democracy, and constitutional rights, 73–74
Majority-voting, 70. *See also* Qualified majority rule
  bargaining and position-trading under, 47–48
  and citizenship, 64, 65, 65–66
  within Commission, 94, 176

Index

on constitution, 219
within Council of Ministers, 52, 94
and double majority of voters and states, 204
increasing recourse to, 57
simple dual (SD), 99, 104, 105n.17
and stability, 101
Market Council, 143
Marxist socialism, demise of, 25
Maximin criterion, 31
Migration. *See also* Immigration
and citizenship, 66
within EU, 67–68, 69–70
and redistribution, 242–43
Military decision-making, 16–17
Mitterrand, François, 52, 59n.15
Mobility. *See also* Migration
across borders, 76, 80
and citizenship, 67–68
Monetary policy, relocation of authority over, 18
Monnet, Jean, 3, 52
Monotonicity, 38, 49, 50, 56–57
Munich conference (2003), xv, xvi, 237

Nash bargaining solution, 152, 162
Nationalism
forces reflecting, 28
and political competition, 12
Nation states, transfer of attachment from, 54
NATO, 16, 17, 22n.12
Negotiation set, 152
Netherlands, and EU budget incidence, 115
Nice reforms, 92–93, 101
Nice Summit (December 2000), 85, 128
Nice Treaty (2000), 151, 169, 173, 181, 195
NOMINATE algorithm, 170, 178–79, 181
Nonrequired referenda, 204
Normalized Banzhaf index (NBI), 88, 100
Nullification option, 250

Objective, of ever-closer union, 42–43, 51, 56
Ochlocracy, 206
Opinion polls, 8, 21n.6
OPOV (one-person–one-vote) principle for EU, 86, 100, 101, 102, 104, 240, 248
Optimal citizenship with dispersed populations and heterogeneous preferences, 66–67

Optimal citizenship with heterogeneous preferences, 63–65
Optimal citizenship with heterogeneous preferences and separated communities, 65–66
Optimal citizenship with homogeneous preferences, 62–63
Opt-out option, 250
Overcrowding, costs of, 67–68
"Own resources," 122, 134

Pakistan, partitioning of from India, 11
Pareto criterion
and *acquis communautaire*, 48
and competitive federalism, 32
Parliamentary method of legislative policy-making, 160
Parliamentary model, 169, 170–71, 172, 192, 194, 195, 196, 198, 198n.1
Penrose-Banzhaf measure (PBM), 87–88, 105n.9
Plebiscites, 222
Policy coordination, competing views of, 159–60
Political failure
European Union as counterweight to, 19
and voting as expressive, 8–9
war as, 5–11, 17
Political legitimacy, under contract theory, 206
Portugal, and redistribution, 122, 123–24
Position-trading, 46–48
Power index approach, 87–89
Pragmatists, 50, 52
Presidential model, 169, 170, 171, 194–96, 241
evolutionary approach toward, 199n.2
Principal-agent relationship
and war-making, 7
and referendum, 249
Prisoner's Dilemma Game, and war, 6, 9–10
Prodi, Romano, 134
Prodi Commission, 173, 176, 197
Public choice theory
and coalitions of interests, 10
and euroscepticism, 40–41
and incidence of budget, 117
and voting procedures, 248
and war impulse, 9
Public economics, and purpose of EU, 3

Public good, in definition of citizenship, 62
Public goods
  and EU budget, 109, 112, 114–15, 130, 134
  EU's failure to provide, 239
  and parliamentary governments, 170
  and parliamentary vs. presidential systems, 196
  question of level of provision of, 241–43
Purpose or goals of European Union, 1, 238
  vs. description of actual policies and practices, 2
  as force for peace, 3–5
  as institutionalizing peace, 4, 16–19
  and public economics, 3
  and purpose of firm, 1–2

Qualified majority rule, 125, 246, 246
  abstruse logic of, 248
  and budget, 124–25, 130
  on constitution, 219
  in European Council, 94, 199n.1
  and secession, 120–21
  supermajority, 18
  and veto power, 132
  and vote weighting, 131

Ratification procedure, for revision, 44
Rational actor analysis, of war, 5–6
Rational choice theorists, and direct democracy, 208
Rawls, John, 207
Rawlsian veil of ignorance. *See* Veil of ignorance
Redistribution
  and EU budget, 109–10, 111–12, 113, 117–28, 134–34
  and EU politics, 211
  and parliamentary vs. presidential systems, 196
  question of level of, 242–43
  in rational actor analysis of politics, 5–6
  regional, 216–17
  tariffs as, 21
Referenda, 45. *See also* Direct democracy in EU decision-making
  in California, 211
  and confederation, 240, 249, 249–50, 250–51
  on constitutional amendments, 250–51
  on EU policies at national level, 249–50
  on European Constitution, 205, 219–21, 254
  in European Union, 210–12, 248–49
  fiscal or budget, 204, 225
  nonrequired, 204
  optional statutory, 222–23
  and representative democracy, 209
  required (mandatory), 204, 205, 221
Religions
  and rights, 76
  and voting rule, 72–73
Required referenda, 204
Right of exit, 128
Rights, 61, 70–74
  in European Union, 74–77, 252–53
  in European Union (national vs. European), 77–80
  and heterogeneous interests, 74
  and immigration or emigration, 67, 68
  and majoritarian democracy, 73–74
  permanence of needed, 207
  as relative, 74, 78
  of religion, 73
  to secede, 249–50
  and structure of European Union, 61
Riviera ownership, as example, 68
Roll-call votes, 181
Rome, Treaty of. *See* Treaty of Rome
Rotating presidency, 241
Rousseau, Jean-Jacques, 206, 207

Santer, Jacques, 197
Santer Commission, 173
Schroeder, Gerhard, 169, 198, 240
Secession
  and autonomy, 20, 22n.15
  and referenda, 249–50
  threat of, 128
Sectoral policy-making in EU, 139–41, 144–47, 158–61
  vs. cabinet policy-making, 145–46, 158
  and countervailing mechanisms for coordination, 147–58, 159
  rise of, 141–44
Separation of powers, 195, 208
Servius, 205–206
Seville European Council (2002), 139, 143, 147, 159
Simple dual (SD) majority voting, 99, 104, 105n.17
Single European Act, 46, 125

Index

compromise leading to, 47
negotiation leading to, 52
Single Market Program, 93
  and counterfactual scenarios, 192, 197
Sinn, Hans-Werner, 243
Social Affairs Council, 139
Social budget, 119–20
Social contract. *See* Contractarian political philosophy
Social Fund, 118, 120, 122
Sovereignty, complexity and division of, 14–15
Spain
  and redistribution, 117, 122, 123–24, 127
  terrorist murders in, 80–81
Spillover (*engrenage*) principle, 52–53
Spillovers
  from political failure, 4
  from provision of goods and services, 242
"Splicing of issues," 46
Square-root dual majorities, 100–101, 104
Square-root rule, 100
Status quo bias, 98
Strategic voting, 21n.7
Structural funds, 227
Structural policy, and EU budget, 114
Subsidiarity principle, 42, 245–46
Supermajority voting, 18
Sweden
  and EU budget incidence, 115
  as "eurosceptic," 203
  threat position of, 124
Switzerland
  and direct vs. representative democracy, 212
  and fiscal curbs on representatives, 225
  and initiative vs. optional referendum, 223
  and national *demos*, 216, 217
  political corruption in, 215
  signature-collection time limits in, 225
  voter turnout in, 213
  and Wicksellian hypothesis, 217–18
Symbolic voting. *See* Expressive voting

Tabellini, Guido, 30, 58n.8, 109, 126
Taxation, 134, 226, 228
  EU level and national, 243–45
  and public services (Wicksellian connection), 217–19, 244
Taxation Matters Council, 143
Thatcher, Margaret, 9, 25, 47, 52, 58n.15

Threat
  as budget influence, 112
  financial concessions from, 123, 124
Tocqueville, Alexis de, 14–15
Trade issues, 10
"Traditional own resources," 122
Transfer of attachment, from nation-state to European entity, 54
Transport Council, 139
Treaty of Amsterdam, 125, 129, 151, 173
Treaty of the European Union. *See* Maastricht Treaty
Treaty of Maastricht. *See* Maastricht Treaty
Treaty of Nice. *See* Nice Treaty
Treaty of Rome, 111, 118–19
  and agricultural fund, 120
  collective decision rules of, 124–25
  as incomplete contract, 111
  preamble of, 42

Unanimous decision making (unanimity rule), 44–45, 70, 93
  and confederation, 246
  deviation from, 94
  in election of European Commission, 172–73
  and EU budget, 119, 125, 126–27, 130
  instability of in Council, 101
  negative assessment of, 57
  and position-trading, 46–48
  and rights, 207
  status quo favored by, 49–52
  Wicksellian, 131
Undercrowding, costs of, 67–68
Unions of nations, conflict between, 10
United Kingdom (Britain)
  and EU budget incidence, 115
  as "eurosceptic," 203
  and EU as state, 40
  and mad-cow disease agreement, 156
  political corruption in, 215
  and redistribution, 117, 122, 123
  referendum in, 211
  and Single European Act, 52
  and Treaty of Maastricht, 42
  voter turnout in, 213
United States
  and direct vs. representative democracy, 212
  and fiscal curbs on representatives, 225
  and initiative vs. optional referendum, 223

United States (cont.)
  political corruption in, 215
  presidential election in (2000), 196
  relationship between politicians and citizens in (vs. Europe), 81
  voter turnout in, 213
  and Wicksellian hypothesis, 217
United States Constitution. *See* Constitution, US
USC (union of states and of citizens) principle for EU, 86, 99, 102, 103, 104

VAT (value added tax), 226–27, 228
"VAT own resources," 122, 123
Veil of ignorance, 21n.8, 64, 65, 75, 76, 242
Veto
  and budget procedure, 130
  by Council formation, 153–54
  referendum as, 209
  and small minorities, 246
  voting by, 131–33, 135, 246–48
Vote-trading, 46
Voting
  and economic model of politics, 14
  as expressive, 8–9, 13, 17, 21n.8, 213, 228
  strategic, 21n.7
  supermajority, 18
Voting rules, 246–48. *See also* Majority-voting; Qualified majority rule; Veto
  choice of, 70–74
  in Commission, 176, 197
  for European Union, 85–86, 101–104
  roll-call vs. secret ballot, 181
Voting by veto, 131–33, 135, 246–48

Wallace, Helen, 141, 143
War
  and domestic democratic politics, 19–20
  EU as preventing, 4–5, 238
  as political failure, 5–11
Weimar Republic, 224
Wicksell, Knut, 34, 207
Wicksellian connection between public services and tax prices, 217–19, 244
Wicksellian unanimity, 131

Yugoslavia
  partitioning of, 11
  top-down federalism of, 20